The Spectral Mother

The Spectral Mother

FREUD, FEMINISM, AND PSYCHOANALYSIS

Madelon Sprengnether

Cornell University Press

Ithaca and London

First published 1990 by Cornell University Press.

Material from Madelon Sprengnether, "Enforcing Oedipus: Freud and Dora," in *The (M)other
Tongue: Essays in Feminist Psychoanalytic Interpretation*, edited by Shirley Nelson Garner,
Claire Kahane, and Madelon Sprengnether, copyright © 1985 by Cornell University; and
Madelon Sprengnether, "(M)other Eve: Some Revisions of the Fall in Fiction by Contemporary
Women Writers," in *Feminism and Psychoanalysis*, edited by Richard Feldstein and Judith Roof,
copyright © 1989 by Cornell University, are used by permission of the publisher, Cornell
University Press.

Excerpts from *Housekeeping* by Marilynne Robinson, copyright © 1981 by Marilynne Robinson,
are used by permission of Farrar, Straus and Giroux, Inc.

The lines from "Transcendental Etude" from *The Dream of a Common Language: Poems, 1974–
1977*, by Adrienne Rich, are reprinted with the permission of the publisher, W. W. Norton &
Company, Inc., and the author. Copyright © 1978 by W. W. Norton & Company, Inc.

International Standard Book Number 0-8014-2387-2 (cloth)
International Standard Book Number 0-8014-9611-x (paper)
Library of Congress Catalog Card Number 89-396881
Printed in the United States of America
*Librarians: Library of Congress cataloging information
appears on the last page of the book.*

⊗ The paper used in this publication meets the minimum
requirements of the American National Standard for
Permanence of Paper for Printed Library Materials Z39.48–1984.

For my mother,
Roberta Christy Lucas,
and in memory of my father,
William Francis Sprengnether, Jr.

Contents

Preface

In a conversation with a friend not long after I started writing
this book, I confided some of my doubts and conflicts
about the project of deciphering Freud's phobic responses to the
figure of the mother. He listened carefully and then told me the
following dream. "I was fishing," he said, "and I made this wonder-
ful catch. As I pulled the fish out of the water, I realized that I had
landed a coelacanth—a species once thought to be extinct. At first I
was elated, but then as I watched it flopping helplessly on the
ground, I began to feel bad about what I had done. I was afraid that I
might be destroying the only living example of this prehistoric fish.
So I threw it back."

At first I took this to be a cautionary tale—a warning about
trespassing against the venerable (and now defenseless) Freud.
Later, however, I decided that the meaning of the dream (for me, at
least) had to do with the power of the unconscious as hidden and as
Other. And that prehistoric entity, I concluded, is wily enough to
take care of itself.

In this book I explore the vicissitudes of a theory that seeks to
establish ground rules for making sense of the irrational and unpre-
dictable aspects of human thinking and behavior. I haven't sought
to eliminate these elements, or to fix and preserve them as a taxi-
dermist might, but rather to investigate the biases built into the
theory (and its various ramifications) which constrain our understanding of women's mobile presence and subjectivity.

   This book has had a long period of gestation, reaching back to the
early 1970s, when I first began reading psychoanalytic theory out of
a mixture of personal and professional interest. From the beginning,
as a woman and as a feminist, I was concerned about the belated-
ness of Freud's thinking about femininity and about his virtual
silence concerning mothers (I already was one). I remember being
proselytized, as a young instructor at Middlebury College, by one of
my male colleagues, who sought to moderate my interest in feminism by recommending that I read Freud on female sexuality and
Helene Deutsch on masochism. One early-morning phone conversation with him began: "All this talk about women as human
beings somehow misses the point." To be fair to him, I suppose that
what he meant was something like "Vive la différence!" but I was
wary.

   I also remember a psychoanalytic seminar at the University of
Minnesota Medical School, during which the professor claimed
that in evaluating a woman over forty for analysis you assess her
ability to attract a man, or her "come hither," as he put it without a
trace of irony. Later at the same seminar, a resident in psychiatry,
reporting on the progress of his treatment of a young woman, spent
considerable time describing her sexual problems. When asked
whether she had ever had an orgasm, he replied nervously, "She
hasn't even had intercourse." No one, not even the professor, remarked on the non sequitur.

   Yet I have found the techniques of psychoanalytic interpretation,
along with many of its underlying assumptions, both valuable and
useful. For me Freud's greatness lies in the process rather than the
product of his interpretations: in his description of the transference
phenomenon, for instance, and of the compulsion to repeat, as well
as his reliance on free association and his bedrock belief in the
hidden agency of the unconscious. The developmental theory that
Freud regarded as essential to his thought introduces a certain warp
into an otherwise neutral array of hermeneutic strategies—a warp
that reproduces some aspects of Freud's own culture. In casting his
fate with that of Oedipus, Freud rationalized an idealized patriarchy, one he may have wished to experience as a child and which
he strove to establish in the context of his own marriage and extended family. But in choosing this story as a basis for understanding his own history, as well as that of his culture, he privileged and

legitimized the status quo, which represses femininity and the figure of the mother, relegating both to a position of subversion. The Oedipus complex formalizes a conflict internal to patriarchy between paternal authority and maternal priority. In this book I argue that Freud was at least dimly aware of this problem, that he was at times even attracted to alternate constructions, but that he shied away from them, just as he balked when confronted with evidence of his own bisexuality, and as he consistently evaded the issue of maternal subjectivity.

Because I believe that Freud's Oedipal model and its implications are central not only to his own system but also to post-Freudian psychoanalytic theory, including the object relations and Lacanian schools, I have given most of my attention to a reading of his texts, under the general heading of "The Spectral Mother." In "Femininity as Subversion: Freud and Post-Freud," I describe Freud's legacy and its unhappy consequences for psychoanalytic feminists, regardless of the current mode of theory they choose. In "Alienating Grace," I offer some speculations about how one might displace Freud's emphasis on Oedipus in order to include the mother as an active figure in the process of enculturation and thus to open new possibilities for imagining and interpreting female subjectivity. My intention in writing this book is not to create a new orthodoxy but rather to offer an intervention into the Oedipus complex (as understood by Freud and as replicated and elaborated by his followers) in order to release its theoretical stranglehold on feminism. Solutions other than the one I offer may well be possible. What I have done in this book is work through, to the best of my ability, my own train of thought concerning Freud's suppression of the figure of the mother and its consequences for his understanding of women. If among my readers some take inspiration for their own creative efforts in this direction, I will be pleased.

It is a pleasure to name the people who helped me in the writing of this book. In Minneapolis, Toni McNaron and Shirley Nelson Garner, both of whom welcomed me to Minnesota in 1971 and have stood by me ever since, supported me with their love and friendship throughout this project. I thank them for their sustained caring as well as their belief in me. I am also grateful to the University of Minnesota, first for a single quarter leave, which gave me time to draft the final chapters of the book, and then for a grant in aid of research, which allowed me to employ Stephanie Athey, a graduate student in English, to help me with crucial details. Stephanie's cheerfulness and efficiency sustained me during a quarter when I was feeling frustration about my lack of writing time. On the West Coast, I give special thanks to Janet Adelman, who talked me through a crisis and who has continued to offer both affection and wise counsel. Elizabeth Abel has also encouraged me and generously offered to let me read parts of her own book then in process. Susan Schweik and Valerie Miner have read my manuscript in its entirety and have helped me at various points to clarify my intent. I turned to them for advice about matters large and small from the start, and they have given freely of their time and energy. The friendship of Janet, Elizabeth, Sue, and Valerie has warmed my stay on the West Coast and helped me to feel at home. Despite their good advice, I alone, of course, bear responsibility for the book's remaining flaws and infelicities. I also thank Bernhard Kendler of Cornell University Press for his clarity and grace as an editor, and for the care with which he has handled this manuscript.

I am especially grateful to two people, both of whom I love very deeply. My daughter, Jessica Gohlke, whose birth coincided with the beginning of my professional academic life, and who turns twenty as I bring this book to a close, has not only inspired my subject but also caused me to take it to heart. More than that, in her funny, talky, self-respecting, beautiful, and high-spirited way, she has given me joy. To my husband, Robert Littlejohn, I give thanks beyond thanks: for the incomparable gift of time, for his faith that I would use it well, for the purchase of a hard disk computer and expert technical assistance, for coffee in the morning and music in the evening, for his love of language, travel, and conversation, but most of all for his deep generosity of spirit and loving presence, both of which have helped to transform my life.

MADELON SPRENGNETHER

Oakland, California

The Spectral Mother

Introduction

In the first of Freud's three essays on the psychology of love, he observes that adult men seek mother surrogates in their love objects. Although this is the case, he claims, in all normal relations, it is especially evident in cases where the "libido has remained attached to the mother . . . even after the onset of puberty" (*SE* 11:169). As if moved by his own description, Freud then offers a startling analogy: "The comparison with the way in which the skull of a newly born child is shaped springs to mind at this point: after a protracted labour it always takes the form of a cast of the narrow part of the mother's pelvis" (*SE* 11:169). In this vivid testimonial to the shaping power of the mother's body, Freud expresses an awareness that he fails to incorporate into his theoretical project as a whole. Whatever our other differences, as human beings we have one thing in common: we are all born of woman. As Freud sees it, "no one possesses more than one mother, and the relation to her is based on an event that is not open to any doubt and cannot be repeated" (*SE* 11:169).[1]

---

1. Despite recent developments in reproductive technology, no one has yet devised a successful artificial womb. The fact that wombs can be "rented," so to speak, or borrowed, however, does complicate Freud's categorical statement that "no one possesses more than one mother." In cases where there is both an egg donor and a womb donor, it is difficult to say (leaving aside the legal issues involved) which woman has the greater claim to the title mother. Current advances in reproductive technology highlight the inadequacy of our cultural assumptions concerning motherhood.

For the most part, however, Freud had trouble thinking about the figure of the mother, as well as the earliest period of development.[2] Surely, in the rearing of his own six children he had the opportunity to observe both, yet (with a few exceptions) he seems generally indifferent to the special character of the mother-infant relationship. At the same time, the figure of the mother is not altogether banished from Freud's work. She appears in the interstices of his argument, a persistent, though suppressed, presence. In the pages that follow I offer a reading of Freud's texts which examines the ways in which he avoided dealing with the mother and the period he finally characterized as "pre-Oedipus," as well as some of the consequences of that avoidance for post-Freudian psychoanalytic theory.[3]

In the process of formulating the Oedipus complex Freud set the parameters for his subsequent treatment of the mother by establishing her position as object rather than subject—the passive recipient of the son's libidinal urges.[4] Evidence of autonomy or desire on

2. Many people have observed this feature of Freud's work. Reviewing Freud's schematic treatment of the mother in his case histories of Dora, Little Hans, and the Rat Man, Iza Erlich says: "It is as if Freud could not bring himself to look closely at the mother, the figure his theory proclaims to be so central" ("What Happened to Jocasta?" 284). Coppélia Kahn regards Freud's inability to confront the importance of the mother as evidence of his "matrophobia," or fear of becoming like her ("The Hand That Rocks the Cradle" 79). Philip Rieff comments on Freud's repression of the preoedipal mother-son relationship from his self-analysis (*Freud* 185), while Peter Gay states succinctly that "there is no evidence that Freud's systematic self-scrutiny touched on this weightiest of attachments, or that he ever explored, and tried to exorcise, his mother's power over him" (*Freud* 505). Estelle Roithe's argument, which in many respects parallels my own, is perhaps the most sweeping. She states: "Freud's theoretical neglect of the mother in the early life of the child and his insistence on the centrality of the phallic, paternal power represents, apart from anything else, a denial of the profound importance of the two-person phase in infantile life; the phase 'before' father when the infant is 'alone' with his mother. I believe that Freud's disturbed relationship to his own mother and thence to women in general was responsible, to a large extent, for this neglect" (*Riddle of Freud* 124).

3. I use the phrase "preoedipal mother" throughout this book to refer to the figure of the mother in the earliest phase of the child's development. Because Freud coined the term "pre-Oedipus" late in his career, my use of the word "preoedipal" may appear at times to be anachronistic. As a matter of convenience, however, I think it is justified.

4. In "Writing and Motherhood," Susan Suleiman discusses psychoanalysis as a theory of childhood which necessarily denies the mother subjectivity. Judith Kegan Gardiner points to the obvious inequity of this situation when she says that "mothers are all persons who resent being treated only through our needs" ("Mind

the part of the mother, as a result, slipped to the margins of his consideration, appearing in the form of digressions or asides. Two other processes appear to accompany this move. While avoiding a direct confrontation with issues of maternal power (seduction, aggression, betrayal) Freud idealizes the mother's devotion to her child, at the same time that he conceives of her as castrated and hence inferior or worthy of masculine contempt. Both strategies seem designed to obscure her relative strength and importance vis-à-vis that of an infant.[5] Finally, in his cultural speculations, Freud maintains that civilization itself depends on the male subject's detachment from and transcendence of the mother. This line of argument nearly effaces her from the drama of human development.

By segregating issues of power from that of motherhood, Freud also allies femininity with passivity, a conjunction that makes it difficult for him to conceive of masculinity apart from aggression. "Feminine" identification on the part of men undergoes repression along with consideration of the mother's subjectivity. Neither vanishes completely, however. Traces of these concerns surface in odd moments, producing gaps and inconsistencies in Freud's argument, to which he himself often calls attention, as if to acknowledge his own bad faith. The result is a form of textual instability that Freud in his discussion of Dora associates with hysteria. The analyst himself, unable to create a coherent narrative, produces instead a symptomatic text, in which the elements he strives to banish from consciousness disrupt the smooth flow of the story he wishes to tell, ultimately calling it into question. In at least one case, the effect of subversion is so great that it appears to unravel the fabric of the argument as it is being woven, as if there were a Penelope principle at the heart of the text, silently undoing the labor of analysis.

Mother" 139). Addressing this problem from another angle, Julia Kristeva attempts to represent maternal subjectivity through a special form of discourse in "Stabat Mater." For Adrienne Rich, freeing the experience of motherhood from its institutional constraints opens new possibilities for women's self-definition (*Of Woman Born*).

5. Estelle Roithe offers a lucid analysis of Freud's defensive posture in this regard. Dorothy Dinnerstein looks at culture as a large-scale reproduction of it (*Mermaid and the Minotaur*).

My reading of these phenomena leads me to the conclusion that Freud's construction of the Oedipus complex obscures as much as it illuminates. Instead of regarding it as a fundamental breakthrough in his consciousness, I see it as a complex compromise formation, which allowed him to proceed with his self-analysis in a way that left unexamined his rather conventional assumptions about women and femininity. In particular, it permitted him to turn aside from the significance of maternal desire, consideration of which might have led him in the direction of a less conservative social theory. Instead Freud's Oedipal construct stands as a monument to patriarchy, sometimes even cited as its authorization.

Freud himself is clear in his own estimation of the role of the Oedipus complex (and its corollary, the castration complex) in human civilization: they are inseparable, if not actually synonymous. For Freud, the incest taboo is upheld by the father and his threat of castration, while the son's renunciation of his mother prepares him for the sacrifices and sublimations that civilization requires. The daughter, in contrast, has less reason to submit to the rigor of the father's law, since she has no basis on which to fear castration. When she has grown to womanhood, her influence is regressive, her personality childlike and even hostile to culture. Civilization, in Freud's account of the evolution of human society, rests on the achievement of phallic masculinity, itself the outcome of the successful negotiation of the Oedipus and castration complexes.

Yet this story, as powerful and seamless as it appears, comes with a subtext that has the effect of a persistent, low-level disturbance. While acknowledging the existence of matriarchy (a period in history which corresponds to that of the preoedipal) Freud can't find a satisfactory explanation of its relationship to the development of patriarchy. To give it priority, as Bachofen does in *Mother-Right* in his progressive chronological scheme, would seem to undermine the authority of the father, to which Freud pays tribute in his concept of the primal horde. But in Freud's account, where matriarchy is sandwiched between two father-dominated periods, which lead to the development of the modern nuclear family, there is no rationale for mother-rule. That he wants to include this phenomenon at all suggests an attraction that equals his uneasiness with the issue of maternal power. In the end, matriarchy remains unintegrated into his scheme, testifying to the problematic nature of his patriarchal paradigm.[6]

As Freud grows older, he associates women not only with the beginning of life but also with its end, so that the figure of the mother fuses with that of death. In his concept of the death instinct, which aims to return the living entity to its inorganic origin, he equates the body of the mother with the ultimate undoing of masculine striving and achievement. Freud's fragmentary accounts of mother-infant separation reinforce this pessimistic view, for the child's games of mastery memorialize the loss they are meant to control. Like the process of mourning, the developmental process that leads the child away from its mother internalizes an absence, so that the subsequent achievements that Freud attributes to the successful passage through the Oedipus and castration complexes appear to rest on a quicksand foundation of loss. Undermined from within, phallic masculinity, the cornerstone of patriarchal culture, is thus inherently unstable.

The preoedipal mother, in Freud's unsystematic treatments of her, emerges as a figure of subversion, a threat to masculine identity as well as to patriarchal culture. Never a major figure in Freud's theory, which revolves around the drama of the father-son relationship, she has a ghostlike function, creating a presence out of absence. Like the spirit of the mournful and unmourned Jocasta, she haunts the house of Oedipus. Her effect is what I call "spectral," in the full etymological sense of the word. Derived from the latin verb *specere*, to see, to look at, "specter" is related to "spectacle," "speculation," and "suspicion," while its immediate source is the Latin *spectrum*, meaning, simply, an appearance. In English a specter is a ghost, a phantom, any object of fear or dread. Freud's representations of the preoedipal mother evoke all of these associations. She is the object of his fascinated and horrified gaze, at the same time that she elicits a desire to possess and to know. In her disappearing act, she evades and frustrates his attempts at grand theory at the same time that she lures him, like a fata morgana, into the mists of metapsychology.

6. My argument in this book concerns not the validity of matriarchal theories of the development of human society but rather Freud's entanglement with the subject and its resonance for him with preoedipal issues.

It seems in Freud's writing that the preoedipal mother, like Medusa, cannot be looked at directly. At the same time, she exercises a fatal kind of attraction that inspires in him a multitude of defensive strategies. Within a range of responses that includes marginalization, denial, splitting, and transcendence, Freud takes up and relinquishes positions that his followers seem to differentiate more carefully and maintain more consistently. The image of the preoedipal mother which one derives from him thus depends to a large extent on the text one chooses for consideration. It is precisely this condition of heterogeneity, on the other hand, that has proven so fruitful for the production of theory. Because Freud's portrayal of the preoedipal mother is so richly suggestive yet problematically undeveloped, his assumptions about the preoedipal period are open to various lines of interpretation. Both Anglo-American object relations and French Lacanian theory, the two branches I am concerned with in this book, locate their points of origin within this field of indeterminacy.

The spectral quality of the preoedipal mother, her alternating presence and absence in Freud's texts, makes it equally possible to emphasize her role in development and to minimize it. Hence object relations theory posits an original maternal presence from which infant subjectivity must differentiate itself, while Lacan invents an umbrella term for the preoedipal period (the Imaginary) which subsumes the figure of the mother, giving her the character of an abstract necessity. Whereas the mother looms large in object relations theory, she is curiously disembodied in Lacan's system of thought. These two dispositions have significant consequences, in turn, for the feminist uses of psychoanalytic theory.

Object relations theory, which emphasizes the body of the mother, also highlights issues of sexual difference, which, in turn, lend themselves to essentialist formulations. Cultural school feminists, such as Nancy Chodorow, who stress the social construction of gender, have difficulty eliminating this bias from their work. Lacanian theory, on the other hand, explains sexual difference as the result of a position taken in language. This apparent rejection of biologism facilitates the cultural view of gender and supports the practice of *l'écriture féminine* as a strategy open to men and women alike. But it also threatens to erase the concerns of women as women. In consequence, some of the female advocates of *l'écriture féminine* vacillate between essentialist and androgynous views. To complicate matters further, neither the French nor the Anglo-American feminist theorists give much indication of appreciating their sisters' dilemmas. Rather, these two sophisticated branches of theory appear to be at odds with each other, threatening an impasse in further development of the field as a whole.[7]

Both object relations theory and Lacanian theory, moreover, retain Freud's hierarchical ordering of the preoedipal and Oedipal periods, a structure that subordinates the role of the mother to that of the father. Both schools as a result tend to view the mother and the femininity that she embodies as subversive. While object relations theorists perceive a threat to masculine identity in the period

7. Alice Jardine's *Gynesis* attempts to bridge this gap, although her method of first explicating French theory and then interrogating it from an Anglo-American perspective reads somewhat schizophrenically to me. Recent editions and translations of French theory have made this complex body of work more accessible to an English-speaking audience and have begun to produce some interesting results. Margaret Homans, for instance, combines aspects of Lacan's theory with that of Nancy Chodorow in order to read women authors (*Bearing the Word*). Yet the notion that Anglo-American literary criticism is primarily thematic, pragmatic, and untheoretical persists, contributing to the existing division between the Anglo-American school of object relations theory (popular among critics in this country) and Lacanian psychoanalysis. Thus as recently as 1986 Mary Jacobus stated that she felt it necessary to repudiate her Anglo-American critical heritage when she encountered French theory. In the preface to her *Reading Woman* she writes: "My own feminist literary criticism began in the early 1970s in the wake of writing by Mary Ellmann and Kate Millett, at a time when feminist literary criticism, however energetic, was relatively untheoretical in its critique of literature and of the assumptions governing conventional criticism. Such criticism attempted to shift the ground, to place the accent elsewhere, to expose the interestedness of phallocriticism, and to privilege the writing, perspective, and experience of women. Elaine Showalter later called this attempt 'gynocritics.' In the course of rereading my own previously published essays for inclusion in this book, it became clear to me that the significant break for many feminist critics, and certainly for myself, occurred as a result of the intellectual and political influence of French feminist thinking from the mid-1970s on. For that reason, I have chosen not to include anything written before 1978" (x).

See Toril Moi's *Sexual/Textual Politics* for a similar evaluation of the relative merits of Anglo-American criticism and French theory. There is no question that the school of object relations theory is included in the dismissal of Anglo-American literary critical practice. Until very recently it has seemed that one must irrevocably choose between Anglo-American and continental modes of criticism as well as psychoanalysis, forging an absolute allegiance to one over the other. See Paul Smith's *Discerning the Subject* (131–51) for an overview of this controversy and an argument for feminism's engagement with the "tensions and contradictions produced by having within itself both these manners of thinking" (135).

of mother-infant symbiosis, Lacan conceives of feminine *jouis-sance* as a means of disturbing the Symbolic order. Whether subversive of male gender identity or the phallocentrism of language, the mother remains marginal to culture, the position she occupies in Freud's thought. The inherent conservatism of this arrangement makes it difficult for feminists to use psychoanalytic theory as a tool for social change. Instead, the stereotypes of masculinity and femininity tend to reemerge under new names, reinforcing the old hierarchies they are meant to disrupt.

Freud's legacy for feminists is mixed. As both Juliet Mitchell, a Lacanian (*Psychoanalysis and Feminism*), and Nancy Chodorow, an object relations theorist (*Reproduction of Mothering*), point out, psychoanalysis offers a means of comprehending the unconscious structure of patriarchy. What it does not provide is a strategy for change. Instead, psychoanalysis tends to reproduce its problematic inscription within patriarchy despite the intent of its user. Freud's Oedipal/preoedipal hierarchy, for instance, may permit a theory of feminine subversion, but it does not allow for transformation.

The path toward a solution which I offer in this book involves an intervention into Freud's account of the preoedipal mother so as to remedy her (theoretical) exclusion from culture while preserving a recognition of her difference and otherness.

As a means of promoting discussion between Anglo-American and French feminist theorists, as well as of dislodging psychoanalysis from its patriarchal base, I suggest that we reexamine Freud's briefly entertained idea of castration as separation from the mother. Lacan, who picks up on this idea, which seems to render the Oedipal threat of castration null, nevertheless regards the *nom du père* (including his *non*) as an essential factor in cultural development.[8] For him, as for Freud, civilization is necessarily a patriarchal

---

8. For Lacan the phallus functions as an agent of division, severing the mother-infant bond and thus shattering the stage of the Imaginary. In this sense, it "castrates" everyone, regardless of sex. At the same time, however, the phallus, because of its role in destroying the mother-infant dyad, plays a privileged role in the child's subsequent relations to language and culture, which bear the marks of phallocentrism, despite the apparent emptiness of the phallus itself as a signifier. From my own point of view, I would say that Lacan wants to have it both ways: to deny that sex difference matters (since everyone is "castrated" or separated from the mother) while affirming the patriarchal order (because the phallus stands for or performs this task). See David Macey for a lucid critique of Lacan's choice of the phallus as a privileged signifier (*Lacan in Contexts* 177–209).

phenomenon. Derrida, who denies the dream of plenitude represented by Lacan's conception of the Imaginary and the object relations formulation of mother-infant symbiosis, sees castration (or radical separation) as a universal condition (see *Of Grammatology* 95–268). The advantage of this position is that it does not endorse the phallus as signifier and hence the equation between patriarchy and culture. Its disadvantage is that it erases the body of the mother. A beneficial conjunction between feminism and psychoanalysis must take account of the fact (as Lacanianism and poststructuralism fail to do) that a woman's body is the carnal origin of every human subject without desubjectifying the mother herself (as object relations theory tends to do). Combining Freud's notion of castration as separation with his understanding of the ego as a product of mourning—"the precipitate of abandoned object-cathexes" (*SE* 19:29)—might make this possible.

If subjectivity, for instance, may be understood as an elegiac construct, the product of an internalized loss that is felt as primary, then one might avoid some of the problems in Freud's portrayal of the preoedipal mother, as well as the worst pitfalls for feminists in Anglo-American and French psychoanalytic theory. Freud's tendency to idealize the mother-son relationship (anticipating the object relations concept of mother-infant symbiosis) suggests a state of original plenitude that subsumes the mother's desire in that of her male offspring.[9] If, however, the ego represents a reactive formation to loss, then separation would seem to be primary and the mother's body itself a focus of mourning. In this memorial or elegiac view of the ego, the loss that precipitates the organization of a self is always implicitly the loss of a mother, whose status as present/absent problematizes her signification. The mother's body becomes that which is longed for yet cannot be appropriated, a representative of both home and not home, and hence, in Freud's terms, the site of the uncanny. As both origin and Other, the preoedipal mother escapes the equally devastating effects of idealization and erasure, allowing for the possibility of maternal discourse as well as a nonphallocentrically organized view of culture.

In Freud's scheme, renunciation of the mother, accomplished through the boy's successful negotiation of the castration complex,

9. I have explored this idea in another way in "(M)other Eve: Some Revisions of the Fall in Fiction by Contemporary Women Writers."

leads to the development of culture. If, however, separation from the mother represents not a secondary but an originary condition, then there is no necessary link between the figure of the father and culture, or, in Lacan's terms, the phallus and the Symbolic order. No longer an exile from the process of signification, the body of the (m)other may actually provide a new, and material, ground for understanding the play of language and desire. Julia Kristeva's meditation on pregnancy as a state of internalized otherness ("Stabat Mater") offers fruitful possibilities for development in this regard. Focusing on the difference within the body of the (m)other,[10] her work suggests an analogy between the process of signification and that of maternity. Pursuing this line of argument, one may regard cultural production as an aspect of, rather than an alternative to, reproduction.

To date, psychoanalytic theory has not challenged the patriarchal status quo. At best, perhaps, it has provided a means of analyzing the internal workings of this social structure and, through a recognition of its particular psychological configuration, its historicity. Because psychoanalysis both grows out of and helps to sustain the patriarchal social order, it is important to understand the strategies by which it operates. Freud's lifelong uneasiness in dealing with the preoedipal mother attests both to his conservatism in matters concerning gender and to the inherent instability of his hierarchically organized model of the family and culture. That he himself failed to revolutionize our understanding of this model is not surprising; that his work suggests a means of doing so is richly ironic as well as empowering.

10. My use of the term "(m)other," which I have also employed in my essay "(M)other Eve," derives ultimately from *The (M)other Tongue: Essays in Feminist Psychoanalytic Interpretation* (ed. Garner, Kahane, and Sprengnether) and an earlier stage of thought as represented by my contribution to the introduction to that collection. In the meantime I have benefited from Jane Gallop's review essay of that volume as well as from Martha Evans's introduction and conclusion of her *Masks of Tradition*.

PART I

The Spectral Mother

I

Anticipating Oedipus

An examination of Freud's early life reveals some interesting material that may have a bearing on his later elaboration of the Oedipus complex. Looking at Freud's own preoedipal phase in Freiberg, for instance, we find a family structure that differs significantly from the one that characterized his subsequent years of development in Vienna. Freud appears to favor the later, more conventional model—a preference that has the effect of displacing or repressing questions regarding his mother's desire.

We know that Jacob and Amalie Freud resided in Freiberg, Moravia, during the first three years of young Sigmund's life. We also know that his father had previously been married to a woman named Sally Kanner, by whom he had two sons who were grown by the time he married Amalie, twenty years his junior.[1] Jacob and

---

1. Every student of Freud must be indebted to Ernest Jones's seemingly exhaustive three-volume study of Freud's life. Even Jones, however, was unaware of the existence of the mysterious Rebecca, Jacob Freud's second wife. Given his closeness to the Freud family and in particular to Anna, to whom he dedicated his biography, moreover, Jones could be expected to portray his subject in a positive light. More recent biographers not only have the benefit of new information but also have the freedom to adopt a more critical perspective. In forming my own views concerning the significant events in Freud's life I have found Ronald Clark's *Freud: The Man and the Cause* and Paul Roazen's *Freud and His Followers* particularly helpful. I have also consulted Peter Gay's *Freud: A Life for Our Time*, although it appeared in print after my own manuscript was substantially completed. In a more speculative vein, I have found Marie Balmary's *Psychoanalyzing Psychoanalysis*, Marianne Krüll's *Freud and His Father*, and several articles by Peter Swales especially stimulating. For

Amalie had two other children during this time: Julius, who died in less than a year, and Anna, reputedly Freud's least favorite sister. On the basis of Freud's memories of his half brother Philipp and his cousins John and Pauline (the children of his other half brother, Emmanuel) we may infer that relations among the brothers and their respective families were fairly close.[2] Emmanuel and his wife, Maria, may actually have shared a maid with the Freud family, a woman named Monica Zajíc,[3] whom Freud refers to as his "nannie." Life in Freiberg was disrupted first by the sudden dismissal of this woman, who was accused of stealing from her young charge, and then by the departure of Freud's family for Leipzig, where they spent a year before moving to Vienna. Philipp and Emmanuel and his family chose at this time to emigrate to England.

Even this minimal narration reveals at least two factors that may have played a role in the formation of Freud's psyche: the existence of what we would now call a "blended family" and the motif of departure, by death or otherwise. Freud's own memories of this period, combined with some information that has come to light in recent years, may help to unfold the significance of these factors, especially in regard to his lifelong inability to theorize maternal desire.

On the basis of an 1852 entry in a Freiberg register, it now appears that Jacob Freud was married not twice but three times; his second wife, Rebecca, was thirty-two years old at the time the entry was

---

an understanding of the political and cultural climate of late nineteenth-century Vienna, I am indebted to Carl Schorske's *Fin-de-Siècle Vienna*, William McGrath's *Politics of Hysteria*, and Allan Janik and Stephen Toulmin's *Wittgenstein's Vienna*. Recent biographies of Melanie Klein and Karen Horney by Phyllis Grosskurth and Susan Quinn, respectively, have illuminated my understanding of the relationship between Freud and his early women followers (*Melanie Klein: Her World and Her Work; A Mind of Her Own: The Life of Karen Horney*). Finally, *The Complete Letters of Sigmund Freud to Wilhelm Fliess 1887–1904*, translated and edited by Jeffrey Moussaieff Masson, has brought many of my thoughts about Freud into focus and helped to shape this study.

2. See, for instance, "Screen Memories," *SE* 3:303–22, which is generally regarded as a recollection from Freud's childhood.

3. While most biographers assume that Freud's nursemaid was Monica Zajíc, Marianne Krüll follows Josef Sajner and Peter Swales in their speculation that she was a woman named Resi Wittek. For the purposes of my argument this is not a critical point, so I have chosen the more usual attribution.

made.[4] By 1855, the date of Jacob's marriage to Amalie, Rebecca must either have died or been divorced. Most biographers assume that Jacob's first marriage ended at the death of Sally Kanner, the mother of Philipp and Emmanuel. If Freud himself knew of Rebecca's existence, he gives no such evidence, referring to his father as having been married only twice. Marie Balmary, in her book *Psychoanalyzing Psychoanalysis*, hypothesizes that Jacob set Rebecca aside, according to Jewish law, on the grounds of infertility, and that Rebecca responded by committing suicide (73). She interprets these events in the light of her thesis that Freud's Oedipal construct obscures what she calls the "hidden fault of the father," displacing the burden of guilt onto the son (7–24). Whether or not one agrees with this line of reasoning, Balmary's attempt to comprehend the role of Rebecca in Freud's imagination is useful in that it directs our attention to the intricacy of Freud's immediate family constellation.

Freud not only had two mothers, alive and present, in Amalie and the woman who was hired to care for him, but he also had two ghost mothers in the women who had previously married his father. While I find Balmary's argument for Rebecca's suicide tenuous, I agree with her assumption that children absorb what is unspoken along with what is spoken, a family's hidden or ghost history along with its official one. Whatever the reasons for the silence around Rebecca, the silence must have impressed itself on the mind of the young Freud.[5] There were yet other mysteries for him to ponder.

When Freud sought analogues for his primary insight into family dynamics, he turned to the stories of Hamlet and Oedipus, focusing on the child's culpability to the exclusion of the parents'. In exploring this evasion, both Balmary and another recent biographer, Marianne Krüll, point to Freud's father as the figure he strove to protect.

---

4. For a discussion of the research leading to the hypothesis of Rebecca as Jacob Freud's second wife, see Krüll 96–97.

5. Ronald Clark offers three possible interpretations of Freud's silence about Rebecca: (1) she did not in fact exist; (2) her existence was kept a secret from him; (3) Freud had some awareness of Rebecca but repressed this knowledge. "This third possibility," he states, "if correct, would, according to Freud's own beliefs, have significantly affected the development of his own mental life, and it would be ingenuous to believe that it would not have affected the course of psychoanalysis" (*Freud* 7).

What both overlook is the possibility of maternal complicity in the web of guilt, just as Freud himself chose to ignore the implications of Gertrude's and Jocasta's desire. His mother's desire must have been evident in some form, however, since the entire family shared a single room in Freiberg. Two other children were born and one died in the same circumstances.

Freud was confronted at an early age by the mysteries of eros and death. That he responded to them is clear from his own recollections of this time. Writing to his friend Wilhelm Fliess on October 3, 1897, he maintains that he greeted the birth of Julius with "adverse wishes and genuine childhood jealousy," and that "his death left the germ of [self-]reproaches" (Masson, *Letters* 268). In the same letter Freud refers to the incident in which his libido was aroused toward *"matrem . . . nudam"* (268). His reference to this event as having taken place when he was two and a half suggests that it occurred at the house in Freiberg rather than on the train from Leipzig to Vienna, as he reports. It seems likely that there would have been an occasion for such an encounter in light of the family's close quarters, which would have facilitated Freud's observation of the coming and going of his sibling Julius as well.

Freud links his mother erotically to the theme of appearance and disappearance in another revealing memory. In attempting to confirm the authenticity of his recollections of his nurse, Freud interrogates himself: "I said to myself that if the old woman disappeared from my life so suddenly, it must be possible to demonstrate the impression this made on me. Where is it then?" The following scene emerged in response to this question:

> My mother was nowhere to be found; I was crying in despair. My brother Philipp (twenty years older than I) unlocked a wardrobe [*Kasten*] for me, and when I did not find my mother inside it either, I cried even more until, slender and beautiful, she came in through the door. What can this mean? Why did my brother unlock the wardrobe for me, knowing that my mother was not in it and that thereby he could not calm me down? Now I suddenly understand it. I had asked him to do it. When I missed my mother, I was afraid she had vanished from me, just as the old woman had a short time before. So I must have heard that the old woman had been locked up and therefore must have believed that my mother had been locked up too—or rather, had been

"boxed up" [*eingekastelt*]—for my brother Philipp, who is now sixty-three years old, to this very day is still fond of using such puns. The fact that I turned to him in particular proves that I was well aware of his share in the disappearance of the nurse. [October 15, 1897; Masson, *Letters* 271–72]

In this passage Freud identifies Philipp as an agent in the absence or departure of the two women who arouse the strongest current of feeling in him: his mother and his nurse. In a later meditation on the same scene he speculates that as a child he also regarded Philipp as having caused his mother's pregnancy with his sister Anna.

The child of not yet three had understood that the little sister who had recently arrived had grown inside his mother. He was very far from approving of this addition to the family, and was full of mistrust and anxiety that his mother's inside might conceal still more children. The wardrobe or cupboard was a symbol for him of his mother's inside. So he insisted on looking into this cupboard, and turned for this to his big brother, who (as is clear from other material) had taken his father's place as the child's rival. Besides the well-founded suspicion that this brother had had the lost nurse 'boxed up', there was a further suspicion against him—namely that he had in some way introduced the recently born baby into his mother's inside. [*SE* 6:51n]

Marianne Krüll takes this passage as partial evidence of the existence of a sexual relationship between Philipp and Amalie (*Freud and His Father* 125). The truth or falsehood of this allegation matters less than the fact that Freud himself looked on his half brother and mother as lovers, complicit in the production of yet another infant rival. The word *eingekastelt*, moreover, pulls Freud's mother into the nexus of association that involves departure. If Philipp and Amalie together were responsible for the appearance of Anna, were they also complicit in the dismissal of Freud's nurse? Who made Julius disappear? Although Freud draws attention to his own death wishes against his brother, it seems likely that he would also have wondered about the role of the adults in his environment, including his mother. And then there is the question of Rebecca.

Marie Balmary regards the disappearance of Freud's nurse as a "figuration of Rebecca's disappearance" (149). She also entertains the possibility that Amalie was complicit with her husband in the setting aside of his second wife (74). Once again, I am less interested in establishing an actual sequence of events than I am in drawing out a train of possible associations. If Freud had any subliminal awareness of the existence of Rebecca, who had mysteriously vanished, he may also have associated her with the departures of his younger brother and his nannie, and finally with the removal of his immediate family from Freiberg to Vienna. Even if one rejects Krüll's hypothesis that this departure was motivated by Jacob's interest in separating Philipp and Amalie (128), no one can disagree that the move had that effect. How might Freud have construed his mother's desire under these circumstances?

When Freud described the preoedipal phase in girls as a "surprise, like the discovery, in another field, of the Minoan-Mycenean civilization behind the civilization of Greece . . . so grey with age and shadowy and almost impossible to revivify—that it was as if it had succumbed to an especially inexorable repression" (*SE* 21:226), he might also have been describing his Freiberg family existence behind that of Vienna. The Oedipus complex, with its streamlined nuclear family structure, seems to be modeled on the family that reconstituted itself around Jacob, Amalie, and their children rather than the one that embraced Philipp, Emmanuel, and Maria and extended itself into that of the Zajíc landlords. By taking this later family configuration as typical, Freud seems to have evaded the questions posed by Amalie's status in relation to Jacob's previous wives as well as her problematic involvement with Philipp. Exploring this material along the lines of Freud's own reminiscences suggests that he associated her with the magic of appearance and disappearance, with the powers of life and death. That Freud allied her with Philipp in his imagination also raises the question at least of Amalie's fidelity to Jacob. This topic appears to have been too threatening for Freud to develop, even in theoretical terms, for when he discusses the mother's infidelity, what he means is her betrayal of her infant for her husband rather than her turning from her husband to another man.

The very young Freud may well have questioned who his father was and felt anxious about missing people. The subject of departure, moreover, was clearly overdetermined, as we know from Freud's own reports of his railway phobia, stemming most likely from the dislocation of his family from Freiberg to Vienna.[6] It seems quite possible that Freud regarded his mother as mysteriously and perhaps threateningly involved in these issues, and that instead of examining them more closely as an adult, he chose to allow them to recede into a shadowy past, "grey with age . . . and almost impossible to revivify" (*SE* 21:226). In this light, it makes sense too that he would wish to pass over in silence the question that plagues Hamlet concerning his mother's complicity in his father's death, and that he would virtually ignore the implications of Jocasta's incestuous desire for her son. If we consider the portrait of Amalie as a strong-willed if not domineering woman which emerges from the comments of friends of Freud and of members of his own family, we have all the necessary elements for Freud's repression of her early influence on him.

According to Estelle Roithe, it is precisely Amalie's strength, in part the heritage of her position within a traditional Jewish family structure, that calls forth her son's need to insist on paternal authority. She suggests that the Oedipus complex "might be a reaction-formation on Freud's part to an opposite constellation, one in which the informal and customary role prescribed that his mother was the dominant and most powerful influence and his father the weaker one" (*Riddle of Freud* 105). Freud himself lends support to such an interpretation when, in *The Interpretation of Dreams*, he describes his disappointment in Jacob's mild and accommodating response to an overt gesture of anti-Semitism.

I may have been ten or twelve years old, when my father began to take me with him on his walks and reveal to me in his talk his views upon things in the world we live in. Thus it was, on one such occasion, that he told me a story to show me how much better things were now than they had been in his days. 'When I was a young man', he said, 'I went for a walk one Saturday in the streets of your birthplace; I was well dressed, and had a new fur cap on my head. A Christian came up to me and with a single blow knocked off my cap into the mud and shouted:

---

6. Jones reports that "through most of his life Freud suffered in varying degrees from *Reisefieber* (anxiety at departing on a journey), which was at its most acute in the nineties," and that even in later life he was "so anxious not to miss a train that he would arrive at a station a long while—even an hour—beforehand." Jones also traces the origins of this phobia to the departure from Freiberg (*Life* 1:181, 305, 13).

"Jew! get off the pavement!"' 'And what did you do?' I asked. 'I went into the roadway and picked up my cap,' was his quiet reply. This struck me as unheroic conduct on the part of the big, strong man who was holding the little boy by the hand. [*SE* 4:197]

In William McGrath's reading of this incident, "Jacob Freud had demonstrated his impotence in the face of the anti-Semitic insult, and that failure blocked the way to his providing a masculine model for his son" (*Politics of Hysteria* 64). Even Freud's daughter Anna, long after his death, in attempting to defend her father against irresponsible biographical speculation, inadvertently corroborates this view. Complaining about Marthe Robert's *From Oedipus to Moses: Freud's Jewish Identity*, she writes in a letter to Masud Khan: "She describes my father's father as an authoritarian figure, orthodox Jewish and in every respect the kind of father against whom a son revolts. The true facts are that he was a freethinker, a mild, indulgent and rather passive man, just the opposite" (quoted in Young-Bruehl, *Anna Freud* 431). Freud may well have felt the need to create a strong paternal presence in theory in order to make up for the perceived deficiencies of his actual father, who appears to have been less forceful in character than his mother.

Yet by all accounts Freud and his mother were close. She evidently referred to him throughout his life as "mein goldener Sigi" (Jones, *Life and Work of Sigmund Freud* 1:3) and was fond of repeating anecdotes that she regarded as prophetic of his future greatness. Freud himself wrote that "if a man has been his mother's undisputed darling he retains throughout life the triumphant feeling, the confidence in success, which not seldom brings actual success along with it" (*SE* 17:156). Outwardly the relationship was one of mutual devotion, expressive of the ideal Freud later elaborated in his essay "Femininity," in which he describes the bond between mother and son as "altogether the most perfect, the most free from ambivalence of all human relationships" (*SE* 22:133). The image of his mother which Freud presented to the world in no way indicates that he feared her or doubted her feelings toward him.[7]

7. Estelle Roithe considers Freud's relationship with his mother profoundly ambivalent (*Riddle of Freud* 89–124). Reports by Amalie's grandchildren, moreover, give us reason to believe that she had a domineering personality and was difficult to

Many readers have observed the obvious idealization of this portrait, which Jim Swan analyzes as the outcome of Freud's experience of being cared for by two women: his young, middle-class
Jewish mother and his old, lower-class Catholic nurse. By attributing aggressive sexuality solely to his nurse, Swan argues, Freud
maintains an image of his mother as beautiful and pure. As the
object of Oedipal desire, moreover, the pure mother appears less
menacing.

> But there is still the remarkable circumstance that Freud had, in
> effect, *two* mothers: his actual mother—whose nakedness he can
> mention only in Latin—and his Nannie whom he remembers in asso-
> ciation with numerous disturbing sexual experiences. Having two
> such mothers, and the luck of having the "bad," ugly mother banished
> from his life when he was only two and a half, allows Freud to main-
> tain a secure split between the internalized good and bad mothers. It
> also allows him to preserve his close relationship with his actual, very
> idealized mother who, in turn, idealizes her first-born and only son.
> ["*Mater* and Nannie" 34]

Freud's nurse becomes a convenient scapegoat for the more disturbing aspects of maternal desire. It is she who both arouses and
shames the young boy, steals from him, and ultimately abandons
him. Questions concerning seduction, aggression, and betrayal
which might otherwise have accrued to Freud's mother (if only in
fantasy) can be disposed of through the nurse. Freud had at hand a
means of dismissing or displacing these issues, which seem naturally to arise out of the circumstances of his birth and early life. By
the time the four-year-old Freud and his family moved to Vienna,
the stage had been set for his subsequent spectral portrayals of the
preoedipal mother.

---

live with. Judith Heller Bernays writes: "She was charming and smiling when
strangers were about, but I, at least, always felt that with familiars she was a tyrant,
and a selfish one. Quite definitely, she had a strong personality and knew what she
wanted" (Ruitenbeck, *Freud as We Knew Him* 338). Freud's son Martin regarded
Amalie as "impatient" and "self-willed" as well as "highly intelligent" (quoted in
Gay, *Freud* 504).

2

Freud, Fliess, and Emma Eckstein

I do not believe it was the blood that overwhelmed me.
—Sigmund Freud

If one wishes to trace the process by which Freud arrived at
his central hypothesis concerning the Oedipus complex
and his characteristic set of responses to the figure of the mother,
the crucial document to examine is *The Complete Letters of Sigmund Freud to Wilhelm Fliess*, translated and edited by Jeffrey
Moussaieff Masson. These letters, first published in abridged form
under the title *The Origins of Psychoanalysis*, provide a day-by-day
account of Freud's struggle to comprehend the etiology of the neuroses, an effort that included a confrontation with his father's death
as well as the labor of self-analysis that prompted his theory of
dream interpretation. Never intended for publication by Freud himself, who twice in his life conducted a purge of his private papers,
these letters, in their complete edition, reveal hitherto hidden aspects of Freud's relationships and thought processes which have a
bearing on his construction of theory. Jeffrey Masson, for instance,
takes the letters as evidence that Freud abandoned his seduction
theory for primarily personal reasons—out of a need to exonerate
his friend Fliess of the charge of malpractice in the bungled nasal
surgery he performed on Emma Eckstein.[1] Masson's somewhat

1. Masson's claim that Freud's abandonment of the seduction theory contami-
nated the entire development of psychoanalysis has provoked fierce opposition from
the psychoanalytic establishment—and for good reason. Masson's insistence on
reality over fantasy *does* make it difficult, if not impossible, to talk about uncon-

hyperbolic attack on Freud, and more recently on the entire psychoanalytic establishment, however, has tended to elicit a pro- or anti-
Freud stance in regard to the letters. A more useful approach is to
read them for insight into Freud's fixation on phallic models of
explanation and hence his attraction to Oedipus. Freud's responses
to Fliess in the aftermath of the Emma Eckstein affair serve as a
focus for these issues, which in turn define the limits of his thinking about the mother.

Before his discovery of *Oedipus Rex* as a dramatic enactment of
his patients' desires, Freud entertained two models of neurosis: one
including neurasthenia and anxiety neurosis (called the "actual
neuroses"), which resulted from the inadequate release of sexual
tension, and the other, including hysteria, obsessional neurosis, and
paranoia (the neuroses of defense), which resulted from sexual
abuse in childhood recollected in later life. The latter became
known as the seduction theory.[2]

---

scious mental processes, a belief in which is necessary to psychoanalytic discourse.
Falsely constructing the argument, Masson forces himself—and his detractors—
into extreme positions. Masson, for instance, has stated that psychotherapy, as a
mode of dominance, is by its very nature abusive (*Against Therapy*). The debate
centering on Masson's controversial allegations has been shaped in part by Janet
Malcolm's journalistic accounts of his conflicts with the Freud establishment, first
published in two articles in the *New Yorker* and later issued under the title *In the
Freud Archives*. By focusing on Masson's personality to the detriment of his ideas,
Malcolm has unfortunately set the tone for much of the succeeding discussion of his
books. I personally don't believe that it is necessary to equate an interest in Freud's
seduction theory with the destruction of psychoanalysis, since "real" events will
always have symbolic resonance for the individual on both conscious and unconscious levels. At the same time, I think that it is naive to assume that Freud's
abandonment of the seduction hypothesis was completely impersonal in its motivation and had no deleterious effects on the future course of his thought.

2. The evolution of Freud's ideas concerning the various types of neurosis is
complicated and uneven—as might be expected under the circumstances. It doesn't
help that his terminology was also in flux during this period. I have introduced an
artificial order into this material as a means of clarifying the phallic emphasis of his
interpretation of the "actual" neuroses and the corresponding repudiation of femininity which attended his abandonment of the seduction theory. For a more thor-
ough discussion of Freud's ideas on anxiety neurosis and the neuroses of defense, see
Krüll (*Freud and His Father* 1–70) and Frank Sulloway (*Freud: Biologist of the Mind*
22–131). Sulloway argues for the importance of Freud's (generally neglected) neuro-
psychological treatise *Project for a Scientific Psychology* in the later development of
his ideas. He emphasizes the biologistic strain in Freud's thought, the legacy of his
nineteenth-century scientific background. William McGrath reads Freud's shifting
perspectives on hysteria as the outgrowth of his stance toward politics, in particular

Freud's assumptions regarding the etiology of the actual neuroses in both women and men revolve around the availability of unimpeded sexual intercourse and hence invoke a phallic perspective. The first cause of neurasthenia in males, for instance, is presumed to be masturbation, and its relief or cure a result of heterosexual activity.

> Neurasthenia in males is acquired at the age of puberty and becomes manifest when the man is in his twenties. Its source is masturbation, the frequency of which runs completely parallel with the frequency of male neurasthenia. One can observe in the circle of one's acquaintances that (at least in urban populations) those individuals who have been seduced by women at an early age have escaped neurasthenia.

The second cause of this type of neurosis is equally straightforward and functional. "This second noxa is *onanismus conjugalis*—incomplete intercourse in order to prevent conception." Even men not predisposed to the first cause of neurasthenia will, in time, fall ill from the second, Freud claims. A form of hysteria in women previously sound can also be traced to this source.

> The *mixed neurosis* of women is derived from neurasthenia in men in all those not-infrequent cases in which the man, being a sexual neurasthenic, suffers from impaired potency. The admixture of hysteria results directly from the *holding back* of the excitation of the act. The poorer the man's potency, the more the woman's hysteria predominates; so that essentially a sexually neurasthenic man makes his wife not so much neurasthenic as hysterical. [February 8, 1893; Masson, *Letters* 40–42]

Freud's perspective on the problem of neurasthenia is predominantly masculine. During the years in which he himself is actively siring children, he does not hesitate, for instance, to speak openly in the presence of a woman patient about "the harmfulness of coitus reservatus" (February 4, 1888; 18), even crediting himself for her subsequent pregnancy, which he believes may complete her cure.

---

toward the growing anti-Semitism in the Vienna of Mayor Karl Lueger (*Politics of Hysteria*). McGrath equates Freud's abandonment of the seduction theory with his adoption of a less rebellious attitude toward authority.

Given the undesirability of the alternatives to unrestricted inter-course (the consequences of which Freud himself felt in his rapidly increasing family), the outlook for reducing the incidence of this kind of neurosis thus seems bleak. In the absence of the discovery of an innocuous means of contraception, Freud concludes: "Society appears doomed to fall victim to incurable neuroses, which reduce the enjoyment of life to a minimum, destroy marital relations, and bring hereditary ruin on the whole coming generation" (February 8, 1893; 44).

Freud's hypothesis concerning parental seduction in the neuroses of defense (hysteria, obsessional neurosis, and paranoia) involves a more complex theory of causation based on the mechanisms of memory and repression.[3] It also mitigates the masculine bias of his interpretation of the "actual" neuroses. Although Freud continues to treat both male and female patients, the issue of father-daughter seduction encourages the analyst to adopt, provisionally at least, the daughter's point of view. More threateningly, the seduction theory, since it applies to both men and women, raises the question of maternal aggression. A number of factors act on Freud at this time, however, to divert his thinking from the subjects of female sexuality, femininity, and maternal desire and toward the myth of Oedipus. These factors reveal themselves through the portrait Freud paints of his friendship with Wilhelm Fliess.

Freud's relationship with Fliess, the Berlin ear, nose, and throat specialist to whom he confided his thoughts on paper and whom he met at designated intervals for intimate exchanges of ideas, provides a dramatic focus for the letters. The evolution of psycho-

---

3. In his footnotes to his translation of Charcot's *Tuesday Lectures* Freud explains the function of memory in a hysterical attack: "The core of a hysterical attack, in whatever form it may appear, is a *memory*, the hallucinatory reliving of a scene which is significant for the onset of the illness. It is this event which manifests itself in a perceptible manner in the phase of '*attitudes passionelles*'; but it is also present when the attack appears to consist only of motor phenomena. The *content of the memory* is as a rule either a psychical *trauma* which is qualified by its intensity to provoke the outbreak of hysteria in the patient or is an event which, owing to its occurrence at a particular moment, has become a trauma" (*SE* 1:137). In "The Aetiology of Hysteria," published a few years later, Freud refines this concept of memory formation by referring to the "mnemic symbols" deposited in the patient's psyche as a result of the original traumatic situation (*SE* 3:193). Here he defines the nature of the trauma, moreover, as "sexual experiences in childhood consisting in stimulation of the genitals, coitus-like acts, and so on" (206).

analysis is so deeply enmeshed in the development and decline of this friendship, moreover, that one cannot readily distinguish the political from the personal. This entanglement becomes critical in the circumstances surrounding Fliess's operation on Freud's patient Emma Eckstein, in which Freud's loyalties, engaged on all sides and complicated by his own medical anxieties, are called into question. Freud's choices during this period not only reflect his predisposition in favor of phallic explanations but also reveal the source of his anxiety about "feminine" identification as fear of castration.

Freud's correspondence with Fliess involves a regular report on his health, including references to frequent headaches, bouts of fatigue and depression, a plethora of cardiac symptoms, and an occasional episode of impotence.[4] Fliess's own theory regarding the nasal origin of sexual disturbances leads Freud to lay special emphasis on the condition of his nose. He responds, in addition, to Fliess's recommendation that he discontinue smoking by reporting his periods of "abstinence" from nicotine as well as his lapses. For a lengthy period of time, Freud also conspires with Fliess to determine his vulnerable "periods" by a series of calculations applied to the female menstrual cycle. Freud even alludes occasionally to Martha's periods and her general state of reproductive health, without, however, extending his confidence to her regarding his own "death deliria" (April 19, 1894; 68).

Freud's entertainment of Fliess's medical theories, however bizarre, supports his disposition to consider his problems organic in nature. In a letter in which Freud describes his own work on hysteria, he also writes: "I really have the impression that the whole

4. Max Schur, Freud's personal physician during the cancer years, disagrees with Jones's estimation that Freud's symptoms were primarily psychoneurotic (see Jones, *Life* 1:311). He thinks it is possible that Freud suffered from an organic heart ailment, "specifically a coronary thrombosis in a small artery" (*Freud Living and Dying* 61). E. M. Thornton, on the other hand, attributes Freud's nasal and cardiac symptoms to his heavy use of cocaine at this time (*Freudian Fallacy* 151–93). Her obvious animus against psychoanalysis as manifested in her claim that Freud's theories were produced by his cocaine addiction, however, tends to detract from her argument. Since Freud's use of cocaine to treat the swellings in his nose was obviously bound up with his relationship with Fliess and his nasal theories, I do not see any absolute contradiction between Thornton's hypothesis and that of Jones. It seems less likely to me on the whole that Freud might have suffered a cardiac episode such as the one that Schur describes. Thornton, moreover, lists tachycardia as one of the common symptoms of cocaine abuse.

business is organic and cardiac; something neurotic would be much harder to take" (December 11, 1893; 63). On another occasion Freud's anxiety about an attack of "severe cardiac misery" leads him almost to plead with Fliess for a diagnosis.

It is too distressing for a medical man who spends every hour of the day struggling to gain an understanding of the neuroses not to know whether he is suffering from a logical or a hypochondriacal mild depression. He has to be helped with this. . . . This time I am especially suspicious of you, because this heart affair of mine is the only one in which I have heard you make contradictory statements. Last time you still explained it as being nasal and said that the percussive signs of a nicotine heart were missing; this time you really show great concern for me and forbid me to smoke. I can understand this only if I assume that you want to conceal the true state of affairs from me, and beg you not to do this. If you can say something definite, just tell me. [April 19, 1894; 67–68]

Freud's cardiac symptoms, including "violent arrhythmia," "constant tension," and "dyspnea" (ibid. 67), are suspiciously similar to ones he describes in his male patients, and suggest (to adapt his phrase) an affair of the heart. Such symptoms, as both Shirley Nelson Garner and Wayne Koestenbaum have argued, in combination with Freud's feelings of strain and depression, his obsessive concern with the condition of his nasal cavities, and his eagerly awaited "congresses" with his friend, all point to a complex and unacknowledged homoerotic attachment to Fliess.[5] In Garner's

5. Later Freud was to identify his former attachment to Fliess as homosexual, although he characterized it, in a letter to Ferenczi, as a tendency he had overcome: "You not only noticed, but also understood, that I *no longer* have any need to uncover my personality completely, and you correctly traced this back to the traumatic reason for it. Since Fliess's case, with the overcoming of which you recently saw me occupied, that need has been extinguished. A part of homosexual cathexis has been withdrawn and made use of to enlarge my own ego. I have succeeded where the paranoiac fails" (quoted in Jones, *Life* 2:83). A few years later, however, Freud evoked Fliess's memory once again, this time as a way of explaining his faint in front of Jung in Munich. Writing to Jones about the incident, he claims that in both cases there was "some piece of unruly homosexual feeling at the root of the matter" (1:317). Shirley Nelson Garner, in "Freud and Fliess: Homophobia and Seduction," interprets Freud's attraction to Fliess as simultaneously homoerotic and homophobic, a position with which I agree. Wayne Koestenbaum, who sees Freud's collaboration with Fliess as designed to celebrate the creativity of men over that of women,

simple and eloquent phrase, Freud's letters to Fliess are "love letters" ("Freud and Fliess"). In this kind of highly charged emotional atmosphere Freud appeals to his friend for medical advice, even if the dread diagnosis concerns the imminence of his own death.

The context in which Emma Eckstein's crisis (as a result of Fliess's operation on her nose) occurs is thus richly overdetermined. It is further complicated by the fact that Freud subjects himself to nasal surgery at the hands of the same physician. Such a similarity of circumstance might well have led Freud to imagine himself in Eckstein's position, if not to identify with her sufferings.[6] Freud's letters to Fliess during this period are in fact replete with the details of his own nasal problems, beginning with his report on the improvement of his condition following his own operation.

> Last time I wrote you, after a good period which immediately succeeded the reaction, that a few viciously bad days had followed during which a cocainization of the left nostril had helped me to an amazing extent. I now continue my report. The next day I kept the nose under cocaine, which one should not really do; that is, I repeatedly painted it to prevent the renewed occurrence of swelling; during this time I discharged what in my experience is a copious amount of thick pus; and since then I have felt wonderful, as though there never had been anything wrong at all. . . . I am postponing the full expression of my gratitude and the discussion of what share the operation had in this unprecedented improvement until we see what happens next. [January 24, 1895; 106]

---

hence privileging the anus (as the organ of intercourse between men) over the uterus, also documents Freud's conflicts regarding his intimacy with Fliess, and thus his homophobia ("Privileging the Anus"). Freud's theoretical stance in respect to homosexuality, I would add, reflects the duality of his response to Fliess; he vacillates between expressions of acceptance and repugnance.

6. Wayne Koestenbaum also makes this point. Though Koestenbaum and I have developed our arguments independently, there are interesting points of overlap. We both, for instance, note the similarity of Freud's position to Emma's, given that each submitted to an operation on the nose at the hands of Fliess. Koestenbaum argues, moreover, that the effect of Freud's collaboration first with Breuer and then with Fliess was to emphasize male creativity at the expense of women's reproductive power, hence to repress the figure of the mother. In other respects, our emphases differ. Whereas Koestenbaum interprets Freud's reaction to the scene of Eckstein's bleeding in terms of his anxiety about anal penetration, I stress the element of castration fear. Although these two positions are not entirely incompatible, they suggest different lines of development.

In a letter that predates Eckstein's bleeding episode Freud reports on nasal discharges experienced by them both. On March 4, 1895, Freud describes Eckstein's condition as "still unsatisfactory": "The purulent secretion has been decreasing since yesterday; the day before yesterday (Saturday) she had a massive hemorrhage, probably as a result of expelling a bone chip the size of a heller; there were two bowls full of pus" (113). In the same mailing, on a separate enclosure, Freud refers to his own continuing difficulties: "On the last day you were here, I suddenly discharged several scabs from the right side, the one not operated on. As early as the next day there appeared thick, old pus in large clots, at first on the right side only and soon thereafter also on the left. Since then the nose has again been flooded; only today has the purulent secretion become somewhat less dense" (115–16). Freud's faith in Fliess at this point, however, remains unshaken. He attributes the persistence of his heart symptoms to a "focal pus accumulation" that produces "eruptions like a private Etna," concluding, in accordance with Fliess's theory, that "the condition of the heart depends upon the condition of the nose" (March 4, 1895; 116).[7]

Eckstein's near-fatal hemorrhage, witnessed by Freud, brings him to a moment of horrified recognition that challenges the structure of his relationship with patient and doctor both. The central drama unfolds as follows:

7. Given Freud's preoccupation during this period with the sexual etiology of the neuroses, his concern that his own complaints might be neurotic in origin and his later speculations in the Dora case history about the displacement of sexual wishes upward (not to mention Fliess's views about the connection between the genitals and the nose), it is surprising that he never seems to have examined the symbolic overtones of his nasal obsession. That he should entrust his nose to his friend's surgical interventions speaks to a level of intimacy that Freud expressed consciously: "I do not share your contempt for friendship between men, probably because I am to a high degree party to it. In my life, as you know, woman has never replaced the comrade, the friend" (August 7, 1901; Masson, *Letters* 447). Freud's horror, then, at the mess Fliess made of Eckstein's nose may well have represented his anxiety about the fate of his own most sensitive organ. For a particularly witty discussion of Freud's failure to make the obvious symbolic connection between the penis and the nose, see Garner's "Freud and Fliess." Koestenbaum also makes the nose/genital equation, although he sees the nose as anus rather than penis. Perhaps the nose, a protuberance that permits entry, signifies or calls up fantasies related to more than one organ. If so, Freud may have been most horrified by the confusion of sexual difference that the violation of the nose implies.

29

There still was moderate bleeding from the nose and mouth; the fetid odor was very bad. Rosanes cleaned the area surrounding the opening, removed some sticky blood clots, and suddenly pulled at something like a thread, kept on pulling. Before either of us had time to think, at least half a meter of gauze had been removed from the cavity. The next moment came a flood of blood. The patient turned white, her eyes bulged, and she had no pulse. Immediately thereafter, however, he again packed the cavity with fresh iodoform gauze and the hemorrhage stopped. It lasted about half a minute, but this was enough to make the poor creature, whom by then we had lying flat, unrecognizable. [March 8, 1895; 116–17]

Freud follows this harrowing description with a statement of sudden revelation, the nature of which he does not immediately disclose. "At the moment the foreign body came out and everything became clear to me—and I immediately afterward was confronted by the sight of the patient—I felt sick" (117). This scene has all the shock value that Freud later attributed to confrontations that unveil the fact of sexual difference. In his essay "Some Psychical Consequences of the Anatomical Distinction between the Sexes," for instance, Freud describes the "storm of emotion" and "horror of the mutilated creature" aroused in a male child whose sight of a little girl's genitals causes him to believe in the reality of castration (*SE* 19:252). Such a moment of frozen recognition also characterizes the reaction to Medusa, who "displays the terrifying genitals of the Mother" (*SE* 18:274). These later constructions suggest that what Freud "saw" in the examining room, causing him to flee in distress, affected him in ways that extend beyond a question of medical practice. It is as if he felt he had witnessed Eckstein's castration.

Masson's hypothesis that Freud's abandonment of the seduction theory was intimately bound up with his need to dissociate himself from culpability in Eckstein's drama of suffering is, I believe, correct (*Assault on Truth* 134).[8] The letters reveal an increasing distance on Freud's part from the open admission of wrongdoing in his first letter concerning Eckstein to Fliess: "So we had done her an

---

8. Marianne Krüll comes close to making the same point in her analysis of Freud's abandonment of the seduction theory (21–24). Her book *Freud and His Father*, first published in German, is far less sensational in tone than Masson's and has received, correspondingly, less critical attention.

injustice; she was not at all abnormal" (March 8, 1895; 117). What Masson does not discuss, however, are some of the less obvious motivating factors in Freud's crucial choice of alliance with Fliess in his gradual reconstruction of Eckstein's illness as one in which she is the agent of her own pathology: "She has always been a bleeder" (March 4, 1896; 186).

A clear contributing element in Freud's exoneration of Fliess is his need to believe in the validity of Fliess's theories concerning the possibility of a nasal cure for his own heart symptoms. "With regard to my own ailment, I would like you to continue to be right—that the nose may have a large share in it and the heart a small one," Freud states, assuring Fliess at the same time of his loyalty to him as a doctor: "For me you remain the physician, the type of man into whose hands one confidently puts one's life and that of one's family" (April 20, 1895; 125). Freud's belief in the treatment of his nose protects him, to some extent, from his anxieties about an early death from heart failure, not to mention a recognition of his own neurotic condition. An even more dangerous line of association proceeding from an assumption of Fliess's fallibility, however, leads to an identification with Eckstein. Both she and Freud, after all, submitted to surgical intervention at the hands of Fliess. It is hard to imagine how Freud could have avoided a comparison between these two events and the possibility of a shared fate. The dramatic scene attended by Freud in which Eckstein nearly bled to death elicited in him a mirror response—"I felt sick." The real terror of this moment may consist not only in the castration fantasy hovering on the edges of Freud's description but also in the collapse of sexual difference which it implies. To be like Eckstein, a victim of Fliess's bungled operation, is not only analogous to being a victim of sexual violation; it is also to be a woman.[9] Given Freud's conventional understanding of sex roles, as evidenced, for instance, by his

9. Koestenbaum describes the fantasy content of Freud's identification with Eckstein: "Blood results from male medical force: such blood would flow from Freud if Fliess fully influenced him, if their congress took place not merely in Freud's 'lubricated temporal lobe' but in his anus. Male menstruation, in this context, seems a figure for the distressing anal bleeding that would have been the likely consequence of their intercourse—if we postulate the existence of a symbolic anal hymen, broken upon first penetration" (74–75). In my reading of this incident, the blood signifies primarily castration.

correspondence with Martha during their engagement, it is hardly surprising that he was not able to sustain an imaginative identification of this kind.[10]

Freud's subsequent letters to Fliess, despite occasional notes of reproach, unfold a process in which he reaffirms his faith in Fliess's theories of nasal etiology at the same time that he convinces himself of the origin of Eckstein's periodic hemorrhages in her sexual fantasies. To do otherwise would necessitate a quarrel with Fliess on professional grounds at the very least. More significant, an acknowledgment of his likeness with Eckstein would lead Freud toward a more open consideration of his own homosexual desires as well as a less terrified examination of the position he regards as feminine. Instead, he chooses a construction of Eckstein's illness in which he plays the part of her imagined lover. As the presumed

10. Freud makes clear to Martha what he expects of her in a letter in which he expresses his opinion of John Stuart Mill's essay on the subordination of women: "I remember that a main argument in the pamphlet I translated was that the married woman can earn as much as the husband. I dare say we agree that housekeeping and the care and education of children claim the whole person and practically rule out any profession; even if simplified conditions relieve the woman of housekeeping, dusting, cleaning, cooking, etc. All this he simply forgot, just as he omitted all relations connected with sex. This is altogether a topic on which one does not find Mill quite human. His autobiography is so prudish or so unearthy that one would never learn from it that humanity is divided between men and women, and that this difference is the most important one. . . . It seems a completely unrealistic notion to send women into the struggle for existence in the same way as men. Am I to think of my delicate, sweet girl as a competitor? After all, the encounter could only end by my telling her, as I did seventeen months ago, that I love her, and that I will make every effort to get her out of the competitive role into the quiet undisturbed activity of my home. It is possible that a different education could suppress all women's delicate qualities—which are so much in need of protection and yet so powerful— with the result that they could earn their living like men. It is also possible that in this case it would not be justifiable to deplore the disappearance of the most lovely thing the world has to offer us: our ideal of womanhood. But I believe that all reforming activity, legislation and education, will founder on the fact that long before the age at which a profession can be established in our society, nature will have appointed woman by her beauty, charm, and goodness, to do something else.

"No, in this respect I adhere to the old ways, to my longing for my Martha as she is, and she herself will not want it different; legislation and custom have to grant to women many rights kept from them, but the position of woman cannot be other than what it is: to be an adored sweetheart in youth, and a beloved wife in maturity" (July 5, 1885; E. Freud, *Letters* 75–76).

For an account of the domestic ideal articulated here and its relation to the transformation of the marketplace brought about by nineteenth-century industrialization, see Bram Dijkstra's *Idols of Perversity* (3–24).

object of Eckstein's conventionally heterosexual "longing," Freud can safely ignore the degree to which he has occupied her place in relation to Fliess.

> When she saw how affected I was by her first hemorrhage while she was in the hands of Rosanes, she experienced this as the realization of an old wish to be loved in her illness, and in spite of the danger during the succeeding hours she felt happy as never before. Then, in the sanatorium, she became restless during the night because of an unconscious wish to entice me to go there; since I did not come during the night, she renewed the bleedings, as an unfailing means of rearousing my affection. [May 4, 1896; 186]

Behind this convenient interpretive screen, Freud maintains his friendship with his male friend, while gradually detaching his sympathies from his female patient. This choice, which reflects his earlier bias in favor of a phallic solution to neurasthenic problems, has important consequences for the future development of his ideas.

"I do not believe it was the blood that overwhelmed me" (117),[11] Freud maintains in his letter to Fliess of March 8, 1895, yet it is precisely the matter of Eckstein's bleeding which requires explanation, and which, in the succeeding letters, undergoes a process of hermeneutic transformation until it appears to be self-generated. In this manner Freud effectively disengages himself from an identification with the suffering female body, a strategic gesture that simultaneously sets the parameters of his Oedipal theory. By absolving his friend Fliess of any wrongdoing in the treatment of Eckstein, Freud prepares the path for his subsequent exoneration of fathers (including himself and his own) of the charge of sexual violation of their children. In his abandonment of the seduction theory, as Masson points out, Freud leaves the structure of patriarchal authority intact (*Assault on Truth* 12). This decision has consequences of equal theoretical importance for his portrayal of the preoedipal mother.

By reconstructing Eckstein's bleeding episodes as hysterical ex-

---

11. Freud evidently had an aversion to the sight of blood, a factor that may have influenced his first choice of medical specialization; he only reluctantly abandoned neurological research for general practice and the treatment of nervous diseases.

pressions of longing, Freud also reinterprets his own role in relation to her in conventional heterosexual terms. His Oedipal theory, by focusing on the boy's phallic love for his mother, accomplishes something similar. Both scenarios, for Freud, involve a rejection of the "passive" position, which he will continue to regard as problematically "feminine." This early "repudiation of femininity" closes off certain lines of interpretation that might have led him to a deeper consideration of bisexuality and of female desire.[12] It is the instability of Freud's position as both doctor and patient which is the most interesting feature of his role in the emotional triangle involving Fliess, Eckstein, and himself. Yet the trauma of Eckstein's bleeding seems to have propelled him toward an identification with the position of agency, which in turn shaped his understanding of the Oedipal triangle.

Freud's theoretical breakthrough to the analogy with Oedipus refigures his problematic relationship with Fliess and Eckstein in a way that emphasizes the active and heroic nature of the boy's sensual love for his mother and jealous rivalry with his father.[13]

> I have found, in my own case too, [the phenomenon of] being in love with my mother and jealous of my father, and I now consider it a

12. In his late essay "Analysis Terminable and Interminable," Freud explains that femininity has an undesirable character (with different consequences) for both men and women. "The two corresponding themes are in the female, an *envy for the penis*—a positive striving to possess a male genital—and, in the male, a struggle against his passive or feminine attitude to another male" (*SE* 23:250). While Freud deplores both manifestations of the "repudiation of femininity," he clearly suffered from the latter himself, attempting to master rather than to explore his own homosexual inclinations. Justifying his lifelong emphasis on the superiority of masculine striving, which necessarily entails a conception of female deficiency, he concludes pessimistically: "We often have the impression that with the wish for a penis and the masculine protest we have penetrated through all the psychological strata and reached bedrock, and that thus our activities are at an end. This is probably true, since, for the psychical field, the biological field does in fact play the part of the underlying bedrock. The repudiation of femininity can be nothing else than a biological fact, a part of the great riddle of sex" (*SE* 23:252).

13. Elizabeth Abel in her *Virginia Woolf and the Fictions of Psychoanalysis* describes the process by which the Oedipus complex came to occupy a central place in Freud's thought. She points out, for instance, that Freud's *Three Essays on the Theory of Sexuality* do not revolve around the Oedipus complex, the full significance of which Freud only gradually came to recognize. In my reading of Freud's struggle with the place of the preoedipal mother, I have collapsed this development somewhat in order to highlight the problems inherent in Freud's first choice of the Oedipus story as an analogue of his own.

universal event in early childhood. . . . If this is so, we can understand the gripping power of *Oedipus Rex*, in spite of all the objections that reason raises against the presupposition of fate; and we can understand why the later "drama of fate" was bound to fail so miserably. . . . The Greek legend seizes upon a compulsion which everyone recognizes because he senses its existence within himself. Everyone in the audience was once a budding Oedipus in fantasy and each recoils in horror from the dream fulfillment here transplanted into reality, with the full quantity of repression which separates his infantile state from his present one.   [October 15, 1897; 272]

However terrible the crime contemplated against the father, the boy's fantasied aggression classes him with such heroes as Hamlet and Oedipus. Even the phase of renunciation brought into play by the castration complex appears as a secondary development, an overlay on a foundation of phallic assertion.

Freud's focus, in the Oedipus triangle, on the vicissitudes of male heterosexual desire effectively masks his earlier empathetic identification with Emma Eckstein. This strategic repositioning also facilitates a process of idealization of maternal love, which supplants a more dangerous train of association regarding the possibility of maternal seduction or aggression.

Not all of Freud's examples of parental seduction implicate fathers; some incidents of sexual abuse involve the woman typically employed in a middle-class household as a mother surrogate—the nurse.[14] Describing the progress of an obsessional patient, Freud

14. In "The Aetiology of Hysteria" Freud makes frequent reference to the sexual seduction of children by women charged with their care. "When I first made enquiries about what was known on the subject," he says, "I learnt from colleagues that there are several publications by paediatricians which stigmatize the frequency of sexual practices by nurses and nursery maids, carried out even on infants in arms; and in the last few weeks I have come across a discussion of 'Coitus in Childhood' by Dr. Stekel (1895) in Vienna" (SE 3:207). Later Freud includes governesses and tutors in the list of possible assailants and comments that even when the aggressor can be proven to be a boy, it is often the case that he "had previously been seduced by an adult of the female sex" so that "afterwards, under the pressure of his prematurely awakened libido and compelled by his memory, he tried to repeat with the little girl exactly the same practices that he had learned from the adult woman without making any modification of his own in the character of the sexual activity" (SE 3:208). Again, in the second of his *Three Essays on the Theory of Sexuality*, Freud notes that "it is well known that unscrupulous nurses put crying children to sleep by stroking their genitals" (SE 7:180n). Late in his career, Freud returns to this motif when he discusses the role of mothers in arousing their infant daughters through the

mentions, almost casually, that "this man traveled to his home-town in order to ascertain the reality of the things he remembered and that he received full confirmation from his seducer, who is still alive (his nurse, now an old woman)" (January 3, 1897; 219). On another occasion, Freud asks Fliess to search for a case history in which childhood abuse by means of "*lictus* [licking] (or finger) in the anus" plays a part. "For my newest finding," he claims, "is that I am able to trace back with certainty a patient's attack that merely resembled epilepsy to such treatment by the tongue on the part of his nurse" (January 12, 1897; 223–24). The most prominent among Freud's examples of seduction by a nurse, however, concerns his own.

In his letter of October 3, 1897, Freud states that this woman, and not his father, was the agent of his sexual awakening. "I can only indicate that the old man plays no active part in my case, but that no doubt I drew an inference by analogy from myself onto him; that in my case the 'prime originator' was an ugly, elderly, but clever woman, who told me a great deal about God Almighty and hell and who instilled in me a high opinion of my own capacities" (268). Freud's following letter to Fliess is at the same time less positive and more explicit about her influence. "She was my teacher in sexual matters," he explains, "and complained because I was clumsy and unable to do anything." Freud then analyzes a dream that deals with his feelings of failure as a therapist.

> (Neurotic impotence always comes about in this way. The fear of not being able to do anything at all in school thus obtains its sexual substratum.) At the same time I saw the skull of a small animal and in the dream I thought "pig," but in the analysis I associated it with your wish two years ago that I might find, as Goethe once did, a skull on the Lido to enlighten me. But I did not find it. So [I was] a "little block-head" [literally, a sheep's head]. The whole dream was full of the most mortifying allusions to my present impotence as a therapist. [October 4, 1897; 269]

---

exercise of routine nursery care (*SE* 21:238), yet he does not want to develop the implications of female aggression which hover around these descriptions. Estelle Roithe also makes this point (*Riddle of Freud* 68–70).

The subject of impotence elicits Freud's next association, which in turn recalls his reaction to the trauma of Eckstein's bleeding and the anxious nature of his alliance with her. "Moreover, she washed me in reddish water in which she had previously washed herself. (The interpretation is not difficult; I find nothing like this in the chain of my memories; so I regard it as a genuine ancient discovery)" (ibid.). The nurse as a figure who arouses and humiliates, who is capable of inducing impotence, also appears to be an agent of castration. To the boy Freud, who shares her reddish bath water, she may physically represent castration as well as threaten it.

If nurses are capable of such disturbing activity, so surely are mothers. Yet Freud's strategy of dissociating the "good" mother from the "bad," as Jim Swan points out in "*Mater* and Nannie," allows him to preserve an idealized image of maternity. In this way, Freud can "forget" the mother's power of castration. His abandonment of the seduction theory (which applies to both men and women as agents of sexual abuse) subjects this awareness to an even deeper level of repression.

In summary, Freud's reactions to Eckstein's bleeding appear as a series of shock waves that set the course of his future theorizing. First he absolves Fliess of culpability by interpreting Eckstein's bleeding as hysterically motivated, while affirming his renewed faith in Fliess's medical diagnoses in regard to his own symptoms. The latent contradiction in this position gives rise, in turn, to a thesis concerning infantile eroticism, which has the double advantage of emphasizing the boy's active desire for his mother and further absolving adult male figures of blame. Maternal aggression, named but not explored in the concept of parental seduction, ceases to have meaning in the new Oedipal theory and slips to the margins of consideration. Eckstein's bleeding, deprived of its traumatic effect, is later reintegrated into the Oedipal paradigm through the concept of female castration, from which its author can safely dissociate himself by virtue of his aggressive masculinity. In the process of reconstructing his relationships with Eckstein and Fliess, Freud finally detaches himself from Fliess, whose ideas he can no longer accept. The remains of his friendship survive in the theory of the castration complex, according to which the young boy, under pressure from an authoritative male figure, must, for a time, suppress his own striving and adopt an attitude of waiting. The net result of this intense mental labor is that Freud disengages himself from the most threatening implications of femininity (suggested by Eckstein's violation) in women and in men. Because of its strategic function in this regard, Freud's focus on Oedipal masculinity effectively obscures his vision of the preoedipal mother. Her presence, for precisely this reason, will haunt his texts.

3

Displacements and Denials

Just as his colleague Josef Breuer fled the scene of simulated childbirth staged by his patient Bertha Pappenheim, Freud took flight from the spectacle of Emma Eckstein's bleeding.[1] Whereas Breuer gave up his psychological researches into hysteria, however, Freud constructed a scaffolding of theory that defended him from the ills it purported to explain. This complex compromise formation produced in turn its own symptoms of unease, which appear in the guise of Freud's inability to account for the role of the preoedipal mother. Her functions are, in Freud's texts, margin-

---

1. We owe this account of the conclusion of Anna O.'s treatment to Freud, who wrote to Stefan Zweig in 1932 that "what really happened with Breuer's patient I was able to guess later on, long after the break in our relations, when I suddenly remembered something Breuer had once told me in another context before we had begun to collaborate and which he never repeated. On the evening of the day when all her symptoms had been disposed of, he was summoned to the patient again, found her confused and writhing in abdominal cramps. Asked what was wrong with her, she replied: 'Now Dr. B.'s child is coming!'" It is curious, given Freud's own avoidance in his writing of the figure of the mother, that he then adds: "At this moment he held in his hand the key that would have opened the 'doors to the Mothers' [an allusion to Goethe's *Faust*], but he let it drop With all his great intellectual gifts there was nothing Faustian in his nature. Seized by conventional horror he took flight and abandoned the patient to a colleague" (June 30, 1932; E. Freud, *Letters* 413). Wayne Koestenbaum argues that this story has the status of a "secret that Breuer passed to Freud and that Freud passed to his disciples," serving as a form of homoerotic bonding among men ("Privileging the Anus" 64).

alized, divided, suppressed, or transcended, yet always problematic and thus in need of continuous reformulation. As an object of both fascination and dread, she is the specter that drives him forth and that compels his return. Late in his career, she will begin to evoke thoughts of death.

Freud's emphasis on the boy's guilty love for his mother causes him, in the early case histories, to neglect consideration of the mother-daughter relation, as well as the power of the preoedipal mother herself. Thus in the treatment of his female patient Dora, he insists on a heterosexual interpretation of her desire, at the same time that he admits the inadequacy of this paradigm to account for her homoerotic love for Frau K. While Freud goes to great lengths to establish Dora's sexual fantasies regarding her father, Herr K., and finally even himself, he has relatively little to say about Dora's intimacy with her woman friend, whose "adorable white body" she praises. His dismissal of Dora's mother as a significant player in this complex network of relations, together with his consignment of speculations concerning Dora's "gynecophilic love" to asides and footnotes, sets up crosscurrents in his argument which disrupt its flow. Ultimately, his own narrative displays the symptoms he attributes to the hysteric, whose pathology, he claims, manifests itself in the inability to construct a coherent story.

Freud's case histories of male subjects exhibit similar problems. In his accounts of Little Hans, the Rat Man, Dr. Shreber, and the Wolf Man, Freud either ignores or actively suppresses evidence that points to maternal signification, while insisting on the exclusively paternal etiology of his patients' illnesses. Such a strategy of enforcing Oedipus, however, creates a degree of hermeneutic instability that Freud associates in his Dora case history with hysteria. His study of Leonardo and his three essays on the psychology of love, which attend more closely to the figure of the mother, idealize her relationship to her male offspring in an attempt to dissociate her from the more disturbing implications of her self-sufficiency and power. The dark side of such idealization is debasement, a split that Freud found sanctioned by his culture in the division between the mother and the whore. Ultimately Freud will institutionalize this split, along with its suppression of the mother's authority, through his account of civilization as an outgrowth of the Oedipus complex.

Dora (1905)

The figure of the nursemaid, as revealed in Freud's choice of a name and a sexual fantasy (fellatio) for Dora, is central to this case history. Her position as servant, surrogate mother, and sexual object in the Victorian household makes her a convenient focus for desire and exploitation at the same time that she evokes fantasies of maternal power.[2] The conflict between these two levels of association in the Dora case history finds textual expression in Freud's attempt to enforce an Oedipal interpretation on Dora's desire, which serves the function of reasserting conventional sex roles and subordinating the figure of the nurse along with her implicit (pre-oedipal) challenge to paternal authority. Freud himself reveals the genesis of the pseudonym Dora.

> Who else was there called Dora? I should have liked to dismiss with incredulity the next thought to occur to me—that it was the name of my sister's nursemaid; . . . I had seen a letter on my sister's dining-room table addressed to 'Fräulein Rosa W.' I asked in surprise who there was of that name, and was told that the girl I knew as Dora was really called Rosa, but had had to give up her real name when she took up employment in the house, since my sister could take the name 'Rosa' as applying to herself as well. "Poor people," I remarked in pity, "they cannot even keep their own names! . . . When next day I was looking for a name for someone *who could not keep her own,* "Dora" was the only one to occur to me. [*SE* 6:241]

To this piece of intimate information Steven Marcus adds the association with David Copperfield's invalid child-wife, Dora ("Freud

2. Many critics have commented on the position of the nursemaid in the Victorian family structure. See, for instance, Leonore Davidoff ("Class and Gender in Victorian England"), Sander Gilman ("Male Stereotypes of Female Sexuality in Fin-de-Siècle Vienna"), Theresa McBride ("As the Twig Is Bent"), and Maria Ramas ("Freud's Dora, Dora's Hysteria"). Jim Swan's essay "*Mater* and Nannie," which explores the origin in Freud's own infancy of the image of the woman split into the idealized mother and the debased object of desire, is once again indispensable to my discussion. Kenneth Griggs ("All Roads Lead to Rome") demonstrates the ways in which the figure of Freud's nursemaid and his mother are conflated in some of his dreams, while Jane Gallop in *The Daughter's Seduction* (132–50) points out that class difference (as well as sexual difference) prevents Freud from consciously identifying with the figure of the governess.

and Dora" 309). Both lines of association are relevant inasmuch as nearly everyone in Dora's family circle occupies the role of nurse or invalid, and sometimes both.

Notable among the ill are Dora's father, who suffers from tuberculosis, syphilis, a detached retina, partial paralysis, confusional mental states, and a nervous cough; Frau K., the victim of some form of paralysis, which renders her unable to walk; Dora's mother, afflicted with a vaginal discharge, presumably gonorrhea contracted from her husband; Dora's aunt, dying from a wasting disease; her uncle, a "hypochondriacal bachelor"; and Dora herself, prey to shortness of breath, coughing, loss of voice, an apparent attack of appendicitis, catarrh, and a vaginal discharge of undetermined origin. In this atmosphere of real and imagined illness, Dora's mother, about whom we know very little, accepts expensive presents of jewelry from her husband, ignores the relationship between her husband and Frau K. as well as the attentions paid by Herr K. to her daughter, locks doors, and otherwise spends her time in obsessive housecleaning.[3] It is significant that she refuses the role of nurse; that role falls first to Dora, whose attachment to her father is based in part on her attentions to him during his various ailments. The extent to which the role of nurse involves service, or more specifically caretaking, links it with that of nursemaid or governess, both positions of subordination and exploitation in this story. While Dora's governess betrays the affection of her charge in her pursuit of the elusive love of Dora's father, the K.s' governess suffers a worse fate, being first seduced and then abandoned by Herr K. It is no

---

3. Arnold Rogow provides some interesting historical information about the Bauer household, including some details of Kathe Bauer's concern for cleanliness ("A Further Footnote to Freud's 'Fragment of an Analysis of a Case of Hysteria'"). The most extensive treatment of the Bauer family that I have encountered, however, is provided by Maria Ramas. Iza Erlich discusses the difference between Freud's vivid treatment of the men in this case history and that of Dora's mother, whom he summarily dismisses. She concludes that "be it Dora's madly cleaning mother, Little Hans's beautiful, seductive mother, or the Rat Man's absentee mother, they all appear as silhouettes against the rich background of other relationships, other entanglements" ("What Happened to Jocasta?" 284). Freud's subordination of Dora's mother may be related to his sketchy treatment of the homosexual element in Dora's affectional life, an element that embraces not only her avowed love for Frau K. but also her apparently conflicted feelings for her mother. Among critics who touch on this subject are Karl Kay Lewis ("Dora Revisited"), Toril Moi ("Representation of Patriarchy"), Philip Rieff (*Dora*), and Maria Ramas.

accident that Freud associates the position of Ida Bauer in her family with that of his sister's nursemaid, a role that confers seeming maternal power firmly fixed within the context of patriarchal control.

Frau K., moreover, repeats Dora's pattern of nursing her father, displacing her in the process. From occupying the privileged position of nurse in relation to her father, Dora is abruptly shifted to that of nursemaid or governess, disappointed in her love for the master. Frau K., in the meantime, trades the role of invalid for that of nurse, and in doing so reveals the extent to which both giving and receiving attention are predicated on illness. Dora's option for the role of invalid might be seen in this light as both a desperate bid for affection and a means of avoiding, temporarily at least, the nurse/governess role, associated in both households with betrayal. Dora's situation is complicated by her role as nursemaid of the K.s' children and her intimacy with Frau K., based on the exclusion of Herr K., until her father's affair with Frau K. shatters those relationships. Deprived of the role (involving for her maternal rather than sexual ministrations) on which she had counted to elicit the affections and attentions of members of both families, Dora, now excluded by her father and Frau K., is offered only one position, that of Herr K.'s mistress—a role that renders her powerless and vulnerable to further rejection. Freud's choice of a name for Dora seems to fix her in her dilemma.

Complicating this situation is Freud's other significant act of naming in regard to Dora, his assertion that she fantasizes fellatio.[4] If there is a "primal scene" in this narrative, it is not the classic one

---

4. Freud's assumption that Dora fantasizes fellatio as the preferred form of sexual activity between her father and Frau K. seems particularly odd, given his conviction that Dora's father is impotent. It would make as much sense for a woman under these circumstances to desire (or to fantasize) cunnilingus. Neil Hertz ("Dora's Secrets, Freud's Techniques") and Sharon Willis ("A Symptomatic Narrative") both comment on the peculiarity of Freud's choice of the fellatio fantasy. Willis relates Freud's "blindness" in this instance to the phallocentrism of his discourse. It is interesting, moreover, that Freud attributes Dora's knowledge of fellatio to her reading of Paolo Mantegazza's *Physiology of Love*, a book that does not deal with specific sexual practices. *The Physiology of Love* (published in 1877), one of three books by Mantegazza dealing with human sexuality, is largely a romantic and sentimental paean to human reproduction. If, on the other hand, Dora had read Mantegazza's more explicit *Sexual Relations of Mankind*, she would have discovered a full sexual vocabulary, including references to lesbian lovemaking.

in which the child imagines a sadistic father inflicting pain on the mother. The scene of seduction focuses rather on Dora's father and Frau K. engaged in a sexual act that Freud himself imagines, names, and then at length defends.[5] Dora herself, he then argues, fantasizes fellatio with her impotent father (*SE* 7:48). This fantasy is remarkable not only for its incestuous character but also in the way it reproduces the structure of the nurse-invalid relationship. Dora's father, by occupying the role of invalid, a curiously passive stance in relation to Freud's orthodox notions of male heterosexuality, compels his partner into the role of nurse, so that the act of fellatio appears as one more ministration to his need. At the same time, the figure of the nursemaid, ever present in this case history, recurs oddly in Freud's defense of his discussion of this "perversion" (*SE* 7:51). In a striking series of analogies, Freud relates fellatio regressively to thumb sucking and ultimately to breast-feeding. The passage culminates in the following observation:

> It then needs very little creative power to substitute the sexual object of the moment (the penis) for the original object (the nipple) or for the finger which does duty for it, and to place the current sexual object in the situation in which gratification was originally obtained. So we see that this excessively repulsive and perverted phantasy of sucking at a penis has the most innocent origin. It is a new version of what may be described as a prehistoric impression of sucking at the mother's or a nurse's breast—an impression which has usually been revived by contact with children who are being nursed. In most instances a cow's udder has aptly played the part of an image intermediate between a nipple and a penis. [*SE* 7:52]

5. Toril Moi states: "It is little wonder that he [Freud] feels the need to defend himself against the idea of fellatio, since it is more than probable that the fantasy exists, not in Dora's mind, but in his alone" (66). Freud's interest in persuading Dora that she fantasizes fellatio raises the issue of his (unacknowledged) countertransference. Many readers have pointed to areas of Freud's unconscious entanglement with Dora. The following commentators find varying degrees of sexual interest on the part of Freud toward his young and attractive patient and corresponding feelings of anger and pain at her noncooperation with the treatment and subsequent departure: Jerre Collins et al. ("Questioning the Unconscious"), Karl Kay Lewis, Janet Malcolm (*In the Freud Archives*), Stephen Marcus ("Freud and Dora"), Toril Moi, Hyman Muslin and Merton Gill ("Transference in the Dora Case"), Arnold Rogow, and Jacqueline Rose ("Dora—'Fragment of an Analysis'"). Whereas these readers stress Freud's implicit alliance with Herr K. in his libidinal involvement with Dora, other commentators suggest an identification with Dora herself—with her hysteria. See Suzanne Gearhart ("Scene of Psychoanalysis"), Neil Hertz, and Maria Ramas.

By the end of this passage there is no clear line of demarcation between the nurser and the nurse. In her sexual activity with Dora's father, Frau K. may be said to "nurse" him in two senses, both of which "feminize" her partner through identification with either the figure of the passive invalid or that of the nursemaid who breast-feeds her charge. The image of the cow's udder, in shape midway between the nipple and the penis, marks the ground of this indeterminacy.

Freud's choice of a name and of a fantasy for Dora lock her into an apparently subordinate relationship to the object of her love. The conjunction of love and illness in the scene of seduction, however, creates a paradoxical source of power in the figure of the nurse. The primary figure in this fantasy is female, just as the primary organ may be said to be the nipple rather than the penis. Against this image of fluid gender identity Freud constructs a more conventional scene of heterosexual seduction, which he then presses Dora to accept. Freud's "interpretation" of Dora's repressed love of Herr K. serves at least two functions. It permits the nurse-invalid structure of sexual relations to survive as a fantasy along with the surrender of an aggressive male role at the same time that it denies the power of the nurse by asserting the more culturally sanctioned role division in the structure of Herr K.'s relation to Dora. If the first structure may be described as preoedipal, focusing as it does on a maternal figure, the second is clearly Oedipal. The Oedipal overlay is the one with which Freud himself identifies, effectively preventing him from exploring the extent to which he also identifies with the figure of the nurse, or with the feminine position generally, which he associates with homosexuality.[6] The power of the nurse to disrupt Freud's Oedipal interpretation persists, however, through refusal, which Freud understands as rejection and ultimately as "revenge." The conflict between the two levels of fantasy in this case history repeats itself in the form of the narrative, appearing symptomatically as Freud's anxiety about filling gaps and completeness.

While Freud displays, from time to time, a skeptical attitude toward Dora's father, admitting to the validity of some of Dora's claims about his lack of straightforwardness, he is remarkably un-

6. Others have proposed different reasons for Freud's avoidance of the feminine position. See in particular Gallop, Hertz, and Collins et al.

critical of Herr K., whom he considers an attractive lover (*SE* 7:29).[7] In the two instances in which Herr K. forces his attentions on Dora, Freud clearly sympathizes with him, regarding her behavior rather than his as inappropriate. When Herr K. maneuvers Dora into a situation in which he can embrace her without fear of observation, Freud comments: "This was surely just the situation to call up a distinct feeling of sexual excitement in a girl of fourteen who had never before been approached." Freud interprets her failure to experience excitement as evidence of her hysteria (*SE* 7:28).[8] Later, referring to the scene by the lake in which Herr K. propositions Dora, Freud observes: "Her behaviour must have seemed as incomprehensible to the man after she had left him as to us, for he must long before have gathered from innumerable small signs that he was secure of the girl's affections" (*SE* 7:46). Freud sees both incidents through the eyes of Herr K., going as far as to provide Herr K. with an erection at the scene of the kiss. The origin of this fantasy, however justified, is clearly signaled in the following passage: "I have formed in my own mind the following reconstruction of the scene. I believe that during the man's passionate embrace she felt not merely his kiss upon her lips but also the pressure of his erect member against her body" (*SE* 7:29–30). On the basis of this fantasy, Freud concludes that Dora's feeling of disgust represents a

---

7. It is perhaps not surprising that Freud was predisposed in favor of Herr K., given the fact that it was Herr K. who introduced Dora's father to him for the treatment of syphilis.

8. Several critics have commented on the inappropriateness of Freud's expectation that Dora should have been aroused. Erik Erikson ("Reality and Actuality"), Mark Kanzer ("Motor Sphere of the Transference"), Steven Marcus, Toril Moi, and Philip Rieff all signal Freud's failure to take into account the full complexity of Dora's dilemma, including the fact of her adolescence. I find Marcus's statement describing Dora's situation in many ways the most poignant and acute: "The three adults to whom she was closest, whom she loved the most in the world, were apparently conspiring—separately, in tandem, or in concert—to deny Dora her reality and reality itself. This betrayal touched upon matters that might easily unhinge the mind of a young person; for all three adults were not betraying Dora's love and trust alone, they were betraying the structure of the actual world" ("Freud and Dora" 256). Maria Ramas calls the process by which Dora's version of events was either undermined or denied "gaslighting." If subsequent accounts of Dora's life are true (see, for example, Felix Deutsch, "A Footnote to Freud's 'Fragment of an Analysis of a Case of Hysteria'"), the "success" of Freud's treatment may be gauged by Dora's inability to throw off her neurosis or to accept the terms within which Freud offered cure.

displacement upward of a sensation on the lower part of her body. While we have no information about the reasons for Frau K.'s preference for Dora's father as a lover, it is interesting that Freud chooses a virile construction of Herr K.'s advances. Herr K. represents in this story "normal"—that is, aggressive—male heterosexuality. By representing Dora's refusal of Herr K.'s courtship as abnormal or "hysterical," Freud protects the Oedipal as opposed to the preoedipal fiction. By attempting to coerce Dora verbally into an acceptance of this structure, he further identifies with Herr K., masking his identification with Dora's father. Dora's perception that she is being handed from one man to another would seem to be accurate. The extent to which Freud occupies the role of father/seducer in this analysis appears at the end of a chain of his associations linking the idea of smoke with the longing for a kiss and Dora's thumb sucking to a desire for a kiss from him. "I came to the conclusion that the idea had probably occurred to her one day during a session that she would like to have a kiss from me" (*SE* 7:74).

Freud's interpretive strategies here bear a resemblance to those he employs with Emma Eckstein, for whom he constructs a conventional heterosexual drama in order to avoid the implications of his own potential "feminine" identification. Similarly, his interpretation of Dora's desire has the effect of repressing the image of her father as the passive, and hence implicitly feminized, partner in his affair with Frau K. Furthermore, if we examine Freud's line of argument as the product of *his* unconscious needs and wishes, applying his own interpretive rules to his narrative, we may see the extent to which he allies himself with Herr K. in his role as seducer. From this point of view, many of Freud's digressions and overstatements make sense as expressions not of his scientific neutrality but of his desire to punish Dora for her noncooperation. In this way, he continues to enforce his own Oedipal interpretation while dissociating the nurse/nursemaid/governess figure from the exercise of maternal power.

It is axiomatic for Freud, in his analysis of Dora's motives, that "there is no such thing at all as an unconscious 'No'" (*SE* 7:57). Denial, from this vantage point, may be interpreted as affirmation, so that " 'No' signifies the desired 'Yes' " (*SE* 7:59). Freud's rule for interpreting accusations, moreover, is to look for self-reproaches.

47

"A string of reproaches against other people leads one to suspect the existence of a string of self-reproaches with the same content. All that need be done is to turn back each particular reproach on to the speaker himself" (*SE* 7:35).

With these two principles in mind, one may interpret Freud's furious denial of the charge of titillating his patient with sexual language, coupled with his anxiety about being so reproached, as an indication that he is doing just that.[9] Freud's attempts to disarm such criticism tend, moreover, only to make matters worse. In anticipating the astonishment and horror of his readers at his attribution of the fantasy of fellatio to Dora, he first appeals to the analogy of the gynecologist. Claiming that it is possible for a man to speak to young women about sexual matters "without doing them harm and without bringing suspicion upon himself," he argues that "a gynaecologist, after all, under the same conditions, does not hesitate to make them submit to uncovering every possible part of their body," thus introducing new associations concerning nudity.[10] Next, in defense of the use of technical language to describe sexual matters, he falls into a syntactical slip whereby he seems to say that if a woman is ignorant of certain physiological processes, he instructs her concerning them. "I call bodily organs and processes by their technical names, and I tell these to the patient if they—the names, I mean—happen to be unknown to her." As if to compound this error, he concludes, appealing to the euphemistic idiom of another language: "J'appelle un chat un chat" (*SE* 7:48).[11] Continuing in this vein, and introducing another set of unwanted associations, he argues that "pour faire une omelette il faut casser des oeufs." If something is to be broken, it would seem to be Dora's innocence. "There is never any danger of corrupting an inexperienced girl," Freud affirms. "For where there is no knowledge of sexual processes even in the unconscious, no hysterical symptom will arise; and where hysteria is found there can no longer be any question of 'innocence of mind' in the sense in which parents and

---

9. Collins et al. also make this point.

10. Mary Daly has also noticed the intrusive and prurient implications of this statement (*Gyn/Ecology* 256).

11. "I call a cat a cat": "to make an omelet one must break eggs." Gallop presents a particularly witty discussion of this resort to euphemism in *Daughter's Seduction* (140).

educators use the phrase" (*SE* 7:49). Having metaphorically un-
dressed and violated Dora, Freud then declares her to be experienced already, a kind of Victorian Lolita, whose early pleasure in
thumb sucking is cited as evidence of her predisposition to the
fantasy of "sucking at the male organ" (*SE* 7:51).[12]

While Freud attributes Dora's unwillingness to continue therapy
with him to a desire for revenge, arguing on the basis of her identification with the rejected governess, he does not perceive the extent
to which he stands in the position of the spurned lover or the extent
to which he may share her feelings of betrayal and consequent
desire for retaliation.[13] At the same time, he feels the need to defend
himself from the reproach of betraying her by writing her history. "I
shall not escape blame by this means. Only, whereas before I was
accused of giving *no* information about my patients, now I shall be
accused of giving information about my patients which ought not
be given. I can only hope that in both cases the critics will be the
same, and that they will merely have shifted the pretext for their
reproaches" (*SE* 7:7). Reading this statement, once again, in the
context of Freud's interpretations of Dora's reproaches and denials,
one arrives at a self-reproach on Freud's part for wishing to expose
and humiliate his client. Such a desire—to pain Dora—appears at
the end of a statement assuring the reader of her anonymity. "I
naturally cannot prevent the patient herself from being pained if her
own case history should accidentally fall into her hands. But she
will learn nothing from it that she does not already know: and she
may ask herself who besides her could discover from it that she is
the subject of this paper" (*SE* 7:8–9). The callousness of this remark,
immediately supplemented by Freud's other invocation of the
rights of the gynecologist, suggests that he fully intends to bare
Dora's secrets and to reveal her intimacies in a manner that would

12. Gilman finds ample evidence in nineteenth-century Vienna of the stereotype
of female children as sexually precocious. He links this attitude to the prevalence of
adolescent prostitutes, the exploitation of lower-class women generally, and the
need of their male clients to blame the victim. He speculates that Freud's ideas
concerning the seductiveness of children may derive in part from prevailing stereotypes of female sexuality and in part from his own need to deny parental seduction of
female children. From this point of view one may well ask to what extent Freud
projects his own sexual desires onto Dora.

13. For Moi, Freud's revenge consists in part of his giving Ida Bauer the name of his
sister's servant.

hurt her. Anticipating a reproach concerning his frank discussion of sexual matters, he says: "Am I, then, to defend myself upon this score as well? I will simply claim for myself the rights of the gynaecologist—or rather, much more modest ones—and add that it would be the mark of a singular and perverse prurience to suppose that conversations of this kind are a good means of exciting or of gratifying sexual desires" (*SE* 7:9).

The interpretation of Dora's two dreams serves at least two functions, that of Oedipal camouflage for a preoedipal fantasy based on the figure of the nurse and that of revenge. It is the combination of these two elements that accounts, I believe, for the coercive quality of Freud's interpretations and for the uneasy tone of the narrative. In his relentless pursuit of a heterosexual interpretation of Dora's desire, Freud often substitutes his own train of associations for hers, a tactic that reveals the extent to which he idealizes the figure of Herr K. in order to blame Dora for her refusal. On an interpretive level, he subjects her to a process of defloration, impregnation, and parturition in an aggressively Oedipal fashion at the same time that he invalidates her rejection by naming it hysteria. Metaphorically, Freud seems to accomplish what he cannot in fact, neatly turning the tables on Dora by seducing and abandoning her, revealing in the process her "dirty secrets"—her habit of masturbation and her catarrh. Thus discredited and shamed, the nurse/nursemaid/governess is deprived of her power.

Given Freud's bias in favor of Herr K. as an unconventional though perfectly acceptable lover, he can interpret Dora's resistance as only "a morbid craving for revenge" and her ultimate rejection of her treatment as an "unmistakable act of vengeance." Revealing his own wounded feelings, however, he describes the effect of Dora's "breaking off so unexpectedly, just when my hopes of a successful termination of the treatment were at their highest," as "bringing those hopes to nothing" (*SE* 7:109). If Dora, in the one gesture permitted the figure with whom she has been identified (the governess), wishes to injure Freud, she seems to have been successful. "For how could the patient take a more effective revenge than by demonstrating upon her own person the helplessness and incapacity of the physician?" (*SE* 7:120).

Dora's flight leaves Freud to wrestle with the specters of self-doubt and impotence, an implicit identification not with the supposedly virile Herr K. but with the invalid father. Freud's attempted camouflage of this figure through his aggressively heterosexual interpretation of Dora's desire is unmasked by her noncooperation. In the face of this refusal, he can only insist repeatedly that she is in error. Freud's own text, however, undermines this strategy by calling attention to itself as fragmentary, incomplete, and thus according to his own terminology "hysterical." Issues concerning female sexuality, including the mother-daughter relationship and woman-to-woman desire, Freud banishes to the margins of his case history, but they refuse to stay in place. Instead they form a core of resistance to the smooth flow of the narrative, disrupting it from within.

Freud himself calls attention to his narrative difficulties when he points to patients' inability to produce a "smooth and precise" history as one of the symptoms of hysteria. "They can, indeed, give the physician plenty of coherent information about this or that period of their lives; but it is sure to be followed by another period as to which their communications run dry, leaving gaps unfilled, and riddles unanswered; and then again will come yet another period which will remain totally obscure and unilluminated by even a single piece of serviceable information" (*SE* 7:16). It is the goal of analysis to restore or to construct "an intelligible, consistent, and unbroken case history" (*SE* 7:18). From this point of view, Freud's "Fragment of an Analysis of a Case of Hysteria" appears to be structured around a central irony—the attempt to complete a story and to achieve a narrative closure rendered forever impossible by Dora's deliberate rupture. Freud's claim that the case would have been fully elucidated had Dora stayed only underscores its actual state of incompletion.

> The treatment was not carried through to its appointed end, but was broken off at the patient's own wish when it had reached a certain point. At that time some of the problems of the case had not even been attacked and others had only been imperfectly elucidated, whereas if the work had been continued, we should no doubt have obtained the fullest possible enlightenment upon every particular of the case. In the following pages, therefore, I can present only a fragment of an analysis. [*SE* 7:12]

Not only does Freud begin his case history with a statement about its "ungratifying conclusion" but he also finds occasion periodically to remind the reader of its deficiencies. "I should like to be able to add some definite information as to when and under what particular influence Dora gave up masturbating; but owing to the incompleteness of the analysis I have only fragmentary material to present" (*SE* 7:79). The gaps in Freud's own narrative cause him to resort to "guessing and filling in what the analysis offers him in the shape only of hints and allusions" (*SE* 7:42). Yet, he assures the reader, "it is only because the analysis was prematurely broken off that we have been obliged in Dora's case to resort to framing conjectures and filling in deficiencies. Whatever I have brought forward for filling up the gaps is based upon other cases which have been more thoroughly analysed" (*SE* 7:85). Freud's anxiety about filling gaps, coupled with his awareness of the impossibility of constructing a seamless case history, reveals the extent to which he participates in the phenomenon he describes as hysterical narrative. As if to emphasize his failure to achieve closure, he writes the last section as a "postscript," beginning it with yet another statement of inadequacy: "It is true that I have introduced this paper as a fragment of an analysis; but the reader will have discovered that it is incomplete to a far greater degree than its title might have led him to expect" (*SE* 7:112).

In a structural sense, Freud's insistence on the fragmentary nature of his narrative, and in particular on his inability to fill all the gaps, points to the failure of his interpretation. In his pursuit of a phallic construction of Dora's desire, urging her toward a heterosexual pact in which her gap will be filled and his case history brought to a suitable conclusion, Freud does not perceive the way in which phallic aggressiveness itself acts as a symptom, masking anxiety. His interpretive choices—fellatio over cunnilingus, the virility of Herr K. in contrast to the impotence of Dora's father, and an identification with the master rather than the nurse or governess—all point to the source of this anxiety as female identification.

Many critics, both feminist and nonfeminist, have found conspicuously wanting in this case history any consistent portrayal of Dora's dilemma from her point of view. Standing in the way of Freud's ability to identify with Dora (or with Emma Eckstein, for that matter) are two sets of associations: one that equates femininity with castration, so that a man who occupies a passive, submissive, or "feminine" position in a sexual relation is subject to the anxiety of castration, and another that equates female sexuality in its clitoral manifestations with the rejection of heterosexual intercourse.[14] Feminine identification for Freud seems to threaten loss of power for the male and a corresponding gain (through refusal) for the female. These two sets of associations appear symptomatically in Freud's references to bisexuality and homosexuality, which he mentions as asides, never integrating them with his main arguments concerning Dora.[15] The reference to bisexuality, the most threatening to Freud's concept of aggressive male heterosexuality, occurs at the end of a list of topics that he declines to develop: "But, once again, in the present paper I have not gone fully into all that might be said to-day about 'somatic compliance,' about the infantile genus of perversion, about the erotogenic zones, and about our predisposition towards bisexuality" (*SE* 7:113–14). When Freud refers to the possibly homosexual element in Dora's relationship with Frau K., he does so as an afterthought at the end of a chapter—making a significant association, moreover, between female homosexuality and masculinity: "These masculine or, more properly speaking, *gynaecophilic* currents of feeling are to be regarded as typical of the unconscious erotic life of hysterical girls" (*SE* 7:63). The most notable reference to female homosexuality appears in a footnote: "I failed to discover in time and to inform the patient that her homosexual (gynaecophilic) love for Frau K. was the strongest unconscious current in her mental life" (*SE* 7:120).

The allusions to both bisexuality and homosexuality, on the margins of the narrative, as it were, and hence only partially repressed, raise again the question of what is accomplished by Freud's shrill insistence on Dora's love for Herr K. The fantasy of vaginal

14. Freud's insistence that the clitoris is a masculine organ and that the little girl's pleasure in it is phallic creates an insuperable barrier to his understanding of female sexuality as anything but an obstacle to the achievement of heterosexual intercourse. He must at some level have understood that he was fighting a losing battle in trying to persuade his female patients to abandon this source of pleasure. Mantegazza, who seems on the whole less conflicted on this subject, nevertheless clearly assumes that a woman who has become accustomed to clitoral stimulation will require her lover to learn how to satisfy her in this way.

15. Alternate explanations of Freud's nervous treatment of bisexuality and homosexuality may be found in Collins et al., Gallop, and Willis.

penetration functions in two ways in this case history: it both allays and maintains the anxiety of castration, as it both permits and denies a fantasy of male passivity. It functions as a sign of virility and a means of filling a gap, of confronting and defeating the fear provoked by the sight of a woman's genitals, at the same time that it establishes a dominant-submissive relation in which a woman's "masculine" autoerotic power is denied. While Freud wishes to maintain the sexually indeterminate position of Dora's father in the fantasy of fellatio, he simultaneously wants to divorce it from associations with male homosexuality and to eliminate the power of the nurse. In order to do so, however, he must win Dora's assent. By withholding that gratification, Dora not only holds out for the possibility of another interpretation of femininity but also stands as a silent witness to the anxieties and repressions of Freud's narrative.

The preoedipal mother appears only obliquely in Freud's analysis of Dora through the figure of the nurse, while the mother-daughter relationship itself remains untheorized. Freud's attempt to comprehend the significance of Dora's relationship with Frau K. does not proceed very far and her mother is simply dismissed as an important figure in her life. Much later in his career, when he attempts to explore the preoedipal period in his efforts to elucidate the development of femininity, the baroque convolutions of Freud's narrative betray his teleological interest. The achievement of normal femininity depends on a girl's turning away from her original love for her mother, the suppression of her active libido, and the development of the passive desire to be loved by her father. As in his analysis of Dora, Freud conceives of the daughter's development in terms of her goal: a receptive heterosexual orientation in preparation for her reproductive role in marriage. The inadequacies of this account have been much commented on, yet they are equally apparent in Freud's analyses of his male patients, where his Oedipal assumption of the primacy of aggressive, heterosexual desire controls his interpretations of the child's early relation to its mother. What is correspondingly missing from these case histories is a convincing representation of maternal desire. Instead, Freud continues to portray the mother's role as marginal, fragmentary, or enigmatic, as though she hovered perpetually on the edge of his vision.

Little Hans (1909)

The mother of the precocious "Little Hans" in Freud's "Analysis of a Phobia in a Five-Year-Old Boy" is a case in point. Though central to Little Hans's sexual investigations and quandaries, she appears only fleetingly in Freud's narrative, which emphasizes instead the interpretive materials gathered by the boy's father, with whom Freud has an alliance based on friendship as well as professional interest. In his introductory remarks, Freud reveals the extent of his sympathetic identification with this man.[16]

> The case history is not, strictly speaking, derived from my own observation. . . . The treatment itself was carried out by the child's father, and it is to him that I owe my sincerest thanks for allowing me to publish his notes upon the case. But his services go further than this. No one else, in my opinion, could possibly have prevailed on the child to make any such avowals; the special knowledge by means of which he was able to interpret the remarks made by his five-year-old son was indispensable, and without it the technical difficulties in the way of conducting a psycho-analysis upon so young a child would have been insuperable. [*SE* 10:5]

The "special knowledge" refers to Freud's own theories, of which both parents, he claims, are adherents. In uniting the "authority of a father and of a physician," Little Hans's father acts on behalf of Freud himself, choosing relevant materials (all of which have to do with the boy's fascination with his "widdler" [*wiwimacher* in German][17] and his bewilderment about sexual difference), transcribing brief bits of conversation, and offering, on occasion, an interpretation. Little Hans himself comes to understand the complicity be-

16. Little Hans's father was Max Graf, an early member of Freud's Wednesday group. His mother had been a patient of Freud's and both parents were among the earliest adherents of psychoanalysis.

17. The word *wiwimacher* contributes to the confusion surrounding the question of sexual difference in the conversations between Little Hans and his parents. Whereas for Little Hans his *wiwimacher* is also his primary organ of sexual pleasure, for his mother and sister this is obviously not the case. When Little Hans's mother says that she too has a *wiwimacher*, she may be answering honestly on one level but misleading him on another. The clear implication is that she claims to possess a penis.

tween these two men. Realizing that there is a third party in his conversations with his father, he evades one of his father's interrogations with a shrewd question of his own: "If I write everything to the Professor, my nonsense'll soon be over, won't it?" (*SE* 10:61).

That Little Hans's phobia of horses should be found to derive from his Oedipus and castration complexes is hardly surprising, given the predisposition of both father and professor to this interpretation. On the single occasion when Freud counsels Little Hans directly, moreover, he does not hesitate to indoctrinate him concerning the appropriate responses to his state of conflict. "I then disclosed to him that he was afraid of his father, precisely because he was so fond of his mother. It must be, I told him, that he thought his father was angry with him on that account; but this was not so, his father was fond of him in spite of it, and he might admit everything to him without any fear." Freud then expands on this analysis by describing the inevitability of Little Hans's condition. "Long before he was in the world, I went on, I had known that a little Hans would come who would be so fond of his mother that he would be bound to feel afraid of his father because of it; and I had told his father this." This startling prophecy elicits from the child the awed response subsequently reported by his father: "Does the Professor talk to God . . . as he can tell all that beforehand?" (*SE* 10:42–43).

The alliance between Freud and Little Hans's father eventually draws Little Hans himself into its orbit, for the future that Freud predicts for him requires the boy to develop along lines of masculine identification. The role of Little Hans's mother in this process is problematic at best. At one point Freud refers to her part as "predestined" and her position as "a hard one" (*SE* 10:28), as though she were consigned to provide the backdrop for her son's struggles.[18] Yet her interventions, as they are reported, suggest another range of interpretive possibilities. If Freud fails to take her fully into account, it is because her participation in the story he weaves to make sense of Little Hans's symptoms does not entirely support his thesis.

18. Iza Erlich says that Little Hans's mother "is not an agent but part of a stage set. . . . Her role is preordained; there is nothing in it she can alter" (282–83). Coppélia Kahn repeats this point with emphasis in "Hand That Rocks the Cradle" (81).

Freud reveals toward the end of his analysis of Little Hans that he had treated the boy's mother for a neurotic ailment during her adolescence and that this acquaintance formed the basis for his involvement with the child's parents. The fact that she had been a patient of his presumably also accounts for the awareness of his theories which Freud attributes to her. At the same time, she behaves unpredictably, and in ways that seem subtly designed to question, if not to obstruct, the treatment process. In the first reported conversation between Little Hans and his mother, she answers his query about whether she has a "widdler too" with an unequivocal "Of course." Freud repeats this conversation as though there were nothing unusual about it, yet it seems hard to imagine that the boy's mother would not have understood her reply as misleading. Later, in response to Little Hans's efforts at masturbation, she threatens him overtly with castration. "If you do that, I shall send for Dr. A. to cut off your widdler. And then what'll you widdle with?" (*SE* 10:7–8). Little Hans's mother herself, it seems, is responsible for his assumptions regarding her power, both as the possessor of a "widdler like a horse" because of her size and as someone capable of depriving him of his own. In response to Little Hans's second attempt to ascertain whether or not she truly has a widdler, she answers once again in the affirmative: "Of course. Didn't you know that?" (*SE* 10:10).

The confusing information offered to Little Hans by his mother about the status of her genitals must later be clarified by his father, who thus sets up a conflict of allegiance for the boy. In direct contradiction to what his wife has said, he explains to Little Hans that "little girls and women . . . have no widdlers: Mummy has none, Anna has none, and so on" (*SE* 10:31). Little Hans, who at first appears to be elated by this piece of news, later refutes it: "I saw Mummy quite naked in her chemise, and she let me see her widdler" (*SE* 10:32). No one in this household, incidentally, seems to bother making a distinction between the urethra and the clitoris, so that Little Hans is led, quite reasonably, to inquire of his father: "But how do little girls widdle, if they have no widdlers?" The response to this question is clearly inadequate: "They don't have widdlers like yours. Haven't you noticed already, when Hanna was being given her bath?" (*SE* 10:31).

A conflict between Little Hans's mother and father surfaces in another significant area.[19] In his first correspondence with Freud concerning his son's phobia, Little Hans's father alludes unfavorably to his wife's demonstrations of affection toward the boy. "No doubt," he claims, "the ground was prepared by sexual overexcitation due to his mother's tenderness" (*SE* 10:22). It appears that Little Hans's mother has the habit of taking him into bed with her in the mornings and to soothe him when he is frightened or lonely. That the boy's father disappoves of this ritual is apparent in his description of it.

> The whole thing is a reproduction of a scene which has been gone through almost every morning for the last few days. Hans always comes in to us in the early morning, and my wife cannot resist taking him into bed with her for a few minutes. Thereupon I always begin to warn her not to take him into bed with her . . . and she answers now and then, rather irritated, no doubt, that it's all nonsense, that after all one minute is of no importance, and so on. [*SE* 10:39]

Freud concurs, to a certain extent, with Little Hans's father on the subject of these ministrations. "We must say a word, too, on behalf of Hans's excellent and devoted mother. His father accuses her, not without some show of justice, of being responsible for the outbreak of the child's neurosis, on account of her excessive display of affection for him and her too frequent readiness to take him into her bed" (*SE* 10:27–28). The struggle between Little Hans's parents regarding his sexual enlightenment and his affectional rituals is replayed on the level of interpretation, where the fathers finally succeed in convincing the boy of the "true" nature of his desires.

Yet in the background of Freud's Oedipal construction of Little Hans's desires, another portrait emerges in which the boy's relationship with his mother takes precedence over his affiliation with

---

19. In a postscript (1922) to his analysis of Little Hans, Freud describes a visit from his former patient, now grown to manhood. He maintains that the young man not only showed no traces of his childhood phobia (of which he actually retained no memory) but also had survived his parents' divorce and subsequent remarriages without undue emotional distress. With the benefit of hindsight, one is tempted to see the strain of submerged conflict between Little Hans's parents which runs through this case history as a prefiguration of the ultimate dissolution of their relationship.

his father. It is Little Hans's mother who most obviously exercises sexual power over him: arousing him through her physical care of his body, indulging him by taking him into her bed, feeding his fantasies about her own endowments through her claim to possess a "widdler," and finally prohibiting his masturbatory pleasures by threatening castration. Freud himself acknowledges, in a footnote, the active role of parents (read mothers) in the development of infantile eroticism. "It is one of the commonest things," he avers, "psycho-analyses are full of such incidents—for children's genitals to be caressed, not only in word but in deed, by fond relatives, including even parents themselves" (*SE* 10:23n). This note, which points back to a comment by Little Hans's Aunt M. while his mother was giving him a bath—"He *has* got a dear little thingummy" (*SE* 10:23)—refers specifically to fond female relations. Evidently sensitive to the erotic overtones in his aunt's observation, Little Hans repeats it coquettishly to his mother.

Little Hans's intense attachment to his mother, coupled with her own misleading responses to his questions, leads him to efface the fact of sexual difference. Watching his mother bathe his baby sister, for instance, he remarks, "She *has* got a tiny little widdler" (*SE* 10:14). He makes a similar comment on another occasion, laughing "because her widdler's so lovely" (*SE* 10:21). Freud makes the case that Little Hans's laughter indicates recognition (of female castration) rather than denial, but the evidence reported by his father suggests a persistent unwillingness on the part of the child to dissociate himself physically and sexually from his mother. He identifies specifically with her capacity to bear children.

Following a conversation about chickens laying eggs, Hans describes a fanciful scene in which he himself lays an egg: "At Gmunden I lay down in the grass—no, I knelt down—and the children didn't look on at me, and all at once in the morning I said: 'Look for it, children; I laid an egg yesterday.' And all at once they looked, and all at once they saw an egg, and out of it there came a little Hans" (*SE* 10:85). This charming fable is succeeded by a more serious interchange concerning Little Hans's wish to give birth. In the course of a conversation about his doll Grete, Hans's father asks whether he would like to have a little girl. Hans's enthusiastic reply, "Oh yes. Why not?" leads into a more extended consideration of this possibility.

I: "But only women have children."
Hans: "I'm going to have a little girl."
I: "Where will you get her, then?"
Hans: "Why, from the stork. . . ."
I: "You'd like to have little girl."
Hans: "*Yes, next year I'm going to have one,* and she'll be called Hanna too." [*SE* 10:86–87]

When Hans's father informs him, once again, that "only women, only Mummies have children" (*SE* 10:87), he refuses to believe it.

Still lacking a precise understanding of the process of biological reproduction, Little Hans assumes, not illogically, that his mother alone is responsible for producing babies. His father, meanwhile, attempts to lead him to a proper Oedipal identification.

I: "Did you often get into bed with Mummy at Gmunden?"
Hans: "Yes."
I: "And you used to think to yourself you were Daddy?"
Hans: "Yes."
I: "And then you felt afraid of Daddy?"
Hans: "*You know everything; I didn't know anything.*" [*SE* 10:90]

Under pressure, Hans appears to revert to his awed conviction that his father and the professor are in league with a higher power. Yet he clings to his presumption of his own ability, like that of his mother, to give birth. When questioned about his fantasy that his children are always in bed with him, he responds with verve and ingenuity.

I: "So you thought you were their Mummy?"
Hans: "And really I *was* their Mummy."
I: "What did you do with your children?"
Hans: "I had them to sleep with me, the girls and the boys."
I: "Every day?"
Hans: "Why, of course."
I: "Did you talk to them?"
Hans: "When I couldn't get all the children into the bed, I put some of the children on the sofa, and some in the pram, and if there were still some left over I took them up to the attic and put them in the box, and if there were any more I put them in the other box." [*SE* 10:94]

In response to his father's repeated assertion that "boys can't have children," Hans steadfastly replies, "Well, yes. But I believe they can, all the same" (*SE* 10:95).

Little Hans's fascination with maternity poses interpretive difficulties for Freud which reveal themselves tellingly in a footnote: "There is no necessity on this account to assume in Hans the presence of a feminine strain of desire for having children. It was with his mother that Hans had had his most blissful experience as a child, and he was now repeating them, and himself playing the active part, which was thus necessarily that of mother" (*SE* 10:93n). This statement manages to affirm what it denies—the desire to have children that attests to a "feminine strain of desire" in Little Hans. By turning this admission into an assertion of activity, however, Freud means to salvage the boy's masculinity. Still he cannot argue in favor of Little Hans's "active part" in his role playing without simultaneously acknowledging that of his mother, whose "femininity" in this account requires her to occupy the passive position as the object of her son's Oedipal love. If Freud is cognizant of the hermeneutic problem he has raised, he does not give evidence of it. Instead, he persists in his interpretation of Little Hans's desire as modeled on that of his father, rather than his mother. At the same time, the conversations reported by Little Hans's father reveal the amount of paternal enforcement it takes to sustain this theory.

On finding his son playing with his imaginary children again, Little Hans's father makes another pedagogical foray.

> " 'Hullo,' I said to him, 'are your children still alive? You know quite
>   well a boy can't have any children.' "
> *Hans*: "I know. I was their Mummy before, *now I'm their Daddy.*"
> *I*: "And who's the children's Mummy?"
> *Hans*: "Why, Mummy, and you're their *Grandaddy.*"
> *I*: "So then you'd like to be as big as me, and be married to Mummy,
>   and then you'd like her to have children." [*SE* 10:96–97]

The program of indoctrination undergone by Little Hans does eventually take effect. He continues, nevertheless, to care for his "children" like a mother, accompanying them to the W.C., where he helps them to widdle and do "lumf," and "everything one does with children" (*SE* 10:97). "An unsolved residue," moreover, remains. Imperfectly enlightened about the process of human reproduction, Little Hans still cannot understand "what a father has to do with his child, since it is the mother who brings it into the world" (*SE* 10:100).

Although Freud finds evidence in this case history of the workings of the Oedipus and castration complexes, he does so by ignoring the implications of some of the material he brings forth to illustrate his theses. The significance of maternal "seduction" and the boy's desire to be *like* his mother undergo repression, with the result that the mother's role in relation to Little Hans's analysis appears subversive, if not hostile, while the paternally endorsed Oedipal interpretation emerges as somewhat precarious. This hermeneutic instability is underscored by Freud's reflections, mostly in the form of asides, on issues that further problematize the question of sexual difference.

Little Hans's negotiation of his Oedipus complex depends, in Freud's interpretation, on his recognition that women and girls do not have a penis, an acknowledgment that gives weight to the threat of castration, which in turn propels him into the next stage of his development. In order to proceed normally through these phases, Little Hans must first identify with his father's phallic love for his mother and then renounce that love through fear of his father's wrath and capacity for retaliation. This is the message that both Freud and his father openly convey to him. Little Hans's own words (as reported), on the other hand, relay a different impression. If he resists the conclusions concerning his mother's lack which confirm his own phallic destiny, it is surely in part because she conspires in this resistance, but also because he admires her reproductive capacity and fears the loss of his attachment to her. At the end of his analysis he is still left wondering what power his father has to match his mother's ability to have children. This uncertainty is reflected in some of Freud's own ruminations about the significance of the infant's loss of its mother's breast and the origins of fellatio fantasies. In each case, the mother's breast (or her nipple) displaces the primacy of the phallus.

Little Hans's excited comment on observing a cow being milked—"Oh, look! . . . there's milk coming out of its widdler!"—prompts an interesting digression from Freud on the fantasy of fellatio, to which he had earlier referred in analyzing Dora: "I once put forward the view that there was no need to be too much horrified at finding in a woman the idea of sucking at a male organ. This repellent impulse, I argued, had a most innocent origin, since it was derived from sucking at the mother's breast; and in this connection, I went on, a cow's udder plays an apt part as an intermediate image, being in its nature a *mamma* and in its shape and position a penis" (*SE* 10:7). In explicating the fantasy of fellatio which he attributes to Dora, Freud focuses on the commonplace nature of its origin as a means of disarming the objections of his readers. In the context of Little Hans's relationship with his mother, however, his emphasis shifts to a recognition of the supplementary function of the penis. By conflating nipple and penis, Freud implicitly concedes priority to the former. The resemblance between a penis and a "mamma," in the "intermediate image" of the cow's udder, moreover, clearly problematizes the question of female castration, adding a further complication to the matter of distinguishing sexual difference, the sine qua non of the castration complex. Although Freud's comment on fellatio appears marginal to his primary investigation of Little Hans's phobia, it contributes to the subversive tendencies in the case history which accrue to the subject of maternity. It is not incidental, in this light, that Freud follows his observation on the maternal origins of the fellatio fantasy with a note added much later on the concept of castration as separation from the mother.

Some of his colleagues, Freud states, have argued that the infant's loss of its mother's breast represents a form of castration, and furthermore that "the act of birth itself . . . is the prototype of all castration." In opposition to this view, Freud maintains that "the term 'castration complex' ought to be confined to those excitations and consequences which are bound up with the loss of the *penis*" (*SE* 10:8n). Here Freud appears to refute the implications of his own fascinated inquiry into the possibilities of comparison between penis and nipple. His repeated attempts, in his metapsychological texts, to distinguish between the issue of castration and that of maternal loss, however, attest to the uneasiness of this formulation. Freud's treatment of this subject, which in this instance takes the form of denial, reveals its character as symptomatic. He invokes the preoedipal mother only to banish her; thus acknowledged and suppressed, she continues to haunt the house of Oedipus.

The Rat Man (1909)

Despite her relegation to the margins of Little Hans's treatment, the preoedipal mother is more in evidence in this case history (owing no doubt to the age of the subject) than she is in Freud's analyses of adult men, where the father-son relationship looms large. His explication of the "Rat Man's" obsessional preoccupations, for instance, hinges on his interpretation of the young man's inability to resolve his Oedipal rivalry with his father. Freud's lack of interest in the role of the Rat Man's mother is all the more remarkable in light of the material he suppresses from his published case history, but records in his process notes, concerning her control of the family finances.[20] Finally, material from the patient's early life which points to active female seduction is passed over in silence in favor of a construction of the boy's desire which brings him into conflict with his paternal imago. As in the case of Little Hans, Freud labors to educate his subject concerning the true nature of his erotic dilemma, emphasizing the Oedipal dynamics of the situation while ignoring evidence to the contrary. The result, if

20. Despite Freud's usual practice of destroying the notes on which his case histories were based, parts of the original record of the analysis of the Rat Man have survived. Some of these notes were published (in translation) for the first time in 1955, in vol. 10 of the *Standard Edition*. For a running critique of this translation, including that of the case history proper, see Patrick Mahony's *Freud and the Rat Man*. Mahony also points out that the Rat Man's mother, as controller of the family's purse strings, was in effect a participant in the analysis. Yet she "appears in only a handful of remarks in the published case" (35). He agrees with Iza Erlich in relating this phenomenon to the general pattern observable in Freud's case histories, in which the woman "appears somewhat as a caricature, as 'odd woman out'" (36). Steven Marcus comments more extensively on this problem: "This contraction or narrowness of focus, one might add, is not merely idiosyncratic on Freud's part, though it does figure in a pronounced way in much of his writing. It was characteristic of his culture as well, and one of the more strongly marked features of both the major novels and major autobiographies of nineteenth-century culture is the consistency with which they place the relation of father and child (particularly, of course, father and son) at the center of the human universe of development, passion and choice, and how relatively infrequently the relation of mother and child (with a few notable exceptions) occupies that paramount position. One can say that one of the themes of nineteenth-century literary culture has to do with the conflict surrounding this tendency to a suppression of the mother" (*Freud and the Culture of Psychoanalysis* 113). Peter Gay, who admits in a footnote that the Rat Man's mother appears "somewhat more prominently in the process notes than in the text" (*Freud* 267), nevertheless asserts (almost perversely, from my point of view) that Freud's case history "generally followed the process notes he made every night" (262).

anything, is even more forced and unstable than his interpretations of Dora's and Little Hans's desires.

The Rat Man's obsessional thoughts, based on his fantasy of rats boring into the anus as a mode of punishment, involve many verbal transformations on the rat theme—*ratten* (rats), *raten* (payments or installments), *spielratte* (gambler), and *hieraten* (to marry)—which serve to connect his difficulty in choosing a wife with his financial problems. He is in love with his cousin Gisela, who has no fortune to speak of, but has the option of making a financially advantageous match pleasing to his family. Freud, stressing the line of paternal identification, points to an analogy with his father, who had long ago abandoned an impoverished young woman he loved in order to marry the Rat Man's mother for her better prospects. While this story is surely relevant, it is also significant that by the time of the acute onset of his illness the Rat Man's father had been dead for some time and his mother as a result was in charge of his financial affairs. It was she, moreover, who had originally, albeit indirectly, been responsible for the family's prosperity. In light of this information, Freud's omission from his published case history of the fact that the Rat Man's mother paid for his treatments seems deliberately designed to diminish her role in his analysis of her son's neurosis.[21]

That the Rat Man's mother controls his purse strings is clearly indicated by Freud's process notes from the end of his first interview: "After I had told him my terms, he said he must consult his mother. The next day he came back and accepted them" (*SE* 10: 255). Under the heading "Arrears," Freud observes in a later session that the Rat Man had left his inheritance with his mother, "who allows him a very small amount of pocket-money. In this way he is beginning to behave like a miser, though he has no such inclination" (*SE* 10:266). On another occasion Freud writes that his client "hands over all his money to his mother, because he does not want to have anything from her; it belongs to her and there is no blessing on it" (*SE* 10:297). At the same time, the Rat Man evidently identifies with his mother, even to the point of repeating her words (*SE* 10:298). Given the Rat Man's clear line of association between rats and money in his play on the similarity between *ratten* and *raten*,

21. Mahony also calls attention to this omission (17).

not to mention his contemptuous phrase for his treatment payments ("So many florins, so many rats" [*SE* 10:213]), it seems genuinely odd that Freud does not connect the series that so obviously offers itself: rats-money-mother. Instead he resurrects the Rat Man's father, conferring on him an authority that appears to have been doubtful even when he was alive.[22]

In spite of the fact that the Rat Man's mother exercises control over both money (hence rats) and marriage, Freud attempts to convince him that his father stands in the way of the accomplishment of his desires. In the published account of his case history Freud tells us that he explained to the Rat Man that "the source from which his hostility to his father derived its indestructibility was evidently something in the nature of *sensual desires*, and in that connection he must have felt his father as in some way or other an *interference*" (*SE* 10:182). Freud's interpretation is protected in this instance by his claim that the situation he describes must date from a period in the Rat Man's life which eludes his conscious memory. "It must have been in his very early childhood," he maintains, "before he had reached the age of six, and before the date at which his memory became continuous; and things must have remained in the same state ever since" (*SE* 10:183). Later Freud declares that "there can be no question that there was something in the sphere of sexuality that stood between the father and son, and that the father had come into some sort of opposition to the son's prematurely developed erotic life" (*SE* 10:201). Armed with this conviction, Freud then proceeds to interpret the Rat Man's neurosis as Oedipal in origin. The evidence he brings forward to support his hypothesis is shaky, however, given that his client has no memory of the events in question and that at least one point central to Freud's construction exists only in his own imagination.

22. The story of the Rat Man's father's unpaid gambling debt presents him in an unfavorable light, and according to Freud, his son's "unconscious was filled with hostile strictures upon his father's character" (*SE* 10:210–11). There is evidence, moreover, that the Rat Man's father's weakness in regard to financial matters extended into his married life. He is reported, for instance, to have urged his son to take money from his mother's purse (*SE* 10:266). From these admittedly isolated references one forms an impression of a man not in control of his destiny but rather dependent on others (first on his friend for paying his debt, then on his wife for establishing his fortune) for his position in life. Finally, if it is true, as the Rat Man claims, that he assaulted his own daughter, his moral authority in the family must have been seriously undermined.

At the crux of his analysis of the Rat Man, Freud offers the following interpretation:

> I ventured to put forward a construction to the effect that when he was a child of under six he had been guilty of some sexual misdemeanour connected with masturbation and had been soundly castigated for it by his father. This punishment, according to my hypothesis, had, it was true, put an end to his masturbating, but on the other hand it had left behind it an ineradicable grudge against his father and had established him for all time in his role of an interferer with the patient's sexual enjoyment.

Latent in this story is the assumption of the father's castration threat. And at first it looks as though Freud has hit the mark. As if on cue, the Rat Man produces a memory (not his own, but his mother's) of just such a scene. It appears that once "when he was very small—it became possible to establish the date more exactly owing to its having coincided with the fatal illness of an elder sister—he had done something naughty, for which his father had given him a beating." Freud describes in some detail the boy's rage against his father for this abuse, including the insults he hurls at him: "You lamp! You towel! You plate!" (*SE* 10:205). But he strategically omits, for the time being, the exact nature of the boy's transgression, which does not precisely fit into his picture of the event. According to the Rat Man's mother, Freud tells us later, the boy had bitten someone, most likely his nurse. "In her account," he admits, "there was no suggestion of his misdeed having been of a sexual nature" (*SE* 10:206). At this point, Freud refers us to a footnote for further discussion.

In the footnote Freud attempts to explain away the fact that he has no corroborating evidence for his view that the Rat Man's offense was sexual. Lacking such information, he reaffirms his conviction that such events are *typical*. Thus: "The uniformity of the content of the sexual life of children, together with the unvarying character of the modifying tendencies which are later brought to bear upon it, will easily account for the constant sameness which as a rule characterizes the phantasies that are constructed around the period of childhood, irrespective of how greatly or how little real experiences have contributed towards them." Reluctantly, however, Freud does acknowledge a "gap in the analysis" (*SE* 10:208), an admission that recalls his apologies for the fragmentary nature of his Dora case history. Freud's relegation of this material to a foot-note suggests his need to mimimize its significance, to disguise (even to himself perhaps) the deficiencies of his argument. Turning once again to Freud's process notes to examine what he left out of his case history, we may understand better the nature of his uneasiness.

Freud records a wealth of information in his analytic notes concerning the Rat Man's sexual experiences and fantasies involving the women in his immediate family environment, including his mother. The cumulative effect of this material suggests that the Rat Man's sexual development occurred in a hothouse atmosphere of female exhibitionism and seduction. Only two incidents relating to the boy's nursemaids, Fräulein Peter and Fräulein Lina, survive the passage into Freud's writing of the case history, where they appear to be irrelevant to his main line of interpretation. Together with the suppressed information regarding his mother and sisters from the process notes, however, these incidents problematize the paternal orientation of Freud's analysis.

Early in the case history, Freud reports the Rat Man as saying that he remembers engaging in sexual activity with his governess Fräulein Peter, crawling under her skirt to finger her genitals. The boy also apparently enjoyed watching her undress at the public baths and was in the habit of observing a second governess treat the abcesses on her buttocks at night. Yet a third woman assigned to care for him (Fräulein Lina) makes disparaging remarks in his presence about his sexual abilities, claiming that " 'it could be done with the little one; but Paul' (that was I) 'is too clumsy, he would be sure to miss it.' " This woman, on other occasions, would allow him "to uncover her and touch her, and she made no objections" (SE 10:161). From these incidents it appears that the Rat Man, much like Freud himself, was both aroused and shamed by his sexual interactions with his nursemaids. Similar activities involving his mother and his sisters elicit equally conflicting emotions.

In the process notes we learn that the Rat Man's mother had once exhibited herself to him, an event that contributes, no doubt, to some of his later fantasies.[23] "When he was a child," Freud tells us,

23. Mahony regards the Rat Man's mother as "dangerously seductive and phallic" (36).

"while his mother was in bed once, she happened to move about carelessly and showed him her behind" (*SE* 10:313). Elsewhere we hear of the Rat Man's describing a "scene in which he actually showed his mother an erection"—as if to respond in kind (*SE* 10:309). There is evidence, moreover, of active sexual relations between the Rat Man and at least one of his sisters. Freud reports, for instance, his patient's "suspicion that it was through his sisters that he was led to sexuality, perhaps not on his own initiative—that he had been seduced" (*SE* 10:274). Later the Rat Man admits to "repeated attacks on his next younger sister, Julie, after his father's death," suggesting that "these—he had once actually assaulted her—must have been the explanation of his pathological changes" (*SE* 10:278). This confession is followed by other indications of incest. Freud traces one of the Rat Man's fantasies to another scene with his sister Julie "which he had forgotten in his confession to me. After their romp she had thrown herself back on the bed in such a way that he saw those parts of her form in front" (*SE* 10:282). Finally, concerning his brother-in-law's open expression of jealousy toward him, the Rat Man acknowledges that "even the servants said that she loved him and kissed him [the patient] like a lover, not like a brother," as he proceeds to make a bad joke of the situation: "He himself, after having been in the next room with his sister for a while, said to his brother-in-law: 'If Julie has a baby in 9 months' time, you needn't think I am its father; I am innocent'" (*SE* 10:314).

There is really no evidence to indicate that the Rat Man's father interfered with his sexual activity. On the contrary, he may actually have provided a model for his son's self-indulgence by abusing his own daughter Julie. At one point the Rat Man recalls that "his father must have done something he shouldn't have to her when she was ten. He heard screams from the room and then his father came out and said: 'That girl has an arse like a rock'" (*SE* 10:307). In this incestuous family, there appear to be virtually *no* effective prohibitions against sexual behavior, with the result that the Rat Man and his sister are equally victimized. If anything, this case history would seem to demonstrate the failure, rather than the effectiveness, of the father's castration threat.

The Rat Man's hostility, moreover, appears to be directed primarily against his mother, as a surrogate perhaps for the sexually seductive nursemaids. Early in the case history, Freud reports one of his patient's most disturbing fantasies. In the absence of his beloved, who has gone to nurse her sick grandmother, the Rat Man finds it difficult to concentrate on his work. Then he thinks: " 'You might manage to obey the command to take your examination at the earliest moment in October. But if you received a command to cut your throat, what then?' He at once became aware that this command had already been given, and was hurrying to the cupboard to fetch his razor when he thought: 'No, it's not so simple as that. You must go and kill the old woman'" (*SE* 10:259–60). In this fantasy, suicide alternates with symbolic matricide, an indication that the Rat Man's deepest feelings of aggression (and of course ambivalence) revolve around his mother. In this light, moreover, his fantasies concerning *Freud's* mother—that she is dead, her children hanged, her genitals eaten up—reveal their character as displacements of his wishes and fears in relation to his own (*SE* 10: 282–84). Discussing some of the Rat Man's less severe compulsions in his affair with a dressmaker, Freud himself acknowledges that "a hostile current of feeling against his mother is present, which he is reacting to with exaggerated consideration for her" (*SE* 10:296). I would argue, for instance, that behind the Rat Man's apparent concern for his mother's reaction to his contemplated suicide there lies a homicidal impulse toward her. "He had been serious," Freud reports, "in his intention to commit suicide, and was only held back by two considerations. One of these was that he could not stand the idea of his mother finding his bleeding remains" (*SE* 10:263). Finally, as Freud rather crudely observes ("Hasn't it ever occurred to you that if your mother died you would be freed from all conflicts"), the Rat Man has a specific motive for wishing his mother dead. It is she (and not his father) who stands in the way of his marrying the woman he loves (*SE* 10:283).

If one traces carefully the Rat Man's verbal associations to the rat theme, all but one lead to his mother, and even that one (*spielratte*), given his father's pecuniary difficulties, implicates her indirectly. For one startling moment, moreover, Freud actually supplies the missing link in this chain. Almost casually, he mentions in his process notes that the Rat Man's mother's "hair is now very thin, and while she combs it he is in the habit of pulling it and calling it a rat's tail" (*SE* 10:313). Evidently unable to pursue the implications of this association, however, Freud insists in his published account of the Rat Man's neurosis that his obsessive thoughts and behavior stem from his father complex.

In the Rat Man case history, Freud actively suppresses information that undermines the paternal emphasis of his interpretation. It is only through an examination of his process notes that we can fully appreciate the hermeneutic struggle that informs the construction of this case history. Freud's studies of Dr. Shreber and the Wolf Man read on the whole less conflictedly, in part because he holds fast to the course he has already set. Even here, however, there are signs of instability, places where the text opens up to reveal the possibility of maternal signification.

Dr. Shreber (1911) and the Wolf Man (1918)

Shreber's unusual memoir, on which Freud bases his commentary, offers an instance of transsexual desire. Unlike Little Hans, who tries to imitate his mother by playing with his "children," Shreber believes that he has actually undergone a sex change. Because Freud understands this delusion only in terms of castration, and because he perceives the threat of castration as one that emanates from figures of paternal authority, he construes Shreber's motivation as homosexual. Both Shreber's fantasy of persecution at the hands of his physician, Flechsig, and his later conviction that he has been transformed into a woman in order to play the role of God's wife, Freud claims, may be traced to his relationship with his father.[24] "The feminine phantasy, which aroused such violent opposition in the patient, thus had its root in a longing, intensified to an erotic pitch, for his father and brother. This feeling, so far as it referred to his brother, passed, by a process of transference, on to his doctor, Flechsig; and when it was carried back on to his father a settlement of the conflict was reached" (*SE* 12:50). Freud's assumption of an exclusively paternal etiology in this case is remarkable in light of Shreber's expressed desire to take on the procreative role of a woman in order to create "a new race of men" (*SE* 12:17). What is signally absent from Freud's line of reasoning is any speculation concerning the import of this maternal identification. By the time Freud comes to transcribe his analysis of the "Wolf Man," his

---

24. Morton Schatzman offers in *Soul Murder* a completely different view of paternal etiology. He explains the content of Shreber's fantasies by reference to his father's bizarre child-rearing practices.

attribution of "feminine" desire on the part of a man to homosexuality subsumes all other evidence, including that which pertains to the patient's mother and to the sexual interventions of women servants.

Whereas the Wolf Man's mother figures only briefly and rather insignificantly in Freud's account, other women, including the boy's sister, his nannie, and a household servant, play more prominent roles.[25] Like the Rat Man, he reports having been seduced by an older sister: "It was in spring, at a time when his father was away; the children were in one room playing on the floor, while their mother was working in the next. His sister had taken hold of his penis and played with it, at the same time telling him incomprehensible stories about his Nanya, as though by way of explanation." Freud's comment on this episode reveals the extent to which he associates it with the kind of sexual humiliation he had experienced at the hands of his own nannie. He characterizes the Wolf Man's memory of this event as "offensive to the patient's masculine self-esteem," and one that elicits a counterfantasy in which he takes the aggressive role. Such defensive measures, Freud concludes, correspond "exactly to the legends by means of which a nation that has become great and proud tries to conceal the insignificance and failure of its beginnings" (*SE* 17:20). Other female agents, Freud maintains, threaten the boy with castration.

Turning away from his sister as an object of erotic interest, the child attempts to "seduce" his Nanya by playing with his member in her presence. But she refuses his advances. "She made a serious face, and explained that that wasn't good: children who did that, she added, got a 'wound' in the place" (*SE* 17:24). A similar scene takes place with a serving maid named Grusha. Through a complex process of reconstruction, Freud decides that the Wolf Man's memory of her kneeling on the floor with a pail and broom represents the following sequence of events: "When he saw the girl scrubbing the floor he had micturated in the room and she had rejoined, no doubt jokingly, with a threat of castration" (*SE* 17:92). The accuracy (or inaccuracy) of this interpretation is not in question. What is inter-

25. Here I concur with Peter Gay, who says that "the Wolf Man's biological mother achieves only severely limited significance as a partner in the primal scene he had observed, or fantasized, as a little boy, though certainly mother substitutes contributed to his neurosis" (505).

esting here is the way in which Freud traces the Wolf Man's associations with Grusha to his mother and then projects them onto the primal scene that he imagines the boy witnessed in his infancy. In representing this scene as intercourse *a tergo*, Freud stresses the passivity of the mother's position, thus divorcing her from the problem of female aggression posed by the serving women.[26]

Freud's construction of the Wolf Man's desire as "feminine" in aim and directed toward his father follows his interpretation of the Shreber case and depends on the transfer of the threat of castration from older women to an authoritative man. At one point Freud explains that the boy "had travelled, without considering the difference of sex, from his Nanya to his father," as though the object of his libidinous urges were a matter of little consequence (*SE* 17:46). Later, it becomes necessary to state more explicitly the paternal focus of both his fear and his desire: "At this point the boy had to fit into a phylogenetic pattern, and he did so, although his personal experiences may not have agreed with it. Although the threats or hints of castration which had come his way had emanated from women, this could not hold up the final result for long. In spite of everything it was his father from whom in the end he came to fear castration." As in the case of the Rat Man, Freud chooses to ignore the evidence in front of him in order to sustain his own theory. In this instance, he makes a circular appeal to his own highly speculative argument in *Totem and Taboo*:

In this respect heredity triumphed over accidental experience; in man's prehistory it was unquestionably the father who practised castration as a punishment and who later softened it down into circumcision. The further the patient went in repressing sensuality during the course of the development of the obsessional neurosis, the more natu-

---

26. Freud's supposition that the Wolf Man actually witnessed his parents' intercourse *a tergo* has even less to support it than his conviction that the Rat Man was beaten by his father for an offense that was sexual in nature. Gay deals with this delicate issue by shifting the ground of his discussion to the question of the relationship between fantasy and reality and Freud's quarrel with Jung over the infantile origin of neuroses (290). Mahony makes the interesting point that "there is greater suggestive evidence . . . for the Rat Man than for the Wolf Man to have witnessed coitus *a tergo*" (467). He wonders to what extent the Wolf Man's case history is derivative of the Rat Man's and concludes that it may represent a return of what Freud repressed in his earlier analysis.

ral it must have become to him to attribute these evil intentions to his father, who was the true representative of sensual activity. [*SE* 17: 86–87]

By naming the Wolf Man's father as the "true representative of sensual activity," Freud further represses the implications of female seduction and aggression. His consistent attribution of agency to the father governs, in turn, his interpretation of the Wolf Man's maternal identification.

When, at the age of four and a half, the Wolf Man repeats a phrase he had originally heard from his mother, "I cannot go on living like this," he associates his own conflicts over bowel control with her abdominal complaints. "Thus his lament," Freud says explicitly, "had the significance of an identification with his mother" (*SE* 17:77). Regardless of the fact that the Wolf Man's organ of identification is the anus (which appears to negate his castration anxiety), Freud understands the boy's maternal fixation as an indication of his desire to take his mother's place in sexual intercourse with his father. The interpretation of the Wolf Man's fantasy of return to his mother's womb finds a similar explanation. This fantasy, Freud claims, derives "from an attachment to the father." It signifies "a wish to be inside the mother's womb in order to replace her during intercourse—in order to take her place in regard to the father" (*SE* 17:101).

For the boy to take his mother's place subjects him to the threat of castration, yet the attribution of agency to the father in this respect also holds out the promise of his future masculinity. The desire to return to the mother's womb as expressive of a wish to be united with her femaleness, on the other hand, can only be regarded as regressive. Such a desire, instead of representing an arrest in the progress toward phallic masculinity, appears to negate its development altogether. By focusing his interpretive efforts on the Wolf Man's father and the spectacular *coitus a tergo*, which he places at the center of the case history, Freud manages to avoid speculation along these lines.[27]

27. The Wolf Man's treatment, of course, did not end with his analysis by Freud. He was later reanalyzed by Ruth Mack Brunswick and maintained for a long time a correspondence with Muriel Gardiner which served therapeutic purposes. For a

Leonardo (1910)

The subject of maternal desire, which is on the margins of Freud's case histories, surfaces in a startling way in his reflections on Leonardo da Vinci. Here several strands of his thinking coalesce briefly to compose a sinister portrait of the mother-son relationship, which he nowhere else depicts so explicitly or intensely.[28] If in his other analyses the presence of the Oedipus and castration complexes sustains the boy's phallic masculinity, first by asserting his aggressive erotic drives, and then by subjecting them to repression through the intervention of his virile father, with whom he will eventually identify, their absence or failure in this account begins to outline a different story. The figure of the preoedipal mother, whose functions in the case histories are divided, obscured, or suppressed, emerges in this instance with such force that Freud's analysis of Leonardo assumes the character of a cautionary tale about the dangers inherent in mother love.

Freud's analysis of Leonardo relies on his interpretation of the artist's note concerning his memory of having been struck on the lips by the tail of a bird of prey when he was still a nurseling. On the basis of a mistranslation in the German rendition of the text, Freud takes this bird to be a vulture (*Geier*) instead of the kite (*nibbio*) to which the Italian clearly refers. This error of attribution (far from invalidating his commentary) is central to his representation of maternal desire.

---

more detailed account of the Wolf Man's lifelong involvement with psychoanalysis, see *The Wolf-Man by the Wolf-Man*, edited by Muriel Gardiner. A few years before the Wolf Man's death Karin Obholzer conducted a series of interviews with him, which she has published as *The Wolf-Man Sixty Years Later: Conversations with Freud's Controversial Patient*.

28. Ernest Jones regards Freud's analysis of Leonardo as derived from his own labor of self-reflection (*Life and Work of Sigmund Freud* 2:78). He even goes further to claim that "much of what Freud said when he penetrated into Leonardo's personality was at the same time a self-description; there was surely an extensive identification between Leonardo and himself" (432). Gay is more reserved on this point, although he does acknowledge that Freud would have identified with Leonardo's passion for scientific research (272). If, on the other hand, what Freud has to say about Leonardo's relationship with his mother has a bearing on his own preoedipal period, then we may begin to compose a different portrait of his early life from the one that Jones and others have proposed.

Freud construes the memory of the vulture as a fantasy rather than a true reminiscence. By substituting the idea of the male organ for that of the bird's tail, he arrives at the specific fantasy of fellatio, which he proceeds to justify once again in light of its "innocent" origin in the situation of breast-feeding. His reasoning follows the pattern established in his case histories of Dora and Little Hans, where he argues that the image of the cow's udder mediates between that of the nipple and the penis. Thus Leonardo's vulture fantasy, which gives expression to a passive homosexual desire, actually derives from his relationship with his mother. This line of argument leads in turn to Freud's consideration of mother as vulture: "We interpret the phantasy as one of being suckled by his mother, and we find his mother replaced by—a vulture. Where does this vulture come from and how does it happen to be found in its present place?" (*SE* 11:87–88).

"At this point," Freud ventures, "a thought comes to the mind from such a remote quarter that it would be tempting to set it aside." Such a prelude can only be meant to disarm the critic who might be skeptical of the train of association that follows. "In the hieroglyphics of the ancient Egyptians the mother is represented by a picture of a vulture. The Egyptians also worshipped a Mother Goddess, who was represented as having a vulture's head, or else several heads, of which at least one was a vulture's. This goddess's name was pronounced *Mut*. Can the similarity to the sound of our word *Mutter* ['mother'] be merely a coincidence?" Having located a source for the mother/vulture image, Freud begins to explore its signification.[29] The Egyptians adopted this symbolic device for motherhood, he maintains, "because only female vultures were believed to exist; there were, it was thought, no males of this

29. Freud's dream of the bird-beaked figures offers another probable source for this visual image along with an intensely personal association. In this "true anxiety dream," Freud sees his "beloved mother, with a peculiarly peaceful, sleeping expression on her features, being carried into the room by two (or three) people with birds' beaks and laid upon the bed" (*SE* 5:583). He locates the source of the bird-beaked image in the illustrations to Phillippson's Bible (an edition of the Old Testament in Hebrew and German) and interprets the dream as a representation of his mother's death. For a discussion of the significance of the Phillippson Bible in Freud's Hebrew education, see Marianne Krüll, *Freud and His Father* 156–63. See also William McGrath, *Politics of Hysteria* 38–44. Freud's bird-beaked dream forges another link between himself and the subject of his analysis.

species" (*SE* 11:88). The mother/vulture as a representation of parthenogenesis, he argues further, must have reminded Leonardo of the circumstances of his own early childhood. By imagining a scene in which Leonardo comes upon this discovery, Freud forges a link between the concept of maternal self-sufficiency and the preoedipal period.

> He once happened to read in one of the Fathers or in a book on natural history the statement that all vultures were females and could reproduce their kind without any assistance from a male: and at that point a memory sprang to his mind, which was transformed into the phantasy we have been discussing, but which meant to signify that he also had been such a vulture-child—he had had a mother, but no father. [*SE* 11:90]

The idea of an exclusive mother-infant relationship elicits a series of reflections in which maternal autonomy becomes synonymous with phallic power.[30] As a first step in this process, Freud returns to his equation: nipple = penis. If the vulture symbolizes the preoedipal mother who suckles her child, and the vulture's tail "cannot possibly signify anything other than a male genital" (*SE* 11:93), then Leonardo's fantasy involves the figure of a "phallic" mother. Just such a figure can be found, moreover, in the Egyptian pantheon: "Now this vulture-headed mother goddess was usually represented by the Egyptians with a phallus; her body was female, as the breasts indicated, but it also had a male organ in a state of erection." Freud offers differing explanations for this image of androgyny. In mythological terms, he argues, it must have been intended "to denote the primal creative force of nature" (*SE* 11:94). In the light of psychological theory, on the other hand, it refers to the boy's original assumption that all creatures, including his mother, possess an organ like his own. Freud prefers the latter interpretation, which he causes to subsume the former: "The child's assump-

30. Sarah Kofman sees Freud as veering away from the implications of the mother's "phallic" power, which she conceives in terms of woman's narcissistic self-sufficiency (*Enigma of Woman* 90–95). Although our conclusions differ, our arguments are similar in many respects. Needless to say, moreover, it is not necessary to imagine a woman with a phallus in order to conceptualize the possibility of maternal self-sufficiency and autonomy. I have adopted Freud's terminology here in order to demonstrate how it functions within his system of thought.

tion that his mother has a penis is thus the common source from which are derived the androgynously-formed mother goddesses such as the Egyptian Mut and the vultures' *'coda'* in Leonardo's childhood phantasy" (*SE* 11:97).

By shifting his ground from mythology to psychology, Freud performs a subtle displacement that affects his subsequent arguments concerning maternal power. His redefinition of the maternal phallus as an illusion directs his attention away from the awesome Egyptian mother goddess and the autonomy of the preoedipal mother which she appears to represent and toward the question of masculine development and the role of paternal authority. Leonardo's mother, Freud maintains, by usurping masculine functions, forced her son into passivity, thus disposing him to homosexuality. Freud finds this experience typical of his male homosexual patients.

> In all our male homosexual cases the subjects had had a very intense erotic attachment to a female person, as a rule their mother, during the first period of childhood, which is afterwards forgotten; this attachment was evoked or encouraged by too much tenderness on the part of the mother herself, and further reinforced by the small part played by the father during their childhood. Sadger emphasizes the fact that the mothers of his homosexual patients were frequently masculine women, women with energetic traits of character, who were able to push the father out of his proper place. [*SE* 11:99]

Unchecked by the presence of a strong father, maternal love turns into aggression. Even Leonardo's celebrated portrait of Mona Lisa warns of this danger. For Freud, her enigmatic smile represents "the contrast between reserve and seduction, and between the most devoted tenderness and a sensuality that is ruthlessly demanding—consuming men as if they were alien beings" (*SE* 11:108). In her promise of "unbounded tenderness and at the same time sinister menace," she evokes Leonardo's mother, whose "violence" of caresses, in compensation for the absence of the boy's father, "determined his destiny" (*SE* 11:115–16). Freud reinterprets the vulture fantasy as active maternal seduction: " 'My mother pressed innumerable passionate kisses on my mouth.' The phantasy is compounded from the memory of being suckled and being kissed by his mother" (*SE* 11:107). This kind of unsolicited love also appears to

threaten castration. "So, like all unsatisfied mothers, she took her
little son in place of her husband, and by the too early maturing of
his erotism robbed him of a part of his masculinity" (*SE* 11:117).

The exclusivity of the mother-infant relationship, maternal seduction, the primacy of the nipple, the threat of castration emanating from a woman—all of these issues, to which Freud gives his
distracted attention in the case histories, coalesce around a single
figure in his analysis of Leonardo. This constellation of features
gives rise in turn to a form of hermeneutic instability which escapes
Freud's attempts at control. Having once evoked the image of the
powerful Egyptian mother goddess, Freud cannot quite banish her
or contain her influence over his text. It is only the figure of the
patriarchal father who can check her authority, yet even he seems a
latecomer to the scene. When Freud is moved to generalize from the
example of Leonardo to the nature of every mother's love for her
infant (son), he places the father on the margins of this magnetic
relationship.

> A mother's love for the infant she suckles and cares for is something
> far more profound than her later affection for the growing child. It is in
> the nature of a completely satisfying love-relation, which not only
> fulfils every mental wish but also every physical need; and if it repre-
> sents one of the forms of attainable human happiness, that is in no
> little measure due to the possibility it offers of satisfying, without
> reproach, wishful impulses which have long been repressed and which
> must be called perverse. In the happiest young marriage the father is
> aware that the baby, especially if he is a baby son, has become his rival,
> and this is the starting-point of an antagonism towards the favourite
> which is deeply rooted in the unconscious.   [*SE* 11:117]

In this unexpected encomium to maternal love, Freud does not at
first distinguish between the mother's fulfillment and that of her
infant. The one appears to subsume the other, erasing the boundaries between them. Freud thus implicitly sustains the concept of
maternal self-sufficiency which he elicits in his portrayal of the
Egyptian mother goddess, whose power of asexual reproduction
makes her independent of men.[31] The idea of the father's exclusion

31. Mary Jacobus makes this point in another way. As she observes, the complete
maternal satisfaction that Freud so positively portrays here "does not merely
threaten the child with homosexuality; it ousts the father and unbalances the

from this "completely satisfying love-relation" seems to have exercised an attraction equal to its repulsion for Freud. At the same time, his characterization of maternal love in this brief instance undergoes a transformation that makes it acceptable in a way that the love of Caterina for her son is not.

Within the same paragraph, Freud shifts his focus from the violent caresses of an unsatisfied mother to one who finds every need fulfilled in her love for her infant. The factor of aggression thus miraculously disappears, and in its place Freud offers an idealized image of maternal love. Through this sleight of hand, he attempts to neutralize the effects of the sinister portrait of mother-son relations he has just painted. In generalizing about the preoedipal mother, Freud excludes conflict, neatly displacing the element of menace or antagonism onto the father. By emphasizing the mutually gratifying aspect of the mother-son relationship, however, Freud admits to the marginality of the father's role, thereby reinvoking the example of Leonardo. The incomplete success of Freud's strategy in this regard does not prevent him from using it again.

Toward the end of his essay "Femininity," Freud restates his conviction concerning the ideal nature of a mother's love for her son. "A mother," he claims, "is only brought unlimited satisfaction by her relation to a son; this is altogether the most perfect, the most free from ambivalence of all human relationships" (*SE* 22:133). This vision of maternal plenitude is all the more remarkable for its location in Freud's narrative of feminine dissatisfaction. Appearing as an island of tranquility in a sea of discontent, it functions here, as in the analysis of Leonardo, to shield the mother-son relationship from consideration of the most threatening aspects of maternal desire. The preoedipal mother in this idealized account does not seduce, overwhelm, or betray. Rather the needs of mother and son neatly dovetail, each a perfect complement to the other. That the father appears superfluous to this unit hardly seems to trouble Freud, yet it is precisely this point that causes him in Leonardo's case to posit the harmful effects of maternal seduction. Ignoring

---

oedipal triangle, rendering separation impossible" (*Reading Woman* 164). Whereas Jacobus, following Kristeva, who in turn follows Lacan, reads in this scenario the necessity of the father's intervention, I am interested in highlighting the conflicts within Freud's own discourse.

these discrepancies in his presentation of the mother-infant relationship, Freud is nevertheless consistent in avoiding a direct examination of maternal power.

Contributions to the Psychology of Love
(1910, 1912, 1918)

The concept of maternal plenitude which Freud evokes as a defense against his darker vision of seduction and aggression, and the disturbing consequences (for a boy) of maternal identification, affect his portrayal of adult sexual relations as well. In creating an image of the ideally satisfying and satisfied mother, Freud suppresses her most troubling characteristics, which reassert themselves elsewhere in altered form. The figure of mother as betrayer, for instance, reemerges in Freud's essay "A Special Type of Choice of Object Made by Men," where he argues that the preference of some men for loose women derives from a complex of feelings associated with the mother's "infidelity." Freud traces the need for "love for a harlot" back to the boy's first shocked recognition of his mother's sexual activity, which causes him to adopt the "cynical logic that the difference between his mother and a whore is not after all so very great, since basically they do the same thing" (*SE* 11:171).

In the male imagination, however, the division between the image of mother and that of whore is so profound that the love object assumes one aspect at the expense of the other. In his essay "On the Universal Tendency to Debasement in the Sphere of Love," Freud institutionalizes this split, arguing pessimistically that "we should be justified in expecting psychical impotence to be a universal affliction under civilization and not a disorder confined to some individuals" (*SE* 11:184). In a characteristic move, Freud attributes this form of impotence to the workings of the incest taboo, thereby invoking an image of paternal authority. But the concept of maternal plenitude itself creates an artificial ideal that marks the mother's sensual activity as degraded. In his hyperbolic praise of maternal love, Freud himself implicitly denies the mother's "infidelity," the existence of an eroticism that exceeds the boundaries of the mother-infant relationship. When he confronts this dimension of maternal desire, however, he theorizes a division in the erotic life of the male subject which cannot be healed. Freud's assumption of a disunion between sensual and tender feelings experienced by virtually all men in their love relations with women reproduces the split that runs through his texts, separating the image of the good mother from the bad. The division in the erotic life of men which Freud finds typical of civilized society thus sustains his idealized image of maternity while revealing the flaw at its heart.

In his essay "The Taboo of Virginity," Freud evokes yet another aspect of the preoedipal mother transposed to the female love object. In this essay Freud returns to woman as a source of castration threat.[32] The taboo of virginity common among primitive peoples, he argues, derives from a fear of woman herself. The danger presumed to attend the first act of coitus symbolizes a more general anxiety that men experience in sexual intercourse. In a remarkable passage relating the feelings of primitive to civilized man, Freud explores the meaning of this "dread of woman."

Perhaps this dread is based on the fact that woman is different from man, for ever incomprehensible and mysterious, strange and therefore apparently hostile. The man is afraid of being weakened by the woman, infected with her femininity and of then showing himself incapable. The effect which coitus has of discharging tensions and causing flaccidity may be the prototype of what the man fears; and realization of the influence which the woman gains over him through sexual intercourse, the consideration she thereby forces from him, may justify the extension of this fear. In all this there is nothing obsolete, nothing which is not still alive among ourselves. [*SE* 11: 198–99]

Freud's point of view here is masculine; it is men who fear a loss of their potency in relation to women.[33] Later, however, he maintains

32. Jacobus provides a subtle Derridean reading of this essay, the main point of which I take to be that the fantasy of the phallic woman serves to maintain the artificiality of the mark of sexual difference when in fact "castration" as representative of an internal division characterizes both sexes (110–36). In the last chapter of this book I treat this issue in terms of Freud's redefinition of castration as separation from the mother.

33. Lou Andreas-Salomé, in a letter to Freud, offers another interpretation of the "dread of woman." She sees it as due to the fact that women were once dominant and later, after the defeat of matriarchy, were feared for their powers of retribution

that the threat of castration emanates from the active hostility that women feel toward men, an antagonism that Freud has no difficulty in tracing to penis envy. The embitterment that women feel at the narcissistic wound of defloration, reminding them of their genital deficiency, he argues, poses a very real danger to their husbands, whom they frequently blame for this injury. Freud cites the example of a newly married woman patient who reports a dream that betrays "spontaneously the woman's wish to castrate her young husband and to keep his penis for herself" (*SE* 11:205). In shifting his focus from male to female psychology, Freud loses sight of the subject of male anxiety, while intensifying his descriptions of female revenge.

Freud offers several literary examples that bear out his assumption regarding the psychological validity of the taboo of virginity. The first concerns a peasant youth who refuses to marry his intended bride because he believes she will cost him his life. Only after she has been married and widowed will he accept her as his wife. The title of this play, *Das Jungferngift*, translated as *Virgin's Venom*, reminds Freud of "the habit of snake-charmers, who make poisonous snakes first bite a piece of cloth in order to handle them afterwards without danger" (*SE* 11:206). The next example is even more extreme. Freud quotes the character Judith in Hebbel's tragedy *Judith und Holofernes*, who claims that "my beauty is like belladonna . . . enjoyment of it brings madness and death." Her sexual motives in the seduction of Holofernes, Freud maintains, are thinly disguised as patriotism.

> After she has been deflowered by this powerful man, who boasts of his strength and ruthlessness, she finds the strength in her fury to strike off his head, and thus becomes the liberator of her people. Beheading is well-known to us as a symbolic substitute for castrating; Judith is accordingly the woman who castrates the man who has deflowered

(January 30, 1919; Pfeiffer, *Sigmund Freud and Lou Andreas-Salomé Letters* 89). Kofman agrees with Andreas-Salomé, though not in a historical sense. On the level of fantasy, she argues, the mother always possesses "the power of life and death over man" (72). Jacobus also discusses Andreas-Salomé's letter to Freud on the question of matriarchy and the delicate sparring with him that ensued—without appearing to take sides (134–36). I discuss Freud's conflicted views on the subject of matriarchy in chap. 4.

her, which was just the wish of the newly-married woman expressed in the dream I reported. [*SE* 11:207]

Try as he may Freud seems unable to effect a permanent divorce between female eroticism and aggression. Two lines of association, moreover, draw his examples of sinister love into connection with the figure of the preoedipal mother. In "A Special Type of Choice of Object Made by Men," Freud describes the lover who requires the presence of an "injured third party" as one who seeks to recreate the Oedipal triangle. In this case, he explains, "the libido has remained attached to the mother for so long, even after the onset of puberty, that the maternal characteristics remain stamped on the love-objects that are chosen later, and all these turn into easily recognizable mother-surrogates." Given the unique and irreplaceable nature of the mother-infant bond, however, all subsequent love objects take on the character of mother-surrogates. "No one," Freud generalizes, "possesses more than one mother, and the relation to her is based on an event that is not open to any doubt and cannot be repeated" (*SE* 11:169). In his essay "On the Universal Tendency to Debasement in the Sphere of Love," Freud expands on the implications of this statement. "However strange it may sound," he muses, "we must reckon with the possibility that something in the nature of the sexual instinct itself is unfavourable to the realization of complete satisfaction" (*SE* 11:188–89). The digressions of desire imposed by the incest barrier result in the fact that "the final object of the sexual instinct is never any longer the original object but only a surrogate for it" (*SE* 11:189). Each love object, in this view, assumes the aspect of a maternal supplement.

When Freud puts forth the notion that a mother's love for her infant (son) has the nature of a "completely satisfying love-relation," through the gratification of "wishful impulses which have long been repressed," he alludes to penis envy. In "Femininity," where he develops this theme at greater length, the idea that a son makes up his mother's lack is more explicit. "A mother," he affirms, "can transfer to her son the ambition which she has been obliged to suppress in herself, and she can expect from him the satisfaction of all that has been left over in her of her masculinity complex." It is a small step from this position to the next: "Even a marriage is not made secure until the wife has succeeded in making her husband her child as well and in acting as a mother to him" (*SE* 22:133–34). The role of mother subsumes that of wife, confronting the male subject once again with the specter of a woman who wants to "keep his penis for herself" (*SE* 11:205). It is not at all clear, moreover, that the mother who desires the penis of her infant son is any less threatening than the woman whose "archaic reaction of hostility" toward the man (*SE* 11:208) is released by her first experience of intercourse.

Questions regarding maternal power have a way of recurring in Freud's texts despite his emphasis on male rivalry and the significance of paternal authority within the Oedipal triangle. The pre-oedipal mother, as Freud himself portrays her, refuses to stay in her place, creating a level of persistent, low-level disturbance that problematizes his attempts to theorize her subordination. Freud's efforts to deflect, obscure, or deny the issues posed by her so-called phallic self-sufficiency, as imaged in her reproductive capacity and the threat of castration imminent in her overwhelming love, only highlight the gaps in his argument. These problems are repeated on a different level when he turns from analyses of individuals and developmental issues to cultural and anthropological speculation.

4

Cultural Transcendence

In *Totem and Taboo* Freud constructs a paradigm for his subsequent reflections on matters of culture and religion. What emerges from this text is the Oedipus complex writ large on the early development of human history. In his elaboration of this hypothesis, however, Freud once again engages in a struggle of interpretation (focused in this instance on a struggle for priority with his chosen successor, Jung) involving the position and importance of the preoedipal mother as represented by the role of matriarchy in the evolution of culture. The traces of this conflict, in turn, unsettle his conclusions concerning the primacy of paternal authority as well as the progress from primitive to civilized behavior which the recognition of a father god represents.

Yet in spite of his discomfort with this account, Freud clings to it, repeating it almost verbatim in *Moses and Monotheism*, where, near death, he reaffirms his faith in the patriarchal origins of culture. Here the battle with Jung continues, displaced, as in *Totem and Taboo*, onto the issue of matriarchy. The results, in this instance, are no more satisfactory than they are in the earlier text. Matriarchy, as representative of a developmental stage (in the individual as well as in culture) in which the mother-infant relationship supersedes the Oedipus complex, remains unintegrated into Freud's evolutionary scheme, threatening to disrupt it from within.

Totem and Taboo (1913)

Just as Freud's major conceptual breakthrough to the Oedipus complex owes much of its flavor to the particular configuration of his relationship with Wilhelm Fliess, his subsequent theoretical leap into the field of evolutionary anthropology is intimately bound up with the vicissitudes and the ultimate dissolution of his friendship with Jung. The second half of *Totem and Taboo* especially seems to have been written in resistance to the younger man's ideas as represented in Jung's own groundbreaking text, *Transformations and Symbols of the Libido* (1911–12), first translated into English as *Psychology of the Unconscious* (1916).[1] Part IV of *Totem and Taboo*, in which Freud unfolds his myth of the primal parricide and the Oedipal origins of human culture, was completed well after the formal break between the two men had taken place and may be construed as Freud's response to Jung's heretical views regarding the significance of the incest taboo and the role of the mother, both of which they had debated in correspondence.[2] It is all the more

1. Most commentators agree on the effects if not the actual intent behind the writing of *Totem and Taboo*. J. N. Isbister maintains that Freud's "most immediate aim" was "to foster the rupture between himself and Jung" (*Freud: An Introduction to His Life and Work* 219). Ronald Clark points to Freud's correspondence with Abraham, Jones, and Ferenczi as evidence that he regarded *Totem and Taboo* as a "weapon against Jung and his supporters" (*Freud: The Man and the Cause* 352). Peter Gay gives this line of interpretation a psychoanalytic twist by saying that in his competition with Jung "Freud was displaying . . . an aspect of the oedipal wars often scanted—the father's efforts to best the son" (*Freud: A Life for Our Time* 326). He sees the last paper, which was published after the break with Jung, as a manifestation of Freud's "sweet revenge on the crown prince who had proved so brutal to him and so treacherous to psychoanalysis" (326). Peter Rudnytsky goes further, stating that "in *Totem and Taboo*, despite having himself become the 'primal father' of psychoanalysis, Freud symbolically acted out the murder of Jung as well as that of his own father" (*Freud and Oedipus* 31).

2. From Jones's *Life and Work of Sigmund Freud* and the *Freud/Jung Letters* (ed. McGuire), it is possible to reconstruct the following chronology for Freud's reading of Jung's texts and the composition of his own. In June 1910, the year in which Freud began reading for *Totem and Taboo*, he received a copy of Part I of Jung's *Transformations* in proof. We know from the correspondence that he received the published text on August 20, 1911. Freud comments on it in his letters to Jung first in September and again in November of that year. By mid-January 1912 he had finished Part I of *Totem*, and he presented Part II on May 15 (immediately following his exchange of letters with Jung on the subject of matriarchy) to his Wednesday group. Both parts

curious from this standpoint that Jung's name appears only once in Freud's text and then only in a footnote concerning word associations. The symptomatic nature of this omission extends to Freud's treatment of Bachofen (best known for his concept of mother-right and an obvious influence on Jung), whose work Freud grudgingly acknowledges in a single reference yet cannot adequately account for in his own patriarchal scheme. Freud's difficulty in placing matriarchy in his evolutionary paradigm comes to stand for everything in Jung's thought and character which he cannot assimilate, fusing the challenge to paternal authority contained in Jung's maternal symbolism with the threat embodied in his personal declaration of independence from his mentor. That Jung's deviation from Freud should take the Bachovian form of a fascination with the realm of the "Mothers" seems designed to elicit, or to focus, Freud's deepest anxieties.[3] As if to confirm the neurotic nature of his reaction to Jung's apostasy, moreover, at the height of his unhappiness with his "crown prince," he faints in his presence, an incident that he subsequently relates to two similar episodes in relation to Fliess, and which also rather uncannily recalls his reaction to Eckstein's bleeding. Under these circumstances, the second half of *Totem and*

----

were subsequently published in *Imago*. During the summer of 1912 Freud wrote to Jones about his difficulty with the issue of matriarchy and by the fall he was hard at work on Part III. By this time relations between Freud and Jung were already strained. On September 10 Emma Jung sent Freud a copy of Part II of her husband's *Transformations*, and the two men met fatefully in Munich in late November at the Park Hotel, where Freud fainted. Freud presented Parts III and IV of *Totem* on January 15 and June 4, 1913, respectively. Both were published that year in *Imago*.

3. Although Jung never refers to Bachofen by name in his *Transformations*, the work is permeated by his influence. George Hogenson, who analyzes in detail the differences between Freud and Jung on the matriarchy-versus-patriarchy issue, states, for instance, that Jung "had begun to develop a theory of primal matriarchy under the influence of J. J. Bachofen's *Das Mutterrecht*, a book that Freud had dismissed as inadequate" (*Jung's Struggle with Freud* 59). From a biographical standpoint it is interesting to note that Bachofen, at age eighty, was still on the faculty at the University of Basel when Jung enrolled there as a medical student in 1895 (Wehr, *Jung: A Biography* 55). In Jung's autobiography, moreover, one can trace his fascination with the realm of the Mothers to his conviction regarding his actual mother's uncanny powers. In *Memories, Dreams, Reflections*, he claims that she had two personalities, "one innocuous and human, the other uncanny. This other emerged only now and then, but each time it was unexpected and frightening. She would then speak as if talking to herself, but what she said was aimed at me and usually struck to the core of my being, so that I was stunned into silence" (48–49).

Taboo reads as a nervous attempt to suppress not only Jung's memory but also the challenge to patriarchal authority that his ideas, filtered through Bachofen, raise.

Freud, as his range of reading in the field of anthropology and evolutionary social theory indicates, had more than enough material to support his insistence on the primacy of paternal authority in the formation of the modern family. Even the concept of mother-right, as popularized by Bachofen in *Das Mutterrecht*, did not present an insurmountable obstacle, since his progressive scheme of social organization affirms the triumph of patriarchy over matriarchy. Subsequent theorists who accepted the concept of matrilineality denied a strictly speaking matriarchal stage in which women exercised power. All such accounts, moreover, assume that the modern form of the patriarchal family is the product of a long evolutionary process, representing a gradual increase in civilized behavior. The existence of matrilineality (and even matriarchy) at an earlier stage of development in these systems, far from posing a challenge to patriarchal control, merely attests to an inferior form of social organization. Yet Freud seems to have been uneasy with this type of explanation, as evidenced in the work of John McLennon (*Primitive Marriage*), Sir John Lubbock (*The Origin of Civilization and the Primitive Condition of Man*), and Lewis Henry Morgan (*Ancient Society*), whose work he read and sometimes cites.[4] For his own theory of the beginnings of human society, he turned to Darwin, whose concept of tribal domination by a single powerful male has the advantage of positing an originary form of masculine, and implicitly paternal, control (*The Descent of Man and Selection in Relation to Sex*). At the same time, throughout the period of composition of *Totem and Taboo* Freud expressed doubts about his project, referring specifically on one occasion to his difficulty in accounting for matriarchy—an indication that he was perhaps not

4. Sir Henry Maine's *Ancient Law* and Bachofen's *Mutterrecht*, both published in 1861, offered competing explanations of the origins of human society. Maine's view that patriarchy represented the natural and inherent structure of the human family ultimately lost out to the evolutionary view expressed by Bachofen, although his concept of matriarchy was replaced by that of matrilineality, for which various explanations were offered. For a more comprehensive treatment of this subject, see Elizabeth Fee ("The Sexual Politics of Victorian Social Anthropology") and Rosalind Coward (*Patriarchal Precedents*). Elizabeth Abel discusses these issues as they relate specifically to Freud in *Virginia Woolf and the Fictions of Psychoanalysis*.

satisfied with his own inclination toward the Darwinian hypothesis.[5] I believe that it is his reading of Jung's work during this period that accounts for both his need to avoid the theoretical implications of a stage of development relatively free of male domination and his ultimate discomfort with his own counterexplanation.

On the day Freud received his copy of the first part of Jung's *Transformations and Symbols of the Libido,* he also coyly announced his own most recent efforts on the work that would ultimately establish the terms of his rivalry and difference: *Totem and Taboo.* "Since my mental powers revived, I have been working in a field where you will be surprised to meet me. I have unearthed strange and uncanny things and will almost feel obliged *not* to discuss them with you. But you are too shrewd not to guess what I am up to when I add that I am dying to read your 'Transformations and Symb. of the Lib.'" (August 20, 1911; Mcguire, *Freud/Jung Letters* 438). Despite some expressions of uneasiness on the issue of priority, Freud at first regards his and Jung's research as complementary. On September 1, 1911, he writes:

> I am glad to release you as well as your dear wife, well known to me as a solver of riddles, from the darkness by informing you that my work in these last few weeks has dealt with the same theme as yours, to wit, the origin of religion. I wasn't going to speak of it for fear of confusing you. But since I can see from a first reading of your article in the *Jahrbuch* (I shall have to reread it; for the moment Ferenczi has made off with the volume) that my conclusions are known to you, I find, much to my relief, that there is no need for secrecy. So you too are aware that the Oedipus complex is at the root of religious feeling. Bravo! What evidence I have to contribute can be told in five minutes. [441]

Freud's jockeying for position in this letter bespeaks a certain anxiety about Jung's essay, which he manages to avoid discussing in a serious way by saying that he no longer has it in hand. Not until November does he mention it again, and then only after a chiding letter from Jung's wife, Emma, who suspects (rightly, as it turns out) that Freud is displeased with the work. After a gloomy letter in which he confesses to Jung that his psychology of religion is giving

5. See Jones, *Life* 1:317.

him "a good deal of trouble," that he has "little pleasure in working and constant *douleurs d'enfantement*" (November 2, 1911; 453), he finally attempts to address his sources of disagreement with him. Beginning obliquely and in a complimentary mode, Freud claims that "one of the nicest works I have read (again), is that of a well-known author on the 'Transformations and Symbols of the Libido,'" but he then moves quickly to some pointed critiques.

> Sometimes I have a feeling that his horizon has been too narrowed by Christianity. And sometimes he seems to be more above the material than in it. But it is the best thing this promising author has written, up to now, though he will do still better. In the section about the two modes of thought I deplore his wide reading. I should have liked him to say everything in his own words. Every thinker has his own jargon and all these translations are tedious.

As if to mitigate the harshness of this comment Freud then tries for a softer tone, betraying in the process, however, his nervousness about preceding Jung as well as being preceded by him.

> Not least, I am delighted by the many points of agreement with things I have already said or would *like* to say. Since you yourself are this author, I shall continue more directly and make an admission: it is a torment to me to think, when I conceive an idea now and then, that I may be taking something away from you or appropriating something that might just as well have been acquired by you. When this happens, I feel at a loss; I have begun several letters offering you various ideas and observations for your own use, but I never finish them because this strikes me as even more indiscreet and undesirable than the contrary procedure. Why in God's name did I allow myself to follow you into this field? You must give me some suggestions. But probably my tunnels will be far more subterranean than your shafts and we shall pass each other by, but every time I rise to the surface I shall be able to greet you. [November 12, 1911; 459]

Freud's plaintive question "Why in God's name did I allow myself to follow you into this field?" marks a turning point for both correspondents. While Jung takes his cue for a bolder presentation of his ideas, pushing, in the next letter but one, for a reevaluation of Freud's concept of the libido as it relates to dementia praecox, Freud begins to attack Jung's mythological bent through the work of his former patient, pupil, and lover Sabina Spielrein.[6] On November 30, 1911, following a Wednesday-night meeting at which Spielrein had presented a portion of her paper "Destruction as a Cause of Coming into Being," Freud writes to Jung virtually identifying her work with his through a near slip of the pen. "Fräulein Spielrein read a chapter from her paper yesterday (I almost wrote the *ihrer* [her] with a capital "i"), and it was followed by an illuminating discussion" (McGuire 469). The next sentence confirms the intended identification. "I have hit on a few objections to your [Ihrer] (this time I mean it) method of dealing with mythology, and I brought them up in the discussion with the little girl. . . . What troubles me most is that Fräulein Spielrein wants to subordinate the psychological material to *bio*logical considerations; this dependency is no more acceptable than a dependency on philosophy, physiology, or brain anatomy" (469). At the meeting in question, Freud had expressed another, quite specific, objection. There he remarked that "the presentation itself provides the opportunity for a critique of Jung because in his recent mythological studies he also uses any mythological material whatsoever, of which there is an abundance in its present version,

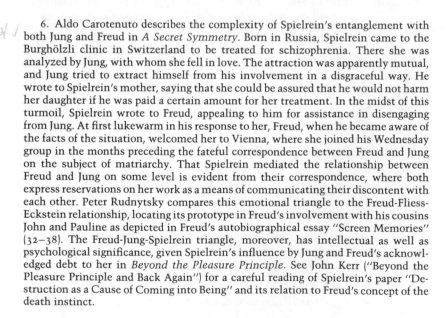

6. Aldo Carotenuto describes the complexity of Spielrein's entanglement with both Jung and Freud in *A Secret Symmetry*. Born in Russia, Spielrein came to the Burghölzli clinic in Switzerland to be treated for schizophrenia. There she was analyzed by Jung, with whom she fell in love. The attraction was apparently mutual, and Jung tried to extract himself from his involvement in a disgraceful way. He wrote to Spielrein's mother, saying that she could be assured that he would not harm her daughter if he was paid a certain amount for her treatment. In the midst of this turmoil, Spielrein wrote to Freud, appealing to him for assistance in disengaging from Jung. At first lukewarm in his response to her, Freud, when he became aware of the facts of the situation, welcomed her to Vienna, where she joined his Wednesday group in the months preceding the fateful correspondence between Freud and Jung on the subject of matriarchy. That Spielrein mediated the relationship between Freud and Jung on some level is evident from their correspondence, where both express reservations on her work as a means of communicating their discontent with each other. Peter Rudnytsky compares this emotional triangle to the Freud-Fliess-Eckstein relationship, locating its prototype in Freud's involvement with his cousins John and Pauline as depicted in Freud's autobiographical essay "Screen Memories" (32–38). The Freud-Jung-Spielrein triangle, moreover, has intellectual as well as psychological significance, given Spielrein's influence by Jung and Freud's acknowledged debt to her in *Beyond the Pleasure Principle*. See John Kerr ("Beyond the Pleasure Principle and Back Again") for a careful reading of Spielrein's paper "Destruction as a Cause of Coming into Being" and its relation to Freud's concept of the death instinct.

without selection. Now, mythological material can be used in this way only when it appears in its original form and not in its derivatives" (quoted in McGuire 591). In writing to Jung himself, however, Freud sounds a less confident and more irritable note: "In my work on totemism I have run into all sorts of difficulties, rapids, waterfalls, sand-banks, etc.; I don't know yet if I shall be able to float my craft again. In any event it is going very slowly and time alone will prevent us from colliding or clashing. I read between the lines of your last letter that you have no great desire for interim reports on my work, and you are probably right. But I had to make the offer." Resuming a more masterly tone, Freud finally takes up the vexed question of the libido, stating unequivocally that "only the power behind the sexual drive can be termed libido" (McGuire 469).

Ignoring Freud's warnings, Jung begins to state his own positions more boldly while Freud reacts overtly through direct disagreement and covertly by finding fault with Spielrein's ideas. Professions of personal difficulty with his work on totemism are interwoven with testy allusions to Jung's prolific output. In a letter in which he once again objects to Spielrein's use of mythological material, he both deplores and defends his own method of investigation as at once different from and implicitly better than that of his rival, Jung.

> My study of totemism and other work are not going well. I have very little time, and to draw on books and reports is not at all the same as drawing on the richness of one's own experience. Besides, my interest is diminished by the conviction that I am already in possession of the truths I am trying to prove. Such truths, of course, are of no use to anyone else. I can see from the difficulties I encounter in this work that I was not cut out for inductive investigation, that my whole make-up is intuitive, and that in setting out to establish the purely empirical science of Ψ A I subjected myself to an extraordinary discipline. [December 17, 1911; 472]

Gradually the two men move toward an open confrontation, heralded by increasing expressions of annoyance on both sides over relatively minor matters: the pace of the correspondence, the conduct of psychoanalytic business, the handling of a treatment case. As Jung's work on Part II of his *Transformations and Symbols of the*

Libido draws to a close, he becomes increasingly explicit about his primary disagreements with Freud over the complexly intertwined issues of incest, the character of the libido, and the place of the mother. The correspondence between February and the end of May 1912 records the struggle between the two men for theoretical control.

On February 25, 1911, Jung writes to Freud explaining his tardiness as a correspondent as an outgrowth of his intense labor on the second part of "Transformations," where he intends to address "all of the problems that arise out of the mother-incest libido, or rather, the libido-cathected mother-imago." "This time," he proclaims, "I have ventured to tackle the mother. So what is keeping me hidden is the κατάβασις [katabasis] to the realm of the Mothers, where, as we know, Theseus and Peirithoos remained stuck, grown fast to the rocks. But in time I shall come up again" (487–88). A few weeks later, he explains that his correspondence with Freud actually interferes with his work and that he had "wanted if possible to write *no letters at all*" in order to save time. This letter ends with what amounts to an open challenge to Freud. "I would never have sided with you in the first place had not heresy run in my blood," Jung declares, concluding his letter with a ringing passage about the dangers of discipleship, from Nietzsche's *Also Sprach Zarathustra* (March 3, 1912; 491). Freud responds to this letter with an invidious comparison between Jung and Adler, an indication that he has already identified him as a betrayer. The correspondence limps along in this fashion until the beginning of May, when the two men finally, and decisively, engage.

In two important letters, Jung announces his divergence from Freud on the incest issue. In the first, he attempts, somewhat confusedly, to redefine incest in a way that is compatible with his line of thinking concerning regression of the libido to the realm of the Mothers. "Like you," he claims, "I am absorbed in the incest problem and have come to conclusions which show incest primarily as a fantasy problem." Jung, it seems, is not interested in the prohibition against biological incest, an essential item in Freud's construction of the Oedipus complex as well as his slowly evolving understanding of the primitive origins of morality. "If biological incest were meant," Jung argues, "then father-daughter incest would have fallen under the prohibition much more readily than that between son-in-law and mother-in-law. The tremendous role of the mother in mythology has a significance far outweighing the biological incest problem—a significance that amounts to pure fantasy" (April 27, 1912; 502). As sketchy as they are, these remarks must surely have alarmed Freud, who would have read in them the degree to which Jung had abandoned the cornerstone of his own theoretical activity.

As if to drive this point home, Jung quickly writes another letter, expanding on his objections to locating the origins of human morality in the prohibition against incest. Although this account (as I read it, at least) is not self-consistent, it does reveal Jung's discomfort with the centrality of the incest taboo in Freud's system, as well as his relative lack of interest in the figure of the father as an agent of enforcement. Jung begins by discussing the role of incest prohibition in "the relatively late period of patriarchy, when culture was sufficiently far advanced for the formation of family ties." The need to prevent incest within the family, he maintains, would apply only to the small boy, who could be expected to desire his youthful mother. Later, when she is less attractive, "with her sagging belly and varicose veins," there would be no need for laws to restrain him. Incest, he then postulates, would constitute more of a real danger in "the early, cultureless age of mother-right, i.e., in the matrilineal family. There the father was purely fortuitous and counted for nothing, so he would not have had the slightest interest (considering the general promiscuity) in enacting laws against the son. (In fact, there was no such thing as a father's son!)" It is hard to imagine an idea less likely to appeal to Freud than that of a matriarchal period in which incest might have been rampant and the father "counted for nothing." It is as though Jung seeks deliberately to anger him. Almost perversely, he continues:

> I therefore think that the incest prohibition (understood as primitive morality) was merely a formula or ceremony of atonement *in re vili*: what was valuable for the child—the mother—and is so worthless for the adult that it is kicked into the bush, acquires an extraordinary value thanks to the incest prohibition, and is declared to be desirable and forbidden. . . . Evidently the object of the prohibition is not to prevent incest but to consolidate the family. [May 8, 1912; 502–3]

By subordinating the incest prohibition to other aims, Jung dismisses its centrality to psychoanalytic theory, hence calling into question the primacy of Freud as founder. That Freud understood what was at stake is evident from the sharpness and the cogency of his reply.

Freud's three main objections, crisply numbered in the text, concern Jung's displacement of the father and corresponding elevation of the mother. In opposition to Jung's notion of a "primordial state of promiscuity," Freud offers "a different hypothesis . . . Darwin's." As for mother-right, it "should not be confused with gynaecocracy. There is little to be said for the latter." Finally in reponse to Jung's assertion that there was a time when the father counted for nothing, Freud states tersely: "It seems likely that there have been father's sons at all times. A father is one who possesses a mother sexually (and the children as property). The fact of having been engendered by a father has, after all, no psychological significance for a child" (May 14, 1912; 504). Having at last defined the shape of their disagreement, the two men quickly begin to fall out with each other, and the tone of the letters degenerates into one of mutual reproach.

Jung's challenge to Freud is both theoretical and personal. By refusing to remain a "son" and a disciple, Jung negates the principle of renunciation embedded in Freud's concept of the Oedipus complex, thus endangering the careful balance of opposing desires sustained by the paternal threat of castration. That Jung should couch his intellectual revolt, moreover, in terms of a disregard for the incest taboo and an open fascination with the issues of matriarchy and mother-right could only have exacerbated Freud's anxiety about the fate of his own Oedipal project. In emotional terms, Freud occupies the position of the betrayed, the less active and hence "feminine" role—an unwelcome reminder perhaps of his alliance with Emma Eckstein in relation to Fliess. As if to concretize this identification, he appears to reenact a piece of that troubled relationship in his climactic confrontation with Jung in Munich, where, after a heated argument with him, he faints.[7]

---

7. Jones calls attention to the parallel between Freud's relationships with Jung and with Fliess (*Life* 1:317), as does Rudnytsky (31). Rudnytsky, speaking of the Freud-Fliess-Eckstein triangle, emphasizes the woman's role as victim but fails to observe the degree to which Freud also identifies with this position. Shirley Nelson Garner interprets Freud's faint as evidence of his unresolved homophobia ("Freud and Fliess"). The friendship between Freud and Jung appears to have been complicated (and ultimately disrupted) by homophobia on Jung's part as well as Freud's. In an early letter to Freud, Jung writes of his ambivalence concerning his feelings for

By the time of the meeting in late November 1912 at the Park Hotel in Munich, Freud had had ample opportunity to gauge the extent of Jung's apostasy. Emma Jung, still attempting to act as mediator between the two men, had sent him a copy of Part II of *Transformations* in early September. There he would have encountered Jung's bald redefinition of "libido" as a generalized type of psychic energy, along with his displacement of paternal authority in favor of a Bachovian romance with the "Great Mother." Central to Jung's account of the hero's regression to the Mother as a struggle with his unconscious that threatens him with death is the cyclical view of emanation from and return to the Mother expressed by Bachofen in his essay on mortuary symbolism. In his chapter "The Three Mystery Eggs," for instance, Bachofen identifies the egg as a maternal principle, representing the origins of all life: "Thus the two conspicuous objects in the Pamphilian grave painting, the eggs and the myrtle wreath, carry the initiation back to the primal material-maternal principle, which also gave rise to Dionysius Dimetor (the two-mothered). The phallic god striving toward the fertilization of matter is not the original datum; rather, he himself springs from the darkness of the maternal womb" (*Myth, Religion and Mother-Right* 29). At the same time death "is not the opposite but the helper of life," so that "the completion of every existence is a coming back to the beginning, and every departure contains a return. The two movements are connected with each other as inexplicably as the two forces to which they correspond. The product of their combined power is the cycle in which all tellurian life eternally moves" (34). Jung would even have found in Bachofen the germ of his idea of the hero's regression to the realm of the Mothers,

---

him, due to his having been molested in his youth by a trusted older man: "Actually—and I confess this to you with a struggle—I have a boundless admiration for you both as a man and a researcher, and I bear you no conscious grudge. So the self-preservation complex does not come from there; it is rather that my veneration for you has something of the character of a 'religious' crush. Though it does not really bother me, I still feel it is disgusting and ridiculous because of its undeniable erotic undertone. This abominable feeling comes from the fact that as a boy I was the victim of a sexual assault by a man I once worshipped" (October 28, 1907; McGuire, *Freud/Jung Letters* 95). Linda Donn, who does not dwell on the specifically homoerotic and homophobic side of the Freud-Jung relationship, does document its intensity for both men and the deep sense of loss that both experienced at its end (*Freud and Jung*).

including the absence of a paternal barrier to incest. "The phallic god," Bachofen maintains,

> stands as a son to feminine matter; bursting the shell of the egg, he discloses the mystery of phallic masculinity that had hitherto been hidden within it, and the mother herself rejoices in him as in her own demon. The phallic god cannot be thought of separately from feminine materiality. Matter, the mother who bore him to the light, now becomes his wife. Bacchus is both the son and husband of Aphrodite. Mother, wife, sister merge into one. Matter takes all these attributes by turns. [29–30]

Jung's main innovation in respect to Bachofen revolves around his concept of the hero's rebirth as a result of his regression not to actual incest with his biological mother but to the mother imago who represents the simultaneously terrifying and renewing powers of the unconscious. Yet there are many passages that sound a direct echo of his predecessor's work. On the cycle of birth and death, for instance, he lyricizes:

> All that is living rises as does the sun, from the water, and at evening plunges into the water. Born from the springs, the rivers, the seas, at death man arrives at the waters of the Styx in order to enter upon the "night journey on the sea." The wish is that the black water of death might be the water of life; that death, with its cold embrace, might be the mother's womb, just as the sea devours the sun, but brings it forth again out of the maternal womb. [*Psychology of the Unconscious* 245]

Concerning the fusion of mother, sister, and wife in the guise of myth, Jung says: "In the morning the goddess is the mother, at noon the sister-wife, and in the evening again the mother, who receives the dying in her lap" (272). Like Bachofen, Jung conceives of the realm of the Mothers as both profoundly attractive and finally destructive. For the hero there is "a deadly longing for the depths within, for drowning in his own source, for becoming absorbed into the mother, his life is a constant struggle with death, a violent and transient delivery from the always lurking night. . . . If he is to live he must fight and sacrifice his longing for the past, in order to rise to his own heights" (390–91).

It is hard to keep in mind Jung's distinction between the biological mother and the mother imago, through whom the hero experiences rebirth and hence an awareness of his destiny. Because Jung also wishes to downplay the literalness of incest as well as the necessity for an incest barrier, the figure of the mother assumes gigantic proportions in his work. In her mythological manifestations, she is both frightening and awe-inspiring—in Jung's term, "terrible." Leaving aside for a moment the issue of Jung's disloyalty, it might be expected, in the light of Freud's own disinclination to attribute either power or authority to the figure of the mother, that he would react with some violence to this portrait.

With the benefit of hindsight we may now read Freud's comment to Jones in the summer of 1912 about his difficulty with the subject of matriarchy as an enormous understatement: "I know of the obstacle or the complication offered by the matter of Matriarchy and have not yet found my way out of it. But I hope it will be cleared away" (quoted in Gay, *Freud* 325). We may only conjecture, however, how he felt on actually receiving Jung's manuscript. The tone of injury in the few letters from this period does suggest, however, how badly the relationship had deteriorated. When the two men finally met in Munich in late November, some kind of quarrel was inevitable.

In Jones's account of this meeting, difficulty first arose during a discussion of a paper by Abraham in which he interpreted Amenhotep's erasure of his father's name from public monuments as a manifestation of Oedipal rivalry. Jung strenuously disputed this view. Then Freud began upbraiding Jung and another Swiss for omitting his name from their recent psychoanalytic publications. Suddenly Freud fell to the floor "in a dead faint" (Jones, *Life* 1:317, 2:147). What happened next was equally extraordinary. "The sturdy Jung carried him to a couch in the lounge, where he soon revived. His first words as he was coming to were strange: 'How sweet it must be to die'" (1:317). To this account Jung adds: "As I was carrying him, he half came to, and I shall never forget the look he cast at me. In his weakness he looked at me as if I were his father" (*Memories, Dreams, Reflections* 157).

Freud's words "How sweet it must be to die" have a resonance in this context that extends beyond his own interpretation—that he reacted to the death wishes directed at him by Jung. George Hogenson reads Freud's faint in the opposite sense, as evidence of his *desire* to die, specifically at the hands of one of his most gifted followers (*Jung's Struggle with Freud* 103). Looked at in the light of Freud's association between this episode and earlier encounters with Fliess, in combination with his reaction to Emma Eckstein's bleeding, we may see perhaps an attraction on Freud's part to a passive or "feminine" position in his intimate relations with men. Writing to Jones shortly after the incident, Freud commented: "I cannot forget that six and four years ago I suffered from very similar though not such intense symptoms in the *same* room of the Park Hotel. I saw Munich first when I visited Fliess during his illness and this town seems to have acquired a strong connection with my relation to that man. There is some piece of unruly homosexual feeling at the root of the matter" (Jones, *Life* 1:317). Did Freud's "unruly homosexual feeling" involve a disposition to be loved as a woman might? Certainly his behavior in this instance was less than conventionally masculine. Jung, perhaps wishing to enhance his own manly role, is later reported to have said: "He could not stand a critical word. Just like a woman. Confront her with a disagreeable truth: she faints" (Clark, *Freud* 328).

While Freud's faint may speak of his repressed bisexuality, what is most startling about the incident is the way in which sex roles quickly become indeterminate. Jung describes Freud as looking at him like a *father*, but in the light of his own representation of the death wish as a desire to return to a maternal matrix, he might just as easily have said *mother*. Freud's words "How sweet it must be to die" would not be out of place in Jung's *Transformations*, where he repeatedly evokes the siren call of death. Did Freud himself make this connection? If so, his writing of the last part of *Totem and Taboo* seems designed to repress such an awareness.

Peter Gay, in his biography *Freud: A Life for Our Time*, claims that *Totem and Taboo* emerged from Freud's "hidden life," productively translating "his most intimate conflicts and his most private quarrels into material for scientific investigation" (335). Gay sees in this work not only Freud's attempt, once again, to engage with the ghost of his father, Jacob, but also his "persistent evasion of his complicated feelings about Amalia Freud" (335). "It is telling," he continues, "that in his reconstruction Freud said virtually nothing about the mother, even though the ethnographic material pointing to the fantasy of devouring the mother is richer than that for devouring the father" (335).[8] This evasion is particularly striking in light of the events I have just described. Freud's quarrel with Jung highlights in a dramatic way the very issues concerning the mother's role in culture that Gay finds lacking in Freud's text. Thus when he came to write his influential account of the evolution of human society, Freud suppressed precisely what he found most troubling in Jung's work—his reliance on matriarchal symbolism, a debt that could easily be traced back to its source in Bachofen. Yet Freud's words "How sweet it must be to die" suggest an attraction to this material perhaps equal to its repugnance for him, a need both to acknowledge and to contain the seductiveness of its appeal. The result of these complex motivating factors is a nervous treatment of the subject of matriarchy in a text that excludes any serious consideration of Jung, while referring only grudgingly to his true intellectual father, Bachofen.

Irrespective of Jung's symbolic reinterpretation, Bachofen's understanding of mother-right in itself poses a threat to Freud's Oedipal scheme. A brief overview of Bachofen's evolutionary model of culture as outlined in his major work, *Das Mutterrecht*, reveals the kind of difficulty Freud encountered in dealing with him even to the extent that he does. The first stage of human society, which Bachofen associates with hunting and gathering, is characterized by what he calls "hetaerism," an unregulated sexual activity, in which mother-right (matrilineal descent) is recognized although men may hold political power. This phase yields to "Demetrian matriarchy," a social system based on the institution of monogamous marriage

8. Gay refers to Freud's use of material provided by Ferenczi in his article "A Little Chanticleer," which analyzes a boy's fear of cocks as an instance of castration anxiety. The boy's fantasies, however, as Gay rightly points out, seem to involve his mother as much as his father. At one point, for instance, little Arpad "said quite suddenly: 'I should like to eat a potted mother (by analogy: potted fowl); my mother must be put in a pot and cooked, then there would be a potted mother and I could eat her.' (He grunted and danced the while.) 'I would cut her head off and eat it this way' (making movements as it [sic] eating something with a knife and fork)" ("Little Chanticleer" 211).

Elizabth Abel also draws attention to the maternal content of little Arpad's fantasy life (*Virginia Woolf*). For the sake of my own argument concerning Freud's indifference to women as a source of castration threat, I should add that Ferenczi reports an incident where a chambermaid, on finding the boy manipulating his penis, threatens to cut it off (213).

which coincides with the development of agriculture, in which women dominate and the principle of maternity is honored by the worship of a female deity. Both mother-right and the mother goddess must be overthrown for the modern form of patriarchy, which includes a recognition of paternity, to appear. Bachofen's assumption of the predominance of mother-right in both hetaerism and Demetrian matriarchy derives, moreover, from the physical nature of the mother-infant bond.

> The mother's connection with the child is based on a material relationship, it is accessible to sense perception and remains always a natural truth. But the father as begetter presents an entirely different aspect. Standing in no visible relation to the child, he can never, even in the marital relation, cast off a certain fictive character. Belonging to the offspring only through the mediation of the mother, he always appears as the remoter potency. [109]

In his analyses of Little Hans and Leonardo, Freud indicates that the child's ignorance of paternity and the absence of paternal authority can be seriously disruptive of masculine development. Thus while Bachofen celebrates the civilizing effects of mother-love, Freud's treatment of the seeming exclusivity of the mother-infant relationship reveals anxiety.

The mother-daughter relationship in Bachofen's scheme, moreover, takes precedence over that of the mother (or father) and son: "This religious primacy of motherhood leads to a primacy of the mortal woman; Demeter's exclusive bond with Kore leads to the no less exclusive relation of succession between mother and daughter; and finally, the inner link between the mystery and the chthonian-feminine cults leads to the priesthood of the mother, who here achieves the highest degree of religious consecration" (87). Unencumbered by the intricacies of the Oedipus complex, Bachofen found no obstacle in his theory of mother-right to the subsequent development of the modern form of patriarchal society. He simply postulated the discovery of paternity, attributing a higher status to father-right on the grounds that the father as "promoting cause" of gestation represents a principle of spirituality in contrast to the material contribution of the mother. Freud's focus on psychological development, on the other hand, requires him to account, in very specific terms, for the nature of paternal authority and the primacy of phallic desire. Freud's consistent marginalization of the mother-daughter relationship speaks to only one aspect of his difficulty in theorizing an independent (much less an omnipotent) female principle. Rather than follow Bachofen's model, which would also have supported Jung's psychologized interpretation of his work, Freud reads Oedipus back into the beginnings of time, displacing the concept of mother-right from the originary position Bachofen hypothesizes and sandwiching the mother goddess in between two patrilineal and patriarchal periods.⁹

Freud's first reference to matriarchy occurs in the middle of a speculation about the institution of the incest taboo as a consequence of the primal patricide. Though united in overcoming their father, he explains, the brothers are divided by their sexual desires: "Thus the brothers had no alternative, if they were to live together, but—not, perhaps, until they had passed through many dangerous crises—to institute the law against incest, by which they all alike renounced the women whom they desired and who had been their chief motive for despatching their father." The taboo on incest with the mother preserves the fraternal organization otherwise threatened by sexual rivalry. As an afterthought, Freud adds: "Here, too, may perhaps have been the germ of the institution of matriarchy, described by Bachofen [1861], which was in turn replaced by the patriarchal organization of the family" (*SE* 13:144).

Freud's nervous evocation of Bachofen is echoed in a later passage, which begins with a seeming concession to the mother goddesses, only to end with a reaffirmation of the originary status of the father of the primal horde.

> I cannot suggest at what point in this process of development a place is to be found for the great mother-goddesses, who may perhaps in general have preceded the father-gods. It seems certain, however, that the

---

9. Judith van Herik makes the acute observation that "Freud's chronological reconstructions of goddesses and gods and patriarchies and matriarchies do not all square with each other," concluding that he never settled the issue to his satisfaction (*Freud on Femininity and Faith* 77–78). See George Hogenson for a another view of the theoretical issues at stake for Freud in the matriarchy-versus-patriarchy debate (58–63).

change in attitude to the father was not restricted to the sphere of religion but that it extended in a consistent manner to that other side of human life which had been affected by the father's removal—to social organization. With the introduction of father-deities a fatherless society gradually changed into one organized on a patriarchal basis. The family was a restoration of the former primal horde and it gave back to fathers a large portion of their former rights. [*SE* 13:149]

Father-right, Freud seems anxious to maintain, existed before mother-right, even if the worship of a female deity preceded that of a father god. Freud's final allusion to mother goddesses in *Totem and Taboo* reveals a possible motivation for this insistence.

In the rituals surrounding Attis, Adonis, and Tammuz described by James Frazer in *The Golden Bough*, Freud found instances of the mother-son incest he postulated as a universal (male) desire. The worship of female deities which anchored these cultic practices, however, not only violates the taboo on incest Freud finds central to his thesis concerning human development but also functions independently of an authoritative father god. By assuming the absence of a barrier to incest, Frazer's work, like that of Bachofen and Jung, undermines the function of the castration complex. Freud's account of this stage of religious formation restores the figure of a father in a way that keeps his own theory intact.

The introduction of agriculture increased the son's importance in the patriarchal family. He ventured upon new demonstrations of his incestuous libido, which found symbolic satisfaction in his cultivation of Mother Earth. Divine figures such as Attis, Adonis and Tammuz emerged, spirits of vegetation and at the same time youthful divinities enjoying the favours of mother goddesses and committing incest with their mother in defiance of their father.

By positing a stage of father-right that forms the basis of the patriarchal family, Freud neatly inserts the concept of paternal prohibition into the seemingly exclusive mother-son relationship that characterizes the worship of the great mother goddess. The full significance of this gesture becomes apparent when Freud alludes to the ritual death of the son-lover. "But the sense of guilt, which was not allayed by these creations, found expression in myths which granted only short lives to these youthful favourites of the mother-goddesses and decreed their punishment by emasculation or by the wrath of the father in the form of an animal. Adonis was killed by a wild boar, the sacred animal of Aphrodite; Attis, beloved of Cybele, perished by castration" (*SE* 13:152–53). When it comes to the subject of castration, paternal authority must quickly be invoked, since the alternative clearly raises the question of maternal aggression. As if to reinforce his point that the threat of castration necessitates a paternal presence, Freud writes in a footnote that "fear of castration plays an extremely large part, in the case of the youthful neurotics whom we come across, as an interference in their relations with their father" (*SE* 13:153n).

What emerges from *Totem and Taboo* is an evolutionary paradigm tracing the path from primitive social organization to the introduction of the prohibitions against incest and father-murder which Freud equates simultaneously with the Oedipus complex and with civilization itself. "At the conclusion, then, of this exceedingly condensed inquiry," Freud states, "I should like to insist that its outcome shows that the beginnings of religion, morals, society and art converge in the Oedipus complex" (*SE* 13:156). Mother-right and the worship of a female deity, by implication, occupy subcultural positions on the scale of human development. The series of analogies that Freud draws here between nature and civilization, matriarchy and patriarchy, and the preoedipal and the Oedipal periods remains stable in his subsequent meditations on the large movements of human history. Having broken with Jung and negated the usefulness of his friendship, Freud will never seriously entertain a view of culture that does not assume the originary status of paternal authority. The uneasiness of his placement of matriarchy in this scheme, with all of its rich suggestiveness concerning the preoedipal period, however, continues to disrupt his narrative enactment of the triumph of patriarchal religion and social structure. *Moses and Monotheism*, a transposed version of *Totem and Taboo*, reads on this account as a thinly disguised enforcement of Oedipus.

Moses and Monotheism (1939)

Moses and Monotheism, which argues the hypothesis that Moses was an Egyptian who adopted the Hebrews as his chosen people and bequeathed them his conception of monotheism, actually repeats the substance of *Totem and Taboo* in an attempt to create a seamless version of the development of patriarchal religion. That the issue of matriarchy remained on Freud's mind in the intervening years, however, is evident from an exchange of letters between him and Lou Andreas-Salomé. In a letter in which Andreas-Salomé ironically inquires whether she should read a recent work by Jung, given the seriousness with which Freud takes it, she offers her own matriarchal interpetation of Freud's "taboo of virginity."[10]

> With regard to the short essay on 'The Taboo of Virginity' it occurred to me that this taboo may have been intensified by the fact that at one time (in a matriarchal society) the woman may have been the dominant partner. In this way, like the defeated deities, she acquired demonic properties, and was feared as an agent of retribution. Also her defloration by deity, priests, etc. points back to a time when she was not the 'private property' of the male, and in order to achieve this she had to shake off the shackles of her impressive past—which may still play its part as the earliest positive basis for the precautionary measures of the male. [January 30, 1919; Pfeiffer, *Sigmund Freud and Lou Andreas-Salomé Letters* 89)

Still uncertain of the exact chronology and sequence of events, Freud nevertheless resists Andreas-Salomé's implicit assumption of the originary status of matriarchy. He offers a counterview based on his stance in *Totem and Taboo*.

> I have long had unexpressed ideas on the question of matriarchy. Where is one to place it? I think, on the basis of the totem-taboo hypothesis, in the period after the fall of the primal father, the period in which the male had not yet brought himself to the point of founding a secondary family, in which therefore the dominant role now fell as a matter of course upon the shoulders of the woman, who had lost her master. Unfortunately, I find it impossible to ascribe a date to the whole early history of the family, although I know that this is essential, if one is to give it its full significance in relation to the other phases of the development of the family. [February 9, 1919; 90]

10. Andreas-Salomé was evidently aware of Freud's distaste for matriarchal ideas. In March 1913 she remarked in her journal that Freud disapproved of a lecture ("The Father Problem") given by Victor Tausk "because Tausk's recourse to Bachofen's views on matriarchy had made the interpretations one sided" (*Freud Journal* 114).

Debate on the question of matriarchy appears to have remained lively among Freud's colleagues as well. In a paper delivered before the British Psycho-Analytical Society in 1924, Jones (a loyal patriarchalist) ridicules a recent book titled *The Dominant Sex.*

> According to the account given there, not only do the children belong solely to the mother, the father being quite unrelated to them either in blood or in kinship, but property belongs only to the women and is inherited only through them. The woman is the active wooer, has as many husbands or lovers as she pleases and as long as she pleases; she can at any time divorce her husband . . . in fact he exists only for the sexual pleasure he gives her, and the work he can do at her bidding, being in all other respects merely tolerated very like a drone in a beehive. The woman has a correspondingly dominating position in society, in counsel and in government. The description reads like a feminist's wish-fulfillment dream, a vision of a paradise out of which she has been driven by the protesting male, but to which she hopes one day to return. ["Mother-Right and the Sexual Ignorance of Savages" 145–46]

While admitting to the existence of matrilineality among primitive peoples, Jones offers his own ingenious interpretation of mother-right as a defense against the Oedipus complex, thus managing to adhere to Freud's system of explanation in the face of embarrassing evidence to the contrary.

Whether or not Freud appreciated Jones's spirited defense is unclear. At any rate he was not moved to adopt its logic. Instead, in his discussions of matriarchy in *Moses and Monotheism*, he returns to his wrestling match with Bachofen, incorporating his argument for the cultural transcendence of patriarchy over matriarchy, while suppressing other aspects of his thought. Bachofen's *Mutterrecht* constitutes a powerfully absent presence in this text, which never seems to arrive at a definitive understanding of the placement of matriarchy or the significance of mother-right. In this respect, this late text echoes the profound uneasiness of *Totem and Taboo* in its radical suppression of Jung's influence, down to the (near) excision of his name.

Toward the end of *Moses and Monotheism*, Freud presents his clearest and most succinct account of matriarchy as occurring in an interval between two periods dominated by father-right. The first patriarchal system, he writes, "ended in a rebellion by the sons, who banded together against their father, overcame him and devoured him in common." Following this institution of a totemistic brother clan, "the victorious brothers renounced the women on whose account they had, after all, killed their father, and instituted exogamy." In this manner, moreover, "the power of fathers was broken and the families were organized as a matriarchy." In the ritual sacrifice of the totem, however, Freud sees "the ceremonial repetition of the killing of the father, with which social order, moral laws and religion had taken their start" (*SE* 23:131). This phase coordinates smoothly with Freud's account of the impact of Moses on the Hebrew worship of a father god.

If Freud seems confident in his placement of matriarchy in this passage he appears less definite at other points in his text, where he clearly regards the issue as problematic. The existence of matriarchy, and the worship of a mother goddess, along with the necessity of their overthrow, continue to present sticking points for Freud's Oedipal construction of the origins of human history and culture. In a long footnote, for instance, he attempts to explain the transition from worship of a mother goddess to that of a father god in ancient Crete on the basis of volcanic eruptions and the association of these geologic disturbances with a male deity.

> In Crete at that period (as probably in the Aegean world in general) the great mother-goddess was worshipped. The realization that she was not able to protect her house against the assaults of a stronger power may have contributed to her having to give place to a male deity, and, if so, the volcano god had the first claim to take her place. After all, Zeus always remains the 'earth-shaker'. There is little doubt that it was during those obscure ages that the mother-goddesses were replaced by male gods (who may originally perhaps have been sons).

Freud concludes this digression with an observation that emphasizes the role of violence in this "replacement." "The destiny of Pallas Athene, who was no doubt the local form of the mother-goddess, is particularly impressive. She was reduced to being a daughter by the religious revolution, she was robbed of her own mother and, by having virginity imposed on her, was permanently excluded from motherhood" (*SE* 23:46). Freud's characterization of the subjugation of Pallas Athena suggests a degree of disenfranchisement which requires a continuous level of enforcement. Is it possible that he recognized, however obliquely, the oppressiveness of his own theory of the development of femininity, in which the young girl is similarly "reduced" in status and "robbed" of a loving relationship to her mother?[11] Evidently unsatisfied, at any rate, with this formulation of mother-goddess worship, Freud attempts the subject two more times before arriving at the relatively seamless version that culminates his study.

In the middle of his discussion of totemism, Freud returns to the subject of matriarchy, inserting it somewhat haphazardly into his argument concerning the slow evolution of patriarchal religion. "At a point in this evolution which is not easily determined great mother-goddesses appeared, probably even before the male gods, and afterwards persisted for a long time beside them. In the mean time a great social revolution had occurred. Matriarchy was succeeded by the re-establishment of a patriarchal order." Freud's uncertainty about the sequence of events here becomes more pronounced as he continues to struggle with the chronology of patriarchy, matriarchy, mother-goddess worship, and the great monotheistic father religions.

> It is likely that the mother-goddesses originated at the time of the curtailment of the matriarchy, as a compensation for the slight upon the mothers. The male deities appear first as sons beside the great mothers and only later clearly assume the features of father-figures. These male gods of polytheism reflect the conditions during the pa-

---

11. As early as 1909 Freud takes a stand on the relationship of patriarchy to matriarchy. In a footnote to the Rat Man case history he states that "a great advance was made in civilization when men decided to put their inferences upon a level with the testimony of their senses and to make the step from matriarchy to patriarchy." It is interesting that he also invokes Athena here as a representative of the latter stage. "The prehistoric figures which show a smaller person sitting upon the head of a larger one are representations of patrilineal descent," he claims, pointing to Athena, who "had no mother, but sprang from the head of Zeus" (*SE* 10:233). Estelle Roithe reminds us that the statuette of Pallas Athena (to which H.D. refers in *Tribute to Freud*) was his favorite among his antiquities and that he regarded it as something of a talisman (*Riddle of Freud* 174). In the light of what H.D. tells us regarding the figure—that Freud considered her perfect, except for the fact that she had lost her spear—one is tempted to interpret his attachment to it as fetishlike. She appears to represent both female castration and the ascendance of patriarchy, two of Freud's most cherished ideas, which served, not incidentally, to sustain his own phallic identity.

triarchal age. They are numerous, mutually restrictive, and are occasionally subordinated to a superior high god. The next step, however, leads us to the theme with which we are here concerned—to the return of a single father-god of unlimited dominion. [*SE* 23:83–84]

Freud seems to breathe a sigh of relief when he arrives at the topic that interests him—the return of the father deity. That he himself recognized the inadequacy of his account of matriarchy and mother-goddess worship is evident in the comment "It must be admitted that this historical survey has gaps in it and is uncertain at some points" (*SE* 23:84).

When Freud addresses the subject of matriarchy at length in *Moses and Monotheism* he links it with a concept that supports his teleological aim and that he would also have found in Bachofen. The prohibition against the worship of an image of God in Mosaic religion signifies the subordination of sense perception to an abstract idea, Freud claims. It was "a triumph of intellectuality over sensuality or, strictly speaking, an instinctual renunciation, with all its necessary psychological consequences." The same triumph of intellectuality characterizes the victory of patriarchy over matriarchy. Freud elucidates this idea in a passage that reveals the influence of Bachofen without, however, acknowledging its debt.[12]

> We can far more easily grasp another process of a later date. Under the influence of external factors into which we need not enter here and which are also in part insufficiently known, it came about that the matriarchal social order was succeeded by the patriarchal one—which, of course, involved a revolution in the juridical conditions that had so far prevailed. An echo of this revolution seems still to be audible in the *Oresteia* of Aeschylus. But this turning from the mother to the father points in addition to a victory of intellectuality over sensuality—that is, an advance in civilization, since maternity is proved by the evidence of the senses while paternity is a hypothesis, based on an inference and a premise. [*SE* 23:113–14]

12. I agree with Philip Rieff, who sees an affinity between Freud and Bachofen in their attraction to myth and art as sources of speculation about prehistory (*Freud: The Mind of the Moralist* 207). My identification of Freud's specific debts to Bachofen parallels that of Peter Rudnytsky, whose book I read after completing my own manuscript (187).

Freud would have found these ideas stated in close proximity to one another in Bachofen's introduction to *Das Mutterrecht*. Allowing for a difference in style, one can see in Bachofen's concept of "triumphant paternity" Freud's "step forward in culture."

> The triumph of paternity brings with it the liberation of the spirit from the manifestations of nature, a sublimation of human existence over the laws of material life. While the principle of motherhood is common to all spheres of tellurian life, man, by the preponderant position he accords to the begetting potency, emerges from this relationship and becomes conscious of his higher calling. Spiritual life rises over corporeal existence, and the relation with the lower spheres of existence is restricted to the physical aspect. . . . Triumphant paternity partakes of the heavenly light, while childbearing motherhood is bound up with the earth that bears all things, the establishment of paternal right is universally represented as an act of the uranian solar hero, while the defense of mother right is the first duty of the chthonian mother goddesses. [109–10]

Freud's allusion to the *Oresteia* can also be traced to Bachofen, who writes:

> In the adventures of Orestes we find a reflection of the upheavals and struggles leading to the triumph of paternity over the chthonian-maternal principle. Whatever influence we may impute to poetic fancy, there is historical truth in the struggle between the two principles as set forth by Aeschylus and Euripides. The old law is that of the Erinyes, according to which Orestes is guilty and his mother's blood inexpiable; but Apollo and Athene usher in the victory as a new law; that of the higher paternity and of the heavenly light. This is no dialectical opposition but a historical struggle, and the gods themselves decide its outcome. [110]

One has to wonder at Freud's failure to name Bachofen among his sources, given the similarity of their points of view on the cultural transcendence of patriarchy over matriarchy. Freud's continuing uneasiness on the subject of matriarchy, however, provides an explanation for his elimination (conscious or unconscious) of Bachofen as an acknowledged influence on his thinking in *Moses and Monotheism*.

Whereas Bachofen posits the priority of mother-right (if not matriarchy per se), Freud's Oedipal construction places a strong father figure at the origins of human social organization. At the same time Bachofen's emphasis on the mother-infant bond finds an obvious parallel with the preoedipal period in Freud's psychoanalytic scheme. For Freud to have confronted the full implications of mother-right as Bachofen understands it (or as Jung redefined it in symbolic terms) would also have required him to revise his Oedipal paradigm. Evidently unwilling to theorize a period of human development (or human history) in which the role of the father is marginal or even irrelevant, Freud appears to adopt only those aspects of Bachofen's argument which suit his own hypothesis of paternal authority suppressed and then restored, while effacing the traces of Bachofen's influence by excluding him from citation. The symptomatic effects of this suppression appear in Freud's repeated attempts to theorize the position of matriarchy, none of which seems to satisfy him.

Near the end of *Moses and Monotheism*, as Freud builds toward his final version of prehistoric events, he begins to associate the triumph of the paternal principle with an increase in masculine self-esteem and with heroism. Without naming the mother directly, Freud explains at length how the renunciation of instinctual desire leads to a heightening of self-confidence. It is clear from Freud's argument that he refers to the male child's deferral of desire for his mother under pressure from a paternal authority, which contributes in turn to the formation of his superego. In attempting to correlate this process with the idea of intellectual progress, however, Freud must engage once again with the thorny issue of mother-right. As an example of intellectual advance, Freud cites the decision "that paternity is more important than maternity, although it cannot, like the latter, be established by the evidence of the senses." This observation elicits a renewed discussion of the recognition of father-right, in which Freud confesses his ignorance of how the shift actually came about. "Moreover, in the case of some advances in intellectuality—for instance, in the case of the victory of patriarchy—we cannot point to the authority which lays down the standard which is to be regarded as higher. It cannot in this case be the father, since he is only elevated into being an authority by the advance itself." In this passage, Freud seems momentarily to lose sight of the fact that he has already posited an originary state in which the father's authority is unquestioned. It is possible, on the other hand, that he acknowledges, however briefly, that he has never fully accounted for the understanding of paternity that underpins his concept of the primal horde. In any event, Freud brushes past this area of confusion in order to affirm the principle of heroic mastery which has drawn him into this discussion. "Thus we are faced by the phenomenon that in the course of the development of humanity sensuality is gradually overpowered by intellectuality and that men feel proud and exalted by every such advance. . . . Perhaps men simply pronounce that what is more difficult is higher, and their pride is merely their narcissism augmented by the consciousness of a difficulty overcome" (*SE* 23:118).

Freud's concept of the "great man" in *Moses and Monotheism* is intimately bound up with the "intellectual progress" that the recognition of paternity represents and, by implication, the ascendance of the Oedipal triangle over the preoedipal dyad. Renunciation of instinctual desire (for the mother), which represents a "set-back to sensuality," thus raises "the self-regard both of an individual and of a people" (*SE* 23:116). Mother-right and matriarchy, if they are to find a place in this scheme at all, must occupy an earlier and lower position on the scale of development, but for Freud the acknowledgment of the priority of the mother-infant relationship suggested by this placement threatens to subvert his Oedipal paradigm. Faced with a theoretical dilemma of this magnitude, Freud wavers in his descriptions of matriarchy, buries the influence of Bachofen, eliminates the word "mother" from his discussion of instinctual renunciation, and finally reasserts his thesis regarding the primal horde as the first (and clearly Oedipal) form of social organization.

The fact that Freud engages with the issues of matriarchy and mother-right to the extent that he does betrays his attraction to these ideas. Clearly, also, Bachofen's theory of the cultural transcendence of patriarchy supports Freud's own construction of heroism as the renunciation of instinctual desire necessary to the development of Oedipal masculinity. Freud's use of the cultural transcendence argument, however, emphasizes the later over the earlier, the Oedipal over the preoedipal phase. In *The Future of an Illusion* and *Civilization and Its Discontents*, two texts that intervene between the publication of *Totem and Taboo* and *Moses and Monotheism*, Freud's scheme of progressive development sets up an analogy between the preoedipal period and the state of nature which suggests yet another reason for the vagueness of his formulations of matriarchy, as well as his inability to look closely at the figure of the mother.

The Future of an Illusion (1927)

In the beginning of *The Future of an Illusion*, Freud presents his thesis that civilization is founded on the renunciation of instinct. That he has the prohibition against incest in mind becomes apparent when he describes the consequences of yielding to the pressure of instinctual demands: "If one imagines its prohibitions lifted—if, then, one may take any woman one pleases as a sexual object, if one may without hesitation kill one's rival for her love or anyone else who stands in one's way, if, too, one can carry off any of the other man's belongings without asking leave—how splendid, what a string of satisfactions one's life would be!" (*SE* 21:15).

But if the state of nature represents one that is free of paternal prohibition, nature begins to resemble a terrible matriarch. Nature herself, Freud claims, "would not demand any restrictions of instinct from us, she would let us do as we liked." Like an indulgent mother, nature does not enforce the taboo on incest. At the same time, such lack of restraint, as in the relationship between Caterina and her son Leonardo, poses a special hazard of its own. Nature, Freud states, "has her own particularly effective method of restricting us. She destroys us—coldly, cruelly, relentlessly, as it seems to us, and possibly through the very things that occasioned our satisfaction." The indefiniteness of Freud's language here renders it highly suggestive. Whereas the father's severity, his threat of castration, holds out the promise of the child's survival, the very permissiveness of nature, her offer of gratification, is deadly. Such sinister amorality must be kept in check. "It was precisely because of these dangers with which nature threatens us," Freud concludes, "that we came together and created civilization. . . . For the principal task of civilization, its actual *raison d'être*, is to defend us against nature" (*SE* 21:15).

The fact that Freud does not allude directly to the Oedipal triangle allows him to expand on the theme of the cruelty of nature without acknowledging the parallel between unrestrained nature (personified of course as female) and the preoedipal mother. Nature, inherently hostile to civilization, moreover, continually threatens its overthrow.

> There are the elements, which seem to mock at all human control: the earth, which quakes and is torn apart and buries all human life and its works; water, which deluges and drowns everything in a turmoil; storms, which blow everything before them; there are diseases, which we have only recently recognized as attacks by other organisms; and finally there is the painful riddle of death, against which no medicine has yet been found, nor probably will be. With these forces nature rises up against us, majestic, cruel and inexorable; she brings to our mind once more our weakness and helplessness, which we thought to escape through the work of civilization. [*SE* 21:15–16]

The theme of human helplessness forms a bridge to Freud's understanding of religion as an expression of the desire for paternal protection. Thus Freud completes the series of analogies that align the father with the development of civilization and with patriarchal religion. The place of the mother is the one conventionally assigned to woman in this scheme: she is allied with nature—materialistic, licentious, and amoral, as well as "majestic, cruel and inexorable."

Civilization and Its Discontents (1930)

The analogy between the preoedipal period and the state of nature recurs with added complications in *Civilization and Its Discontents*, where Freud discusses the death instinct and its relationship to aggression. He begins by repeating his parallel between individual psychic history and the origins of civilized development: "At this point we cannot fail to be struck by the similarity between the process of civilization and the libidinal development of the individual. . . . Sublimation of instinct is an especially conspicuous feature of cultural development; it is what makes it possible for higher psychical activities, scientific, artistic or ideological, to play such an important part in civilized life" (*SE* 21:97). So far the emphasis on paternal prohibition is firmly allied with a view of cultural progress which includes a control over nature. In keeping with his

Oedipal paradigm, moreover, Freud sees women, whose interests revolve around maternity, as hostile to the aims of civilization.

> Women represent the interests of the family and of sexual life. The work of civilization has become increasingly the business of men, it confronts them with ever more difficult tasks and compels them to carry out instinctual sublimations of which women are little capable. Since a man does not have unlimited quantities of psychical energy at his disposal, he has to accomplish his tasks by making an expedient distribution of his libido. . . . Thus the woman finds herself forced into the background by the claims of civilization and she adopts a hostile attitude towards it.   [*SE* 21:103–4]

Women not only do not contribute to the work of civilization, but they actively oppose it, exercising a "retarding and restraining influence" (*SE* 21:103). Their position in this regard is not unlike that of nature itself—resistant, if not destructive.

Women and nature, moreover, are associated through dirt. Freud correlates progress in civilization with an increase in demands for cleanliness.

> Dirtiness of any kind seems to us incompatible with civilization. We extend our demand for cleanliness to the human body too. We are astonished to learn of the objectionable smell which emanated from the *Roi Soleil*; and we shake our heads on the Isola Bella when we are shown the tiny wash-basin in which Napoleon made his morning toilet. Indeed, we are not surprised by the idea of setting up the use of soap as an actual yardstick of civilization.   [*SE* 21:93]

At the same time Freud maintains that "the fateful process of civilization would . . . have set in with man's adoption of an erect posture" (*SE* 21:99n), entailing a devaluation of olfactory stimuli which inhibits sexual pleasure. The strong smells associated with the organs of excretion, according to this view, give rise to a repugnance that includes the genitals. The example Freud quotes to support this argument refers specifically to the female genitals, however, suggesting that the "sublimations and libidinal displacements" he describes represent the responses of a male subject to the female body.

All neurotics, and many others besides, take exception to the fact that *'inter urinas et faeces nascimur* [we are born between urine and faeces]'. The genitals, too, give rise to strong sensations of smell which many people cannot tolerate and which spoil sexual intercourse for them. Thus we should find that the deepest root of the sexual repression which advances along with civilization is the organic defence of the new form of life achieved with man's erect gait against his earlier animal existence. [*SE* 21:106n]

The association of women with nature through their hostility to civilization and their closeness to the beginnings of life points to an area of conflict in Freud's argument for cultural transcendence. If civilization has evolved as a defense against nature, then the Oedipus and castration complexes, by implication, act as a check on the preoedipal mother-infant relationship, which threatens the structure of patriarchal authority. Yet Freud is everywhere reluctant to attribute power to the figure of the preoedipal mother. When confronted with what seem the inevitable consequences of his own argument, he shifts his ground, evading the necessity of altering this stance. The result is a textual instability, which speaks more clearly than Freud himself of his ambivalence.

The analogy between the preoedipal period and the state of nature allies the figure of the preoedipal mother with hostile or threatening forces. In his discussion of the death instinct, however, Freud takes care to exempt the mother-son relationship from the universal rule of aggression. In attempting to account for the failure of civilized society to control aggression, Freud posits "an independent aggressive instinct," which he derives from the death instinct he had earlier hypothesized in *Beyond the Pleasure Principle*. The death instinct itself operates "silently within the organism towards its dissolution." But when a portion of it is diverted toward the external world it "comes to light as an instinct of aggressiveness and destructiveness" (*SE* 21:119). The existence of this "original, self-subsisting instinctual disposition," in turn, disrupts the progress of civilization. "And now," Freud claims, "the meaning of the evolution of civilization is no longer obscure to us. It must present the struggle between Eros and Death, between the instinct of life and the instinct of destruction, as it works itself out in the human species" (*SE* 21:122).

The stumbling block in this argument concerns the role of aggression in the mother-infant relationship. If, as Freud maintains, the instinct of aggressiveness is innate in the human species, then it must play a part in preoedipal as well as Oedipal dynamics. While Freud is willing to entertain the notion of aggression in the desire of a male child for his mother, however, he does not want to acknowledge it as a component of maternal eroticism. The best he can do under the circumstances is state that the mother's love for her son constitutes an exception: "Aggressiveness was not created by property. It reigned almost without limit in primitive times, when property was still very scanty, and it already shows itself in the nursery almost before property has given up its primal, anal form; it forms the basis of every relation of affection and love among people (with the single exception, perhaps, of the mother's relation to her male child)" (*SE* 21:113). Freud has already made use of this claim in his analysis of Leonardo, where his musings on the menace of Caterina's caresses led him into similar difficulties. When faced with the bald possibility of maternal aggression, Freud abandons the logical consequences of his argument in favor of a simple form of idealization.

Freud employs a number of different strategies to avoid a direct examination of the preoedipal mother. At the same time, he does not succeed in banishing her completely from consideration. His struggles to incorporate matriarchy and mother goddesses in his system of cultural and religious progress attest to the fascination she holds for him as well as the threat she embodies to his construction of patriarchal authority and the Oedipal masculinity on which it rests. Her presence and her influence in Freud's texts are subversive, unsettling the smooth system of hierarchies which maintains the superiority of patriarchy to matriarchy, and Oedipal to preoedipal development, as reflected in the ascendance of civilization over nature.

Civilization and Its Discontents, in particular, represents the idea of such progress as at war with itself. In addition to the threat that nature poses to the goals of civilization, the death instinct within human nature itself acts to undermine the process of cultural ascendance. Because Freud links these issues to the development of Oedipal masculinity, he cannot help associating the instability of phallic achievement with the influence of women and ultimately with the preoedipal mother. When he turns from his meditations on religion and culture to metapsychological specula-tion, this structure of relationship emerges more clearly. In *Beyond the Pleasure Principle* and *Inhibitions, Symptoms and Anxiety*, in particular, which focus on questions of origins (the infant's first separation from its mother) and conclusions (death), the progressive model of human and cultural development virtually disappears, effaced by another movement that emphasizes instead the element of straying, in form as well as content. The kind of textual conflict that characterizes Freud's attempts to deal with the place and sig-nificance of the preoedipal mother in the works that I have de-scribed intensifies in these essays to the point where his arguments appear almost to cancel themselves. There is something like a Penelope principle at the heart of these texts, which seems to unravel what it creates. It is femininity, as embodied in the preoedi-pal mother, the specter that continues to inspire both awe and dread, that Freud associates with this condition.

5

Undoing

Freud refers to the mother-infant relationship in *Civiliza-tion and Its Discontents* when he describes the oceanic feeling that is derived from breast-feeding. At this stage, an infant "does not as yet distinguish his ego from the external world as the source of the sensations flowing in upon him" (*SE* 21:67). Freud's interest in this stage is brief, however, and he quickly dismisses its importance to the origins of religious feeling, which he attributes instead to the infant's helplessness and consequent longing for a father.

> I cannot think of any need in childhood as strong as the need for a father's protection. Thus the part played by the oceanic feeling, which might seek something like the restoration of limitless narcissism, is ousted from a place in the foreground. The origin of the religious attitude can be traced back in clear outlines as far as the feeling of infantile helplessness. There may be something further behind that, but for the present it is wrapped in obscurity. [*SE* 21:72]

Freud reveals his predilection here for relegating the preoedipal period to a state that is so dim and hoary with age that it cannot properly be examined. This displacement of the mother-infant rela-tionship from the area of discussion, moreover, helps to insulate it from Freud's subsequent speculations on the death instinct. In an earlier essay, however, he reveals a clear line of association between these two subjects. "The Theme of the Three Caskets" joins the figure of the mother with that of death, an imaginative conjunction that also informs the movement and preoccupation of *Beyond the Pleasure Principle*.

In his explication of the fort/da game in *Beyond the Pleasure Principle*, Freud exposes the instability of Oedipal masculinity, based as it is on a renunciation of the desire for union with the mother, a desire that persists throughout life and that can only be fulfilled in death. Later, in *Inhibitions, Symptoms and Anxiety*, Freud returns to the issue of the child's first separation from its mother, in part to refute the birth trauma thesis of his disciple Otto Rank, and in part to affirm his own interest in the preoedipal phase of development. Freud's treatment of these issues, however, can at best be described as one of approach/avoidance. At once fascinated and repelled by the implications of Rank's concept of the birth trauma, which displaces the Oedipal father in favor of the preoedipal mother, Freud circles nervously and inconclusively around the idea of castration as separation—not of the phallus from the male body, but of the infant from the maternal body—a radical transposition of theory from which he subsequently retreats.

"The Theme of the Three Caskets" (1913)

According to Jones, Freud conceived the idea of writing his essay on the theme of the three caskets in the spring of 1912, which would associate it with the period of intense intellectual rivalry with Jung which preceded their final break. It was precisely during this time that the two men exchanged views on the significance of matriarchy in relation to the incest taboo. Jones himself states that "whatever uncertainty may exist about the workings of Freud's unconscious mind about this time there can be no doubt about what most occupied it consciously. That was the approaching break with Jung" (*Life and Work of Sigmund Freud* 2:362). Yet he makes no connection between Freud's personal preoccupations and the writing or the subject matter of "The Theme of the Three Caskets." The reason for Jones's neglect in this regard may stem from the embarrassing resemblance between Freud's main thesis regarding the triple goddess and a very similar idea expressed in Jung's *Trans-*

formations, which he in turn borrows from Bachofen. It would seem illogical, after all, for Freud to express his indebtedness at this time to the very man whose ideas he considered anathema, and whose influence he aimed to suppress through the publication of *Totem and Taboo*. The fact that Freud echoes Jung so closely, however, suggests an attraction to Jung's (and ultimately Bachofen's) matriarchal symbolism which perhaps equaled his antagonism. But because Freud never admits this directly, it cannot affect his conscious theorizing. As a result, "The Theme of the Three Caskets" stands as something of an anomaly, testifying to a strain of Freud's thinking which finds only indirect expression in his more ambitious work.

In "The Theme of the Three Caskets" Freud interprets the casket scene in Shakespeare's *Merchant of Venice* as a representation of a choice among women. The lead casket, by association with silence, signifies death, as does the muteness of Lear's daughter Cordelia. "Gold and silver are 'loud,'" Freud explains, whereas "lead is dumb—in fact like Cordelia, who 'loves and is silent'" (*SE* 12:294). In fairy tales, moreover, dumbness "is to be understood as representing death." Thus the choice that confronts both Lear and Bassanio includes the Goddess of Death. "But if the third of the sisters is the Goddess of Death," Freud reasons, "the sisters are known to us. They are the Fates, the Moerae, the Parcae or the Norns, the third of whom is called Atropos, the inexorable" (*SE* 12:296). This line of speculation, in turn, leads first to the ancient mother goddesses, and finally to each man's relationship to his biological mother.

Freud traces the division of the original Moera of Greek mythology into a trinity of goddesses and their relationship to the more benignly conceived Hours, who stand for the natural cycle of seasons and, by implication, human mortality. Rebelling against the awareness of his fate, however, man substitutes another myth in which the Goddess of Love takes the place of the Goddess of Death, so that "the third of the sisters was no longer Death; she was the fairest, best, most desirable and most lovable of women." This device finds a parallel, moreover, in the character of the great mother goddess of the East, who displays the dual aspect of creator and destroyer.

The Goddess of Love herself, who now took the place of the Goddess of Death, had once been identical with her. Even the Greek Aphrodite had not wholly relinquished her connection with the underworld, although she had long surrendered her chthonic role to other divine figures, to Persephone, or to the tri-form Artemis-Hecate. The great Mother-goddesses of the oriental peoples, however, all seem to have been both creators and destroyers—both goddesses of life and fertility and goddesses of death. [*SE* 12:299]

The mother goddess that Freud has such difficulty integrating into his scheme of cultural development achieves a prominence in this essay which is remarkable. Given his general reticence on the subject of the preoedipal mother, not to mention his hostility to Jung, the boldness with which he climaxes his exposition of the meaning of the three caskets is even more extraordinary: "We might argue that what is represented here are the three inevitable relations that a man has with a woman—the woman who bears him, the woman who is his mate and the woman who destroys him; or that they are the three forms taken by the figure of the mother in the course of a man's life—the mother herself, the beloved one who is chosen after her pattern, and lastly the Mother Earth who receives him once more" (*SE* 12:301). Freud's expression here, while more eloquent than that of Jung, is otherwise quite close to his: "In the morning the goddess is the mother, at noon the sister-wife and in the evening again the mother, who receives the dying in her lap" (*Psychology of the Unconscious* 272). "Woman," in Freud's series, is synonymous with "mother," whose aspect changes according to one's stage in life until it is identical with that of death.[1] "It is in vain," Freud concludes somberly, "that an old man yearns for the love of woman as he had it first from his mother; the third of the Fates alone, the silent Goddess of Death, will take him into her arms" (*SE* 12:301).

There is another occasion on which Freud forms an associative link between mother and death through the intermediary of the

1. In Sarah Kofman's reading of "The Theme of the Three Caskets," the mother stands for several realities that Freud wished to evade: "law and necessity . . . time, Death, *difference*" (*Enigma of Woman* 74). Ernest Becker sees Freud's fear of death as providing the motivation for his heroism (*Denial of Death* 93–123).

Fates. A dream of a woman in a kitchen making dumplings, which Freud relates in *The Interpretation of Dreams*, elicits from him a recollection of a novel that ends with the hero calling out the names of three women. "In connection with the three women," Freud explains, "I thought of the three Fates who spin the destiny of man, and I knew that one of the three women—the inn-hostess in the dream—was the mother who gives life, and furthermore (as in my own case) gives the living creature its first nourishment" (*SE* 4:204). The image of the mother as one of the Fates superimposed on that of the woman in the kitchen evokes a childhood memory that identifies Freud's own mother as the source of these associations.

> When I was six years old and was given my first lessons by my mother, I was expected to believe that we were all made of earth and must therefore return to earth. This did not suit me and I expressed doubts of the doctrine. My mother thereupon rubbed the palms of her hands together—just as she did in making dumplings, except that there was no dough between them—and showed me the blackish scales of *epidermis* produced by the friction as a proof that we were made of earth.

Persuaded as a child by his mother's demonstration, Freud affirms the truth of her conviction through a phrase discovered in later life: "Du bist der Natur einen Tod schuldig" [Thou owest Nature a death] (*SE* 4:205). Generally speaking, Freud does not explore the kind of insight he reveals here. Both the dream of the three Fates and "The Theme of the Three Caskets" prepare the ground, however, for Freud's extended and convoluted meditation on separation from the mother and the role of the death instinct in *Beyond the Pleasure Principle*.

Beyond the Pleasure Principle (1920)

Some recent research on the relationships among Freud, Jung, and Sabina Spielrein has cast new light on Freud's brief citation of Spielrein's paper "Destruction as a Cause of Coming into Being" as one of the sources of his idea of the death instinct.[2] Spielrein,

2. In a footnote to his discussion of the death instinct as it relates to sexual instincts, Freud pays ambivalent tribute to Spielrein's work: "A considerable portion

fleeing Zurich as a result of an unhappy love affair with Jung, arrived in Vienna in October 1911 and quickly became a member of Freud's inner circle, participating in the Wednesday-night meetings at his home and presenting portions of her own psychoanalytic papers. While sympathetic to her plight, Freud did not at first respond favorably to her work, which he associated with that of her former mentor, the increasingly troublesome Jung. Jung himself, whether wishing to find some area of agreement with Freud or wanting to dissociate himself from his ardent pupil, also tended to find fault with her writing. Concerning "Destruction as a Cause of Coming into Being," which he had been charged to edit for the *Jahrbuch für psychoanalytische und psychopathologische Forschungen*, he writes:

> I was working on Spielrein's paper just before my departure. One must say: *desinat in piscem mulier formosa superne* [what at the top is a lovely woman ends below in a fish]. After a very promising start the continuation and end trail off dismally. Particularly the "Life and Death in Mythology" chapter needed extensive cutting as it contained gross errors and, worse still, faulty, one-sided interpretations. She has read too little and has fallen flat in this paper because it is not thorough enough. . . . Besides that her paper is heavily overweighted with her own complexes. [April 1, 1912; McGuire, *Freud/Jung Letters* 498]

In a curious way, Spielrein bears the brunt of the deteriorating relationship between the two men. Both find themselves engaged with her ideas (Jung through their previous collaborations and Freud through his attraction to her concept of destruction at the heart of creation) yet neither can simply praise her work. At the height of their quarrel, both men appear to use her as a means of communicating their dissatisfaction with each other. But Spielrein acts as a mediator in a more positive sense as well.[3] Her way of

---

of these speculations have been anticipated by Sabina Spielrein (1912) in an instructive and interesting paper which, however, is unfortunately not entirely clear to me" (*SE* 18:55).

3. Spielrein's role in the relationship between Freud and Jung is obviously complex and cannot be reduced to a simple formula. Yet Eve Sedgwick's analysis of the role of women in sustaining homosocial relationships among men is surely il-

thinking, profoundly influenced by Jung, offers Freud a means of responding to his rival without acknowledging him directly. Over time, her credit appears to rise with Freud, who seems to have completely dissociated her from the Swiss theorist by the time he recognizes her paper in *Beyond the Pleasure Principle*.

It is interesting that Spielrein does not actually hypothesize a death instinct.[4] Instead she focuses on the conflict between the drive for self-preservation of the individual and of the species, seeing the latter as compounded of both creative and destructive impulses. Summarizing her position, she states:

> The drive for self-preservation is a simple drive consisting of only one positive; the drive for the preservation of the species, which has to dissolve the old in order to create the new, is in its nature ambivalent, consisting of one positive and one negative component. Therefore the arousal of the positive component at the same time evokes the negative one, and vice versa. The drive for self-preservation is a "static" drive, inasmuch as it must protect an already existing individual from alien influences; the drive for the preservation of the species is a "dynamic" drive which strives for change, for the "resurrection" of the individual organism in new form. No change can happen without destruction of the old statues.   [Quoted in Kerr, "Beyond the Pleasure Principle and Back Again" 28]

Spielrein's dynamic interpretation of the drive for preservation of the species bears a certain resemblance to Jung's concept of the regression of the libido to the realm of the unconscious, which in turn owes much to Bachofen's cyclical view of life processes. Ultimately Freud's own working out of these issues through the idea of the death instinct is closest to that of Bachofen. Not wishing to affiliate himself with the theorist of mother-right or with the discredited Jung, however, Freud cites Spielrein, the obscurity of

---

luminating (*Between Men*). Spielrein, who tried to act as a mediator between the two men, attempting to soften their differences as well as to interpret their ideas to each other, provided Freud with a means of communicating with his onetime friend long after their official rupture. The ambivalence Freud evinces toward her in his footnote serves to express (in a highly deflected way) his equally divided responses to Jung.

4. I am indebted here to John Kerr's fine analysis of Spielrein's ideas as expressed in her essay on the topic in question ("Beyond the Pleasure Principle and Back Again").

whose work renders her unthreatening. Still the very existence of the note bears witness to a certain process of repression, calling attention in abbreviated form to a buried train of thought, which leads Freud back into his problematic engagement with the figure of the mother.

Freud's preoccupation with progressive development in religious, cultural, and individual terms undergoes a significant transformation in *Beyond the Pleasure Principle*, which emphasizes instead the profound and regressive attraction of death. Whereas Freud stresses the role of phallic masculinity in the process of cultural ascendance in such works as *Totem and Taboo* and *Moses and Monotheism*, here he neglects consideration of the Oedipus complex in favor of the earlier relationship of a child to its mother and the undertow exerted by that first attachment throughout one's life. The "advance" in terms of instinctual renunciation and mastery of frustration that the fort/da game represents in Freud's dense and tortuous exposition turns out, finally, to be indistinguishable from the desire to retreat. Mother, the child's point of origin, is also its goal and destiny, but as Freud states in "The Theme of the Three Caskets," it is the "silent Goddess of Death" who alone "will take him into her arms" (*SE* 12:301).

In both its structure and its argument, *Beyond the Pleasure Principle* negates forward motion. The result is not calculated to "raise the self-regard" of either a person or a nation. Unlike the idealized heroic past of *Moses and Monotheism*, which appears to carry its narrator to heights of self-confidence of his own, the confusing present of *Beyond the Pleasure Principle* reveals a narrator who is unsure of himself as well as the path he is traveling. His concluding quotation evokes an image of Oedipus as lame or "castrated," rather than tragic or heroic. The impulse to return to a state of organic diffusion and quiescence which Freud attributes to the death instinct is also bound up with feelings of fear and desire attached to the preoedipal mother. As his most serious and extensive meditation on this subject, *Beyond the Pleasure Principle* stands out among Freud's works for the darkness of its vision, as well as its mood of resignation.[5]

5. Freud's favorite daughter, Sophie, his "Sunday child," died of pneumonia, on January 25, 1920, many months before the publication of *Beyond the Pleasure*

There are two movements in *Beyond the Pleasure Principle*, each of which proposes an opposition between two terms which later resolves itself into an identity of aim. In the course of this argument, moreover, eros and the death instinct change positions, as though Freud were attempting to alter the outcome of his speculation that "all instincts tend towards the restoration of an earlier state of things" (*SE* 18:37). The essay as a whole, however, bears out the truth of this claim, which Freud derives from his observations on the efforts of a small child to gain mastery over the condition of separation from his mother. The fort/da game as a representation of an advance that also signifies retreat stands at the heart of this paradoxical essay, in which "mother" as one's point of origin can only be recovered in death, and life as a result appears at any given stage to be going backward.

The pleasure principle, Freud maintains at the outset, aims at the reduction of tension or excitation.[6] "We have decided to relate pleasure and unpleasure to the quantity of excitation that is present

---

Principle. That Freud was profoundly affected by this death is clear from his correspondence in the days following (E. Freud, *Letters of Sigmund Freud* 326–28). Evidently not wanting others to read his text as disguised autobiography, however, he asked his friend Max Eitingon to testify to the fact that he had seen the manuscript virtually complete in the summer preceding Sophie's death. Freud later objected to Fritz Wittels's biographical speculation that the text of *Beyond the Pleasure Principle* betrayed his grief. Jones, who recounts these events, seems to accept Freud's view that his writing was not affected by his personal tragedy (*Life* 3:40–41). Gay is more skeptical. After pointing out that the word for death drive, *Todestrieb*, entered Freud's correspondence a week after Sophie's death, he concludes that "the loss can claim a subsidiary role, if not in the making of his analytic preoccupation with destructiveness, then in determining its weight" (*Freud* 395). Gay also cites the horrors of the experience of the Great War as contributing to the somber quality of Freud's writing at this time.

6. Freud's discussion of pleasure, unpleasure, the aim of the reduction of tension, and the principle of constancy stems ultimately from his early (and subsequently abandoned) attempt to discover a neurological basis for the psychoneuroses. His letters to Fliess from April through December 1895 document his enthusiasm for the work that he titled "Sketch of a Psychology" (Entwurf Einer Psychologie) in manuscript and that has been published in English as "Project for a Scientific Psychology." Because Freud never requested the return of this manuscript from Fliess, it disappeared from view until well after his death, finally making its way into print in 1950. Frank Sulloway draws parallels between the arguments of Freud's "Project" and his metapsychological work *Beyond the Pleasure Principle*, emphasizing the continuity in his writing of his preoccupation with the biological foundations of mental activity (*Freud: Biologist of the Mind* 394–415). Jones, in his chapter on *Beyond the Pleasure*

in the mind but is not in any way 'bound'; and to relate them in such a manner that unpleasure corresponds to an *increase* in the quantity of excitation and pleasure to a *diminution"* (*SE* 18:7–8). Whereas pleasure accompanies the condition of stability, unpleasure involves a deviation therefrom. "The pleasure principle follows from the principle of constancy" (*SE* 18:9), Freud states unequivocally. This principle, however, does not dominate mental life, since the reality principle imposes restrictions on the fulfillment of desire. As an example of a process that embodies a renunciation of instinctual gratification and thus acts independently of the pleasure principle, Freud offers his interpretation of the fort/da game. Noticing that his one-and-a-half-year-old grandson, Ernst, has the habit of throwing a small reel with a string tied to it into his cot with the exclamation "o-o-o-o," which Freud understands to mean "fort" (gone), and then pulling it back with a "joyful da" (there), Freud concludes that the game represents the going away and return of the boy's mother.[7] The child makes up for the loss of his mother by a game in which he pretends to control both her departure and her reappearance. Freud casts this strategy at first in a progressive light: "It was related to the child's great cultural achievement—the instinctual renunciation (that is, the renunciation of instinctual satisfaction) which he had made in allowing his mother to go away without protesting. He compensated himself for this, as it were, by himself staging the disappearance and return of the objects within his reach" (*SE* 18:15). The game, though motivated by a condition of unpleasure, ultimately contributes to the boy's maturation. "At the outset he was in a *passive* situation—he

---

Principle, makes the nonspecific observation that "Freud revived many ideas dating from his neurological period or even earlier, passing swiftly from these to the impressions of his years of analytical experience," concluding in a psychological vein that "this mode of writing in itself indicates that the ideas propounded must be transmuted from some personal and profound source, a consideration which greatly adds to their interest" (*Life* 3:266). There is a curious phenomenon here in which Freud's return to his earlier ideas concerning the organism's tendency to avoid unpleasure and thus to sustain or restore a state of inertia seems to exhibit the very workings of the death instinct.

7. Derrida makes the fort/da game the center of his analysis of Freud's speculative activity in "Coming into One's Own," where he interprets Freud's writing activity as analogous to the play of disappearance and return that his grandson so obsessively enacts.

was overpowered by the experience; but, by repeating it, unpleasurable though it was, as a game, he took on an *active* part" (*SE* 18:16).

Freud speculates that the mastery Ernst achieves through his game may offer a pleasure all its own, so that it cannot be regarded as conclusive evidence of an impulse to repetition that precedes and overrides the pleasure principle. Turning to other examples that he finds more persuasive, however, Freud states that such a motive force does exist, and that it embraces children's games. "Now too we shall be inclined to relate to this compulsion the dreams which occur in traumatic neuroses and the impulse which leads children to play" (*SE* 18:22–23).

Having established his hypothesis of a compulsion to repeat which is "more elementary, more instinctual than the pleasure principle" (*SE* 18:23), Freud begins a long digression on the impact of external and internal stimuli on living organisms, in which he emphasizes the means of binding or disposing of such excitations. This discussion also stresses the disagreeable or unpleasurable nature of stimuli, especially ones that are internal. It is the task of the mental apparatus to bind these stimuli, a process that takes precedence over the operations of the pleasure principle. By a circuitous route Freud thus returns to the issue with which he began the essay—the aim of the reduction of tension—only this time, he ascribes this aim to the compulsion to repeat, as opposed to the pleasure principle. The compulsion to repeat, Freud claims, has the character of an instinct that inheres in all organic life.

> At this point we cannot escape a suspicion that we may have come upon the track of a universal attribute of instincts and perhaps of organic life in general which has not hitherto been clearly recognized or at least not explicitly stressed. *It seems, then, that an instinct is an urge inherent in organic life to restore an earlier state of things* which the living entity has been obliged to abandon under the pressure of external disturbing forces; that is, it is a kind of organic elasticity, or, to put it another way, the expression of the inertia inherent in organic life. [*SE* 18:36]

If Freud's conception of instinctual aims is circular, so is his argument. Although his focus has shifted from the pleasure principle to the compulsion to repeat, his interest remains the same—the reduction of disturbing excitations. Now, however, he takes this notion to its logical conclusion. The ultimate state of quiescence is death.

> The attributes of life were at some time evoked in inanimate matter by the action of a force of whose nature we can form no conception. It may perhaps have been a process similar in type to that which later caused the development of consciousness in a particular stratum of living matter. The tension which then arose in what had hitherto been an inanimate substance endeavoured to cancel itself out. In this way the first instinct came into being: the instinct to return to the inanimate state.

Freud's account of the origins of life as a whole might also be taken to describe the process by which individual human beings come into the world. Looked at this way, the preceding passage resonates with Freud's earlier exposition of the fort/da game, which is called into play as a result of little Ernst's consciousness of separation from his mother. What the game enacts is not only the child's desire for control over her departure, but also his wish for her return. In this light, however, the boy's attempts at mastery reveal their self-canceling aspect. Freud himself makes this point in reference to the compulsion to repeat, which creates only the illusion of forward motion. "Those instincts," he states, "are therefore bound to give a deceptive appearance of being forces tending towards change and progress, whilst in fact they are merely seeking to reach an ancient goal by paths alike old and new" (*SE* 18:38). Freud goes even further, asserting that the self-preservative instincts themselves serve the same end. Seen in this light, the theoretical importance of the instincts of self-preservation, self-assertion, and mastery greatly diminishes. "They are component instincts whose function it is to assure that the organism shall follow its own path to death, and to ward off any possible ways of returning to inorganic existence other than those which are immanent in the organism itself" (*SE* 18:39). What looks like progress is in fact only a devious route to death.

Freud's exposition of the repetition compulsion links little Ernst's game with the condition of separation from one's mother which characterizes the beginning of life itself and with the state of undifferentiation which accompanies death. The desire hidden in this childish amusement is one that elicits an almost lyrical out-burst on Freud's part as well as a certain measure of resistance. In his description of the ease with which primitive forms of life returned to their original state, Freud sounds almost envious.

> It was still an easy matter at that time for a living substance to die; the course of its life was probably only a brief one, whose direction was determined by the chemical structure of the young life. For a long time, perhaps, living substance was thus being constantly created afresh and easily dying, till decisive external influences altered in such a way as to oblige the still surviving substance to diverge ever more widely from its original course of life and to make ever more compli-cated *detours* before reaching its aim of death. These circuitous paths to death, faithfully kept to by the conservative instincts, would thus present us to-day with the picture of the phenomena of life. [*SE* 18:38–39]

At this point in the argument, the aim of the pleasure principle is in accord with that of the compulsion to repeat. Something in this equation, however, causes Freud to attempt a different means of formulation. "But let us pause for a moment," he interjects sud-denly, "and reflect. . . . It cannot be so," he muses, for the sexual instincts "appear under a very different aspect" (*SE* 18:39). This speculation initiates the second movement of the essay, which opposes eros to the death instinct, until even this distinction col-lapses into the all-pervasive desire for return to an earlier state. Freud's narrative asides, which begin to proliferate in this section, mirror the ideological conflicts that he unfolds.

Freud's long digression on the role of eros in instinctual life seems motivated by a recoil from his conclusions regarding the aim of all life as death. At any rate, it constitutes a significant interruption of this train of thought and introduces a new level of complexity by transposing the set of categories with which he began his inquiry. Although Freud does not explicitly identify the aims of eros with those of the pleasure principle, the relationship between them (through reference to instinctual gratification) is obvious. Whereas he begins by associating the compulsion to repeat with an un-pleasurable stimulus against which he sets the pleasure principle (which aims at the reduction of excitation), here Freud sees eros as providing a stimulus that thwarts the goal of the death instinct (and repetition compulsion) to return to a state of quiescence. Having precisely reversed his initial position on these forces, he then sets out to explore their interaction. It is not surprising, under the circumstances, that Freud finds in favor of the death instinct, given what seems to be his preference from the outset for the binding of stimulation. He himself, however, seems not to anticipate this conclusion, at which he appears to arrive with some reluctance. The drama of advance and retreat encoded in the dilemma of little Ernst, whose attempts at mastery only reveal the depths of his desire to regress to his point of origin, is replayed in Freud's own theoretical activity, whose goal appears to be its own undoing. This conflict reveals itself perhaps most dramatically in his narrative metaphors, which set images of progress against ones of backward turning or obscurity.

Sections VI and VII of *Beyond the Pleasure Principle* conclude with Freud's finding that "the pleasure principle seems actually to serve the death instincts" (*SE* 18:63). The process by which he reaches this melancholy truth, however, is particularly convoluted, as if to replicate the circuitous path to death which he has already hypothesized as the universal aim of life. Beginning this new line of inquiry, Freud expresses the hope that it will lead to a denial of the dominance he has attributed to the compulsion to repeat. "Let us turn back, then," he proposes, "to one of the assumptions that we have already made, with the expectation that we shall be able to give it a categorical denial." Questioning his assumption that "all living substance is bound to die from internal causes" (*SE* 18:44), he then considers the evidence offered by biological science, where he claims to seek "a firm footing" (*SE* 18:48). This route, however, leads to a dead end. "At this point," Freud muses, "the question may well arise in our minds whether any object whatever is served by trying to solve the problem of natural death from a study of the protozoa" (*SE* 18:49). Concluding that biology fails to resolve the issue of the dominance of instincts, he tries a new tack. "Let us make a bold attempt at another step forward" (*SE* 18:50). This metaphor of advance is quickly countered, however, by subsequent expressions of uncertainty.

Images of obscurity characterize the next movement, in which Freud takes the opportunity to review some of his own theories.

Discussing the relationship between sexual instincts and ego instincts, he observes that "in no region of psychology were we groping more in the dark" (*SE* 18:51). This question is particularly thorny, moreover, and a lengthy treatment of it seems to give rise to even greater uncertainty. "In the obscurity that reigns at present in the theory of the instincts," Freud concludes somewhat wearily, "it would be unwise to reject any idea that promises to throw light on it." This statement is followed by a reformulation of the original issue and a new objective: "We started out from the great opposition between the life and death instincts. . . . If only we could succeed in relating these two polarities to each other and in deriving one from the other!" (*SE* 18:53).

The last, most speculative part of Freud's argument is riddled with expressions of doubt.

> Apart from this, science has so little to tell us about the origin of sexuality that we can liken the problem to a darkness into which not so much as a ray of a hypothesis has penetrated. [*SE* 18:57]

> But here, I think, the moment has come for breaking off. [*SE* 18:58]

> My answer would be that I am not convinced myself and that I do not seek to persuade other people to believe in them. . . . It is surely possible to throw oneself into a line of thought and to follow it wherever it leads out of simple scientific curiosity. [*SE* 18:59]

> One may have made a lucky hit or one may have gone shamefully astray. [*SE* 18:59]

> We need not feel greatly disturbed in judging our speculation upon the life and death instincts by the fact that so many bewildering and obscure processes occur in it. [*SE* 18:60]

> We may expect it [biology] to give us the most surprising information and we cannot guess what answers it will return in a few dozen years to the questions we have put to it. They may be of a kind which will blow away the whole of our artificial structure of hypotheses. [*SE* 18:60]

As the book draws to a close, Freud's tone grows more harsh and somber. Near the end, he appears ready to abandon the whole of his preceding endeavor. After characterizing the life instincts as "breakers of the peace" and postulating that the death instinct keeps watch over every source of stimulation, which it labors to subdue, Freud breaks off with the abrupt comment: "This in turn raises a host of other questions to which we can at present find no answer. . . . We must be ready, too, to abandon a path that we have followed for a time, if it seems to be leading to no good end" (*SE* 18:63–64). The confidence born from the mastery of instinctual gratification which Freud sets at the heart of civilized development is nowhere in evidence here. A more puzzling mechanism has intervened between the male child's negotiation of the Oedipus and castration complexes, one that appears to thwart or unravel the achievement of masculine identity. The fort/da game, based on a little boy's memorialization of his loss of his mother, institutionalizes both the act of renunciation and the impulse toward regression that inheres in it. The structure of mastery that underpins Freud's concept of masculinity is thus profoundly ironic. As if to acknowledge the degree to which he has shaken the foundations of his own Oedipal theory, Freud concludes with an almost parodic allusion to his swell-foot hero: "We may take comfort, too, for the slow advances of our scientific knowledge in the words of the poet: 'Was man nicht erfliegen kann, muss man erhinken. . . . Die Shrift sagt, es ist keine Sünde zu hinken' [What we cannot reach flying we must reach limping. . . . The Book tells us it is no sin to limp]" (*SE* 18:64).

The concept of return to one's origin as a return to one's mother clearly underlies Freud's exposition of the death instinct. Here as elsewhere, however, he manages to avert his gaze from the figure of the preoedipal mother herself, as though it were possible to dissociate her from the processes through which human life comes into being. Freud's *Inhibitions, Symptoms and Anxiety* bears traces of this struggle, though waged on somewhat different grounds owing to Otto Rank's theory of the birth trauma.

Inhibitions, Symptoms and Anxiety (1926)

Toward the end of *The Ego and the Id*, published in April 1923, Freud describes birth as the "first great anxiety-state" (*SE* 19:58), an apparently favorable reference to Rank's thesis, with which he was acquainted, although *The Trauma of Birth* did not appear in print until December of that year. Jones reports Freud's reaction to Rank's theory when he first heard of it in the summer of 1922:

"Anyone else would have used such a discovery to make himself independent." Later Freud remarked to Ferenczi that "it is the most important progress since the discovery of psychoanalysis" (*Life* 3:59). The concluding paragraphs of *The Ego and the Id* link the subject of birth anxiety with that of the death instinct, although Freud fails to develop this train of association. His reference to "anxiety due to separation from the protecting mother" leads to a statement about the "fear of death, like the fear of conscience, as a development of the fear of castration," which in turn evokes a discussion of the death instincts that "desire to be at peace and (prompted by the pleasure principle) to put Eros, the mischief-maker, to rest" (*SE* 19:58–59). This series of juxtapositions reads mother-castration-death—a conjunction that haunts the later essay *Inhibitions, Symptoms and Anxiety,* in which Freud actively opposes Rank.[8]

During the period between the publication of *The Ego and the Id* in 1923 and the appearance of the essay on anxiety in 1926, Freud's initially favorable reaction to Rank's ideas about the trauma of birth underwent a dramatic alteration. According to Jones, who documents this period of transition, the appearance in print of Rank's book caused Freud a "shock of alarm—lest the whole of his life's work on the etiology of the neuroses be dissolved" (*Life* 3:59). Later, though, he regarded the idea of the birth trauma as one of "fundamental importance" and labored to integrate it into his own theoretical structure. The misgivings of the Berlin group seem to have moved him to reconsider this view, and a circular letter to the members of his Committee, dated February 15, 1924, expresses both his attraction to the book and the focus of his disagreement with it. A careful reading of this letter reveals the nature of the conflict that informs *Inhibitions, Symptoms and Anxiety* and that accounts for its peculiarly obsessive tone and repetitive structure.

After affirming his support of independent research among members of the Committee and discussing a question of analytic technique raised by Ferenczi, Freud addresses the main topic of the letter, Rank's *Trauma of Birth,* which he describes as a "highly significant" work, although he has not yet arrived at a "definitive

---

8. Gay notes that "while the name of Rank appears in it [*Inhibitions, Symptoms and Anxiety*] only a few times, Freud was carrying on a silent debate with him throughout" (485).

judgment" of it. Then he moves directly to the point of greatest interest: "We have long been familiar with womb phantasies and recognized their importance, but in the prominence Rank has given them they achieve a far higher significance and reveal in a flash the biological background of the Oedipus complex. To repeat it in my own language: some instinct must be associated with the birth trauma which aims at restoring the previous existence" (Jones, *Life* 3:61). In this brief statement, Freud makes the connection between the impulse to return to one's point of origin embodied in the death instinct and the figure of the preoedipal mother which eludes him in *The Ego and the Id*. This conjunction, however, elicits resistance, as his next series of reflections and objections reveals. The primacy that Rank attributes to the birth trauma, as Freud rightly perceives, undermines the structure of the Oedipus and castration complexes, on which the production of masculinity and the patriarchal social order as a whole depend. For Rank, the prohibition against incest mandated by the father is a secondary development, a displacement of the earlier experience of birth anxiety, which in itself acts as a deterrent to incestuous desire, preventing the fulfillment of the fantasy of return to the womb (through intercourse). In a lengthy response, Freud makes clear his opposition to this view.

> Obstacles, which evoke anxiety, the barriers against incest, are opposed to the phantastic return to the womb: now where do these come from? Their representative is evidently the father, reality, the authority which does not permit incest. Why have these set up the barrier against incest? My explanation was an historical and social one, phylogenetic. I derived the barrier against incest from the primordial history of the human family, and thus saw in the actual father the real obstacle, which erects the barrier against incest anew. Here Rank diverges from me. He refuses to consider the phylogenesis, and regards the anxiety opposing incest as simply a repetition of the anxiety at birth, so that the neurotic repression is inherently checked by the nature of the birth process. This birth anxiety is, it is true, transferred to the father, but according to Rank he is only a pretext for it. Basically the attitude toward the womb or female genital is supposed to be ambivalent from the start. [Jones, *Life* 3:62]

Freud's own speculations on the death instinct in *Beyond the Pleasure Principle* predispose him to Rank's thesis concerning the traumatic nature of the emergence of life and the desire it engenders to return to the mother's womb as the representative of a previous state of quiescence. By making explicit some of the latent elements in Freud's own argument, however, Rank threatens to explode the Oedipal construction that systematically obscures the figure of the mother. Regardless of the weakness in Rank's argument (deriving from his need to attribute every manifestation of neurosis to the birth trauma), his focus on birth itself brings into the foreground issues that Freud himself has assiduously avoided, relegating them to footnotes and to the margins of his theory. It is no surprise, then, that Freud insists on returning to his own (equally questionable) phylogenetic account, which has the virtue of reinstalling the father as a figure of authority, whose prohibition against incest assures both the progress of masculine development and of Western civilization. Freud's letter, however, did not resolve his ambivalence, which is rooted in his own increasing interest in the preoedipal period. *Inhibitions, Symptoms and Anxiety* reflects this ambivalence in its obsessive preoccupation with the subject of birth, along with its failure to work through the associations it brings forward.

The Trauma of Birth acts as a subtext to *Inhibitions, Symptoms and Anxiety*, which revolves around Rank's thesis at the same time that it represses the most disturbing elements in it. The resulting narrative effect is something like running in place. Like a dog worrying a bone, Freud keeps returning to the same subject, without arriving at a satisfactory formulation. Several addenda in which he readdresses points raised in the body of the work attest to his continuing discontent. At the same time, his statements about his own theoretic endeavor, like those of *Beyond the Pleasure Principle*, express doubt and confusion. *Inhibitions, Symptoms and Anxiety* is itself an inhibited, anxious, and symptomatic text, which betrays in its structure the simultaneous fascination and dread that characterizes Freud's most consistent stance in relation to preoedipal issues. In this essay, for instance, he returns to his study of Little Hans, one of his earliest attempts to comprehend the mother-child relationship, as though to reconsider the primacy of his castration theory in the light of the child's first "castration," or separation from its mother. Every time he approaches this subject, however, he veers away from it again, a gesture that recalls his previous strategies of dealing with the preoedipal period, dating from his first traumatic recoil in response to Emma Eckstein's bleeding. A brief consideration of the main ideas of *The Trauma of Birth* reveals the substance of Freud's attraction and his opposition to the book, and helps to explain the peculiarly unstable nature of the essay he wrote in reaction to it.

Although Rank takes pains to argue for the compatibility of his own ideas with those of the architect of psychoanalysis, he diverges from Freudian orthodoxy in some important respects. For Rank, the birth trauma takes center stage in the drama of human development. All subsequent nervous disorders can be traced back to this event, and analysis as a result takes on the character of an abreaction or reworking of this experience. The analyst in this process becomes the object of the patient's mother transference, and the successful conclusion of the analysis involves a feeling of rebirth. Even a schematic statement of Rank's ideas draws out the obvious—the extent to which his theory revolves around the figure of the mother.[9] Jones, who tends to trivialize this aspect of Rank's thought, reports an incident that emphasizes the fascination it held for the dissident analyst. "It stayed in my mind," he relates, "that in March, 1919, when I met him with his pregnant wife in Switzerland, he had astonished me by remarking in a dismal tone that men were of no importance in life; the essence of life was the relation between mother and child" (*Life* 3:58). It is easy enough, as Jones does later, to disparage Rank's claim to have discovered the root of all neurotic disturbances, and thus to sweep aside some of the more interesting offshoots of his theory, which derive from his preoccupation, dismal or otherwise, with the mother-child relationship.

Rank's transgression against classical psychoanalysis, one that led in 1926 to a permanent rupture with Freud, consists in his emphasis on the primacy of the mother-child bond and its subversive relationship to the Oedipus and castration complexes. Rank's explication of animal phobias demonstrates this tendency. Large animals, he claims, evoke images of the mother's pregnancy, while beasts of prey elicit a fantasy of returning to the mother's womb

9. Gay remarks succinctly that "Rank was elevating the mother's role at the expense of the father's, and the prototypical anxiety of birth at the expense of the Oedipus complex" (475). See also Paul Roazen, who points out that much of post-Freudian psychoanalytic theory has focused on the mother's role in development (*Freud and His Followers* 398).

through the desire to be eaten. When animal phobias relate to the father (as Freud maintains in his case study of Little Hans) they do so through a process of substitution. Rank's attempt to reconcile his theory with that of Freud, as expressed in *Totem and Taboo*, can only have aroused suspicion regarding his orthodoxy.

> The significance of animals as a father substitute, which in the psychology of neuroses Freud has emphasized for the understanding of Totemism, remains not only undisturbed by this conception, but maintains a deepened biological significance, showing how, through the displacement of anxiety on to the father, the renunciation of the mother, necessary for the sake of life, is assured. For this feared father prevents the return to the mother and thereby the releasing of the much more painful primal anxiety, which is related to the mother's genitals as the place of birth, and later transferred to objects taking the place of the genitals. [*Trauma of Birth* 13]

Rank effectively removes the father as the source of castration threat, making him into a kind of bogus authority whose primary function is to act as a screen for a deeper dread in relation to the mother's body. It follows that "the importance of the castration fear is based . . . on the primal castration at birth, that is, on the separation of the child from the mother" (20). If castration occurs at birth, however, the father's role in prohibiting an incestuous mother-child union is clearly secondary. The trauma of birth itself, which makes the mother's genitals a locus of fear as well as desire, bars the child's access to the maternal body. The seeming authority embodied in the father's threat simply eases the child's passage out of the incestuous circuit.

Rank's reinterpretation of the father's role in the castration complex affects all levels of his theory. While civilization still rests on the incest taboo, it is a precarious construct, subject to the undertow of regressive urges focused on the desire to repair the first rupture from the mother's body. Thus, Rank maintains that "the so-called advance in the development of civilization has proved to be a continually repeated attempt to adjust to the enforced removal from the mother the instinctive tendency to return to her" (103). Whereas Freud, in *Totem and Taboo* and later in *Moses and Monotheism*, emphasizes the mastery achieved through renunciation, without which culture cannot exist, Rank lyricizes the intrauterine

state, as well as the siren call to death which resides in the desire to
return to it. In this regard he echoes Freud's own speculations in
Beyond the Pleasure Principle but in such a way as to conjoin the
idea of mother with that of death, an association that Freud himself
avoids stating directly.

Even children, Rank maintains, connect the thought of death
with "a strong unconscious sense of pleasure associated with the
return to the mother's womb" (24). In support of this idea, he turns
to literature and mythology, where he enlists the aid of Bachofen, a
theorist whom Freud had little use for.

> Everyone born sinks back again into the womb from which he or she
> once came into the realm of light, roused by the deed of man. Indeed,
> the ancients recognized in this taking back of the dead the highest
> expression of mother love which keeps faith with her offspring at the
> moment when it stands there abandoned by all (Bachofen). Bachofen
> has demonstrated this very beautifully in the death-bringing Nemesis
> springing from the (bird's) egg, as well as in a number of other ancient
> goddesses of the underworld and of death. [114–5]

Rank goes further, quoting a passage from Bachofen himself: "Everywhere Woman appears as bearer of the law of death, and, in this
identification, at the same time appears as affectionate and as a dark
threatening power, capable of the deepest sympathy but also of the
greatest severity, like the maternally formed Harpies and the Egyp-
tian-Phoenician Sphinx who bore in herself the law of all material
life" (115). Through the medium of Bachofen, Rank challenges
Freud's almost exclusive emphasis on the role of the father in
processes of individual and cultural development at the same time
that he puts pressure on the most vulnerable area of his theory—his
dissociation between maternal love and maternal power. Taking
his clue from *Beyond the Pleasure Principle*, which virtually identifies the figure of the mother with that of death, Rank lifts the
repression that attends this line of thought and extends its implications in ways that Freud seems to have regarded as both seductive
and threatening. Rank brings to the surface of his text precisely
those issues relating to the preoedipal period which Freud has labored to transcend, to marginalize, or to subdue.

Rank's sympathy for Bachofen's studies of ancient symbolism
and mother-right leads to an understanding of religious develop-

ment which also differs from Freud's. Like Bachofen, Rank assumes that mother-right preceded father-right, and that the veneration of a male deity resulted from a displacement of mother-goddess worship. This emphasis on the primacy of maternity leads to a concept of patriarchal religion as an advance based on repression, and hence one that is inherently unstable. Whereas Freud never found a comfortable resolution of the problem of mother-right and mother-goddess worship within his accounts of religion and culture, Rank adopts Bachofen's scheme while attempting to fit it into the structure of *Totem and Taboo*. The pastiche that results is only superficially supportive of Freud's theory. In its deeper implications, as Freud seems to have divined, judging from his earlier reaction to Bachofen, it is subversive. Rank focuses throughout on the magnetic attraction of the mother-relation, which continues to exert its influence despite the transference of primal anxiety onto the father.

> The father-God has been put in the place of the primal mother charged with anxiety and desire, in order, in the Freudian meaning of "Totemism," to create and to guarantee social organization. Every relapse to the veneration of the mother, which can only be accomplished sexually, is therefore anti-social and is persecuted with all the horror of so-called religious fanaticism. But this, like social revolution, finally results in the preservation and strengthening of the father-like power for the protection of the social community. [126]

The father god who guarantees social organization, like the father who threatens castration, is a sham. It is the mother, instead, like one of the ancient goddesses of creation and destruction, who looms large in this study. Oedipus is subordinate to the Sphinx.

By the time Freud published *Inhibitions, Symptoms and Anxiety* he had quarreled with Rank, reconciled, and was on the verge of a final break. The vicissitudes of this friendship are reflected in the vacillations and repressions of the text in which Freud attempted to address the challenge he detected in Rank's ideas. The result of this labor, however, far from resolving the issues in question, intensifies the underlying conflict between Oedipal and preoedipal interpretation. In its narrative effects, *Inhibitions, Symptoms and Anxiety* resembles *Beyond the Pleasure Principle*, where an agent of undoing (what I have called the Penelope principle) continually undercuts the possibility of forward motion. This undoing action creates a condition of textual instability that derives ultimately from the specter of the preoedipal mother, the figure whom Freud alternately invokes and suppresses throughout his writing career.

James Strachey's comment in his introduction to *Inhibitions, Symptoms and Anxiety* that Freud had "an unusual difficulty in unifying the work" is an understatement (*SE* 20:78).[10] Freud himself refers repeatedly to his own uncertainties. He compares himself to a "benighted traveller," who cannot "see an inch further beyond his nose" (*SE* 20:96), describes the humiliation of having worked so long still to "be having difficulty in understanding the most fundamental facts" (*SE* 20:124), dissolves his own reasoning at the end of one chapter with the succinct "*Non liquet*" (*SE* 20:110), and ends another with the pessimistic comment that "we are as much in the dark about this problem as we were at the start" (*SE* 20:149). Finally he brings the book to a close with the unresounding statement: "Further than this, I believe, our knowledge of the nature and causes of neurosis has not as yet been able to go" (*SE* 20:156).

In these comments, as well as others, Freud acknowledges the problem at the heart of this work, the repetitive tendency that causes him to return again and again to his point of departure—the subject of birth and the separation from the mother, which offers a prototype for all other anxiety situations. Although he refers explicitly to Rank on only three occasions, his preoccupation with the issue of birth anxiety manifests itself in four other discussions, the last two of which appear in addenda. Despite his care to distinguish his own views from those of Rank, mainly on the basis of the psychical as opposed to the purely physiological content of anxiety, Freud's obsession with the birth situation betrays his fascination with the preoedipal issues raised by the former Committee member. In this regard, *Inhibitions, Symptoms and Anxiety* is written as much in sympathy with Rank as against him.

Freud had originally understood anxiety as resulting from repression. *Inhibitions, Symptoms and Anxiety*, in contrast, designates anxiety as a reaction to a situation of danger, thus tying it more closely to the ego than the id. It is this new reactive concept of anxiety, in turn, which prompts Freud's first allusion to the birth

10. Gay calls the book "shaggy" in appearance and states that Freud seems "wearily indecisive about just how to order the sheer masses of his material." Yet he defends the essay as crucial to Freud's thought, despite its dishevelment (485–89).

trauma. "In man and the higher animals," he offers, "it would seem that the act of birth, as the individual's first experience of anxiety, has given the affect of anxiety certain characteristic forms of expression." Without naming Rank, or his disagreement with him, Freud then hastens to qualify this statement.

> But, while acknowledging this connection, we must not lay undue stress on it nor overlook the fact that biological necessity demands that a situation of danger should have an affective symbol, so that a symbol of this kind would have to be created in any case. Moreover, I do not think that we are justified in assuming that whenever there is an outbreak of anxiety something like a reproduction of the situation of birth goes on in the mind. It is not even certain whether hysterical attacks, though they were originally traumatic reproductions of this sort, retain that character permanently. [*SE* 20:93–94]

Freud's uneasiness proliferates throughout the essay. The association between hysteria and the birth trauma, moreover, becomes increasingly problematic, as he begins to link the concept of birth anxiety with his redefinition of castration as loss of an object, a radical revision that has the effect of obviating the distinction between masculinity and femininity. First, however, he returns to his case study of Little Hans in order to reaffirm his view of the child's phobia (and consequent anxiety) as a result of castration fear.

In contrast to Rank, who emphasizes the mother's role in animal phobias, Freud reasserts his conclusion that Little Hans's fear derived from the threat of castration embodied in the figure of his father. Thus Little Hans "gave up his aggressiveness towards his father from fear of being castrated. His fear that a horse would bite him can, without any forcing, be given the full sense of a fear that a horse would bite off his genitals, would castrate him." For the sake of completeness, perhaps, Freud includes the case of the Wolf Man in his reaffirmation of the etiological significance of the castration complex. The problems he encounters here are the ones he had earlier finessed, the fact that the Wolf Man had reported an incidence of female seduction and that his fear of being devoured by a wolf does not in itself contain "any allusion to castration." Freud explains these anomalies by maintaining first that the Wolf Man developed a passive (or feminine) attitude toward his father, and that he subsequently repressed his fear of castration, so that it emerged transformed in the wolf fantasy. A simpler line of analysis might connect the experience of seduction with the fear of being devoured by a woman, as another interpretation of Little Hans's phobia might emphasize his fantasy of his mother as the possessor of "a widdler like a horse." Yet Freud, faced with Rank's explicit emphasis on the mother-infant relationship, chooses to maintain his own faith in the explanatory power of the castration complex. "Here, then," he explains, somewhat disingenuously, "is our unexpected finding: in both patients the motive force of the repression was fear of castration. The ideas contained in their anxiety . . . were substitutes by distortion for the idea of being castrated by their father" (*SE* 20:108).

Freud's insistence on the role of castration fear in the generation of anxiety begins to assume a symptomatic character of its own, as he repeats it in opposition to the idea of the birth trauma. In a chapter that emphasizes the process of symptom formation in obsessional neurosis, and which includes mention of conversion hysteria, he states that the "motive force" for both is "the fear of castration" (*SE* 20:122). A note at the end of this chapter, however, suggests an area of disturbance in Freud's argument which comes increasingly into the foreground as he writes. A doubt arises as to whether "fear of castration is the only motive force of repression. . . . If we think of neuroses in women," Freud claims suddenly, "we are bound to doubt it. For though we can with certainty establish in them the presence of a castration *complex*, we can hardly speak with propriety of castration *anxiety* where castration has already taken place" (*SE* 20:123). Whereas castration anxiety attests to the process of masculine development, castration itself (attributed to women) obliterates that possibility. To identify the body of the mother, as Rank does, as the source of anxiety is also to locate the condition of castration at the heart of human development. The series of associations which Freud attempts to avoid through his emphasis on the father's authority begins slowly to coalesce around the figure of the mother as the site of castration, as well as the focus of its threat.

When Freud readdresses the subject of animal phobias, he turns the question of castration in a new direction. "Castration," he claims, "can be pictured on the basis of the daily experience of the faeces being separated from the body or on the basis of losing the mother's breast at weaning" (*SE* 20:129–30). This redefinition of castration as separation applies equally to the birth situation, as Freud himself acknowledges. Without invoking Rank, he considers this notion: "The first experience of anxiety which an individual goes through (in the case of human beings, at all events) is birth, and, objectively speaking, birth is a separation from the mother. It could be compared to a castration of the mother (by equating the child with a penis)." Freud's conception of birth as a castration of the mother recalls his earlier emphasis on female castration as a reality, at the same time that it masks the full implications of the radical reappraisal undertaken here. If the scene of birth is one of castration, the sword may be said to cut both ways. The infant, too, experiences such separation as castration. Yet Freud hastens to divert the reader's attention from this disturbing possibility. "Birth," he states categorically, "is not experienced subjectively as a separation from the mother, since the foetus, being a completely narcissistic creature, is totally unaware of her existence as an object" (*SE* 20:130). That his argument is directed against Rank becomes apparent when he denies that birth anxiety is repeated whenever a separation takes place. Pain and mourning, he claims, are more common and appropriate reactions. A strategic relocation of the threat of castration from the Oedipal to the preoedipal realm has already taken place, however, through the fundamental equation between separation and castration.

The shift from an Oedipal to a preoedipal emphasis characterizes the remainder of Freud's essay. Reviving the question of birth anxiety, which he addresses now for the third time, Freud finally discusses *The Trauma of Birth* directly. He begins by arguing against the notion that infantile phobias reproduce the anxiety experienced at birth, given that "birth has as yet no psychical content" (*SE* 20:135). This observation leads, however, back to a consideration of anxiety due to separation, a subject that evokes an image reminiscent of the opening of *Beyond the Pleasure Principle*. "Only a few of the manifestations of anxiety in children," Freud maintains, "are comprehensible to us. . . . They occur, for instance, when a child is alone, or in the dark, or when it finds itself with an unknown person instead of one to whom it is used—such as its mother" (*SE* 20:136). A child's longing for its absent mother converts into anxiety, which "has all the appearance of being an expression of the child's feeling at its wits' end, as though in its still very undeveloped state it did not know how better to cope with its cathexis of longing" (*SE* 20:137). Anxiety, here, takes the place of little Ernst's game, which has the virtue of a coping mechanism, at the same time that it acts as a ritual memorial to the loss it is meant to master.

In his next reflection, Freud neatly connects the associations he elsewhere labors to disjoin: birth, separation from the mother, and castration anxiety. "Here anxiety appears as a reaction to the felt loss of the object; and we are at once reminded of the fact that castration anxiety, too, is a fear of being separated from a highly valued object, and that the earliest anxiety of all—the 'primal anxiety' of birth—is brought about on the occasion of a separation from the mother" (*SE* 20:137). The experience of the loss of a highly valued object begins with the first separation from the body of one's mother, is repeated subsequently as the infant recognizes its dependence on her for the gratification of its needs, and issues finally in the fear of castration, or loss of one's penis. Despite Freud's disagreements with Rank, he follows him here in the displacement of paternal authority from the primary stages of development and, more important, in the emphasis on castration as always already having taken place. The fort/da game creates only the illusion of mastery. In reality, it attests to the inevitability of a loss that Freud chooses in this essay to call "castration." Jacques Lacan and, in a more radical fashion, Jacques Derrida develop some of the theoretical implications of this realignment of focus and terminology. Freud, however, appears to have been more conflicted about his discoveries. He continues, in this essay, to oppose Rank's thesis regarding birth anxiety at the same time that he muses further on the redefinition of castration as separation. This double focus allows him, paradoxically, to pursue the line of thought begun in *Beyond the Pleasure Principle* as well as to avoid acknowledging the extent to which it undermines his other endeavors.

Freud's persistent opposition to Rank's thesis regarding the trauma of birth as the origin of all other anxiety states, in combination with his inability to let the subject rest, attests to the problematic status of the preoedipal period in his own theoretical system. The result is a symptomatic text in which the issue of anxiety acts as a screen for deeper questions concerning the status of the preoedipal mother. It is as though Freud were returning in fantasy to the scene of Emma Eckstein's bleeding, to the drama of symbolic castration which set the parameters of his emphasis on phallic masculinity. Freud's description of this incident in his letters to Fliess indicates that his sympathetic identification with Eckstein's dilemma was traumatic. To suffer like her, Freud implies, is to submit to the condition of femininity—castration. That he nearly fainted in her presence and subsequently labored to dissociate himself from her difficulties suggests that he could not sustain such a notion. Yet the redefinition of castration as separation from the mother (at birth or later through the experience of her absence) locates femininity as the point of departure for human development. Freud circles around this idea, without confronting it directly. The effect of this evasion manifests itself in repetition—of Rank's thesis, its refutation, and the redefinition of castration from loss of the penis to loss of an object.

Some of Freud's uneasiness about the implications of his theoretical reorientation surfaces in a renewed discussion of the relationship between hysteria and femininity. Resuming the line of thought that castration anxiety cannot have great force where castration has already taken place, he argues that fears regarding the loss of love play the same role for women that fears of losing one's penis do for men. Thus the concept of castration as separation from a loved object (originally the mother) has explanatory force for the etiology of hysteria. This distinction has the virtue of seeming to sustain Freud's phallically organized concept of sexual difference. "It is precisely in women," he claims, "that the danger-situation of loss of object seems to have remained the most effective." The line of reasoning that follows clearly associates the idea of castration as separation with femininity.

> All we need to do is to make a slight modification in our description of their determinant of anxiety, in the sense that it is no longer a matter of feeling the want of, or actually losing the object itself, but of losing the object's love. Since there is no doubt that hysteria has a strong affinity with femininity, just as obsessional neurosis has with masculinity, it appears probable that, as a determinant of anxiety, loss of love plays much the same part in hysteria as the threat of castration does in phobias and fear of the super-ego in obsessional neurosis. [*SE* 20:143]

By reinvoking the issue of phobias, and by extension his problematic discussion of Little Hans, Freud seems anxious to mark a distinction that is increasingly in danger of collapse. As if to rescue masculinity from the field of preoedipal signification, Freud distinguishes between hysteria and obsessional neurosis on the basis of the reality of the threat of castration. It is women, he seems to insist, who suffer from separation anxiety. In having established the priority of this form of anxiety, however, he has already in some sense acknowledged that the guarantee of masculinity is a phantom. The quicksand foundation of Freud's emphasis on the phallic mark of sexual difference becomes apparent as he slips back into discussions of the birth trauma and the question of castration as separation.

As Freud refines his concept of anxiety as a reaction to a situation of danger, he begins to focus on the state of helplessness which precedes it. Symptom formation, he argues, defends the ego against anxiety through a process of displacement. But "if the symptoms are prevented from being formed, the danger does in fact materialize; that is, a situation analogous to birth is established in which the ego is helpless in the face of a constantly increasing instinctual demand—the earliest and original determinant of anxiety" (*SE* 20: 144). In the next chapter Freud repeats his points of agreement with Rank, paying him uncharacteristic tribute in the process.

> We have already traced the line of development which connects this first danger-situation and determinant of anxiety with all the later ones, and we have seen that they all retain a common quality in so far as they signify in a certain sense a separation from the mother—at first only in a biological sense, next as a direct loss of object and later as a loss of object incurred indirectly. The discovery of this extensive concatenation is an undoubted merit of Rank's construction. [*SE* 20:151]

The condition of helplessness, against which the ego attempts to protect itself, through inhibition, repression, and symptom formation, clearly derives from the infant's first cleavage, and subsequent experiences of separation, from its mother. While continuing to argue against Rank's exclusive emphasis on the trauma of birth, Freud offers his own speculations on the role of human biology in contributing to the persistence and pervasiveness of anxiety.

The biological factor is the long period of time during which the young of the human species is in a condition of helplessness and dependence. Its intra-uterine existence seems to be short in comparison with that of most animals, and it is sent into the world in a less finished state.... Moreover, the dangers of the external world have a greater importance for it, so that the value of the object which can alone protect it against them and take the place of its former intra-uterine life is enormously enhanced. [*SE* 20:154–55]

Although Freud stresses the protective role of the father in *The Future of an Illusion* and *Civilization and Its Discontents*, the "object" here seems clearly to refer to the one most intimately related to the infant's intrauterine life—its mother. In an unusual acknowledgment of vulnerability, moreover, he concludes that these conditions of helplessness "creat[e] the need to be loved which will accompany the child through the rest of its life" (*SE* 20:155). Here Freud comes close to Rank in his emphasis on the infant's incompleteness or state of lack, conditions that fuel the ego's desire for mastery without effacing their cause.[11] In this respect, moreover, anxiety and mourning give evidence of the same root problem—the infant's originary state of castration, or separation. Both function as reactive formations to loss. As such, they memorialize or institutionalize that which they seek to control. Addendum B and Addendum C return Freud to the subject of repetition compulsion as the mechanism that subverts the progressive model of human and cultural development by attesting to the lifelong condition of helplessness which is repaired only in death.

Addendum B repeats with added emphasis the concept of anxiety

---

11. Judith van Herik analyzes Freud's negative attitude toward religion as based on his aversion to the position of helplessness or dependency, which he also associates with femininity (*Freud on Femininity and Faith*). Ernest Becker sees Freud's rejection of helplessness as a fundamental aspect of his heroic self-conception, which made it difficult for him to acknowledge any force outside of his control, including that of nature. Such a project leads, in Becker's view, not only to a denial of death but also to a repression of the mother's role in creating life. "It is only logical, then, that if the genius is going to follow to the letter the *causa-sui* project, he comes up against one large temptation: to bypass the woman and the species role of his own body. It is as though he reasons: 'I do not exist to be used as an instrument of physical procreation in the interests of the race; my individuality is so total and integral that I include my body in my *causa-sui* project'" (118). Luce Irigaray, in *Speculum of the Other Woman*, makes a case for viewing all of Western philosophy as founded on this kind of mentality.

as a reaction to a condition of helplessness, originally perceived as traumatic: "Taking this sequence, anxiety—danger—helplessness (trauma), we can now summarize what has been said. A danger-situation is a recognized, remembered, expected situation of helplessness. Anxiety is the original reaction to helplessness in the trauma and is reproduced later on in the danger-situation as a signal for help" (SE 20:166–67). In representing anxiety as the ego's attempt at mastery, Freud evokes an image of the fort/da game, by offering the example of children's play: "The ego, which experienced the trauma passively, now repeats it actively in a weakened version, in the hope of being able itself to direct its course. It is certain that children behave in this fashion towards every distressing impression they receive, by reproducing it in their play. In thus changing from passivity to activity they attempt to master their experiences psychically." In a final backhanded tribute to Rank, moreover, Freud admits that "if this is what is meant by 'abreacting a trauma' we can no longer have anything to urge against the phrase" (SE 20:167). Addendum C, which introduces the subject of mourning, reveals the extent to which the entire essay revolves around the issues raised in *Beyond the Pleasure Principle*.

Although different in affect, anxiety and mourning have a common origin. Both derive from the experience of separation. "Our starting-point," Freud offers, "will again be the one situation which we believe we understand—the situation of the infant when it is presented with a stranger instead of its mother." Under these circumstances an infant will exhibit pain as well as anxiety.

> As soon as it loses sight of its mother it behaves as if it were never going to see her again; and repeated consoling experiences to the contrary are necessary before it learns that her disappearance is usually followed by her reappearance. Its mother encourages this piece of knowledge which is so vital to it by playing the familiar game of hiding her face from it with her hands and then, to its joy, uncovering it again. In these circumstances it can, as it were, feel longing unaccompanied by despair. [SE 20:169–70]

Freud's reference to the child's despair at its mother's loss recalls the situation of his grandson Ernst faced with his mother's departure. Yet the emphasis here falls on the child's experience of helplessness, and the game invoked is one played by its mother to mimic the process of her removal and return. Indeed, Freud claims, "the situation of missing its mother is not a danger-situation, but a traumatic one," that is to say, "if the infant happens at the time to be feeling a need which its mother should be the one to satisfy." The absence of such a need produces a danger situation, which in turn gives rise to anxiety. "Thus," Freud concludes, "the first determinant of anxiety, which the ego itself introduces, is loss of perception of the object (which is equated with loss of the object itself)" (*SE* 20:170). Mourning, in contrast, results from an actual loss, demanding "from the bereaved person that he should separate himself from the object, since it no longer exists" (*SE* 20:172). The prototype for this experience, however, is the originally traumatic one of "missing mother."

In one last attempt to dissociate his own theoretical endeavors from those of Rank, Freud differentiates the "traumatic situation of missing mother" from "the traumatic situation of birth." Repeating his earlier assertion that the infant's narcissism prevents it from experiencing its mother as a being in her own right, Freud states flatly that "at birth no object existed and so no object could be missed." One has to wonder at the need Freud exhibits throughout this essay to refute the idea of the birth trauma. The impulse to dispose of Rank arises, in this instance, after an uncharacteristic reflection on the mother's emotional power over her child. Fear of maternal loss, Freud maintains, precedes fear of loss of love. "Later on," however, "experience teaches the child that the object can be present but angry with it; and then loss of love from the object becomes a new and much more enduring danger and determinant of anxiety" (*SE* 20:170). Maternal anger, virtually a taboo subject in Freud's writing, surfaces here only momentarily. The digression on Rank that follows serves to deflect both the writer himself and the reader from speculating further along these lines. Freud's obsession with Rank in this essay represents both sides of his ambivalence regarding the mother-infant relationship. It acts simultaneously as a denial and as an acknowledgment of his interest. By assiduously refuting the concept of the birth trauma, Freud feels freer, it seems, to focus on the issue of castration as separation. Dealing with these subjects in tandem, however, has the effect of preventing his own theoretical efforts from proceeding very far. *Inhibitions, Symptoms and Anxiety* as a text exhibits the characteristics of repetition compulsion and as such bears silent witness to the subject it systematically evades—the instability of phallic masculinity and the illusion of mastery to which it aspires.

Like the earlier text *Beyond the Pleasure Principle*, Freud's essay on anxiety elicits powerful associations regarding the preoedipal period without exploring their implications. If I am right that Freud's horror in response to the spectacle of Emma Eckstein's bleeding proceeded from his own castration anxiety as well as his perception of her as already castrated, and that this dual reaction to her "femininity" contributed to his inability to focus on the figure of the preoedipal mother, then it is not surprising that he would be reluctant to unfold the theoretical consequences contained in the idea of separation as castration. To have done so would have allied him once again with Eckstein in a state of helplessness and dependence. Yet the condition of radical and primary loss which Freud posits as the result of "missing mother" places everyone, regardless of sex, in this location. Anxiety, repetition compulsion, and mourning all attest to the irreparable nature of this cleavage and to the impossibility of its repair as long as life itself deflects the subject from the fulfillment of its desire. To return to mother, as Rank and Bachofen assert, is to die.

6

Compromising Women

Thou owest Nature a death.

—Sigmund Freud

The first of Freud's three essays on femininity, "Some Psychical Consequences of the Anatomical Distinction between the Sexes" (1925), was published prior to his essay on anxiety. "Female Sexuality" and "Femininity," published in 1931 and 1933 respectively, succeeded it. All three essays give evidence of a retreat from the kind of speculation that informs the structure and content of *Beyond the Pleasure Principle* and *Inhibitions, Symptoms and Anxiety*. Like the late work *Moses and Monotheism*, these essays seem designed to protect the concepts of phallic masculinity and patriarchal control from the elements of subversion contained in the structure of the mother-infant relationship. Rather than pursue the line of thought concerning castration as separation, which stresses a condition of universal helplessness in relation to a maternal figure, Freud ties the notion of femininity as passivity most firmly to the female sex. In doing so, he effectively separates the notion of phallic power from "normal" womanhood, rupturing the mother-daughter bond at the same time that he domesticates the figure of the preoedipal mother. Yet conflicts in Freud's argument concerning bisexuality and the role of female castration attest to the bad faith that informs it. All three essays feature strategies of avoidance. Taken together, they represent yet another flight from the specter of the preoedipal mother. An examination of the circumstances of Freud's life during the period in which he was writing these essays sheds light on the reasons for his retreat from the radical implications of his preceding work.

"Some Psychical Consequences of the Anatomical Distinction between the Sexes" (1925)

Freud establishes the essential outlines of his theory concerning femininity in "Some Psychical Consequences of the Anatomical Distinction between the Sexes." For infants of both sexes, the mother is the original love object. While this situation favors the onset of the Oedipus complex in boys, it acts against a similar development in girls. "Normal femininity," for Freud, requires a heteronomual orientation.[1] In accounting for the process of the girl's detachment from her mother and adoption of her father as a love object, Freud reveals the anxiety elicited in him by the image of a simultaneously castrated and "phallic" mother.[2] His intricate account of feminine development emerges as a complex compromise formation designed to mute or displace such anxiety.

Freud describes the little girl's masturbatory activity as "phallic" on the basis of his association of activity with masculinity and his assumption of an original bisexual disposition in both boys and girls.[3] The task he sets himself is how to disrupt the daughter's love for her mother and suppress her habit of masturbation in favor of the development of femininity, which he understands as both heterosexual and passive in aim. It is the concept of castration which supplies him with this theoretical tool. The small girl's discovery of her castration, Freud argues, disillusions her regarding her mother

1. Adrienne Rich offers a searching critique of Freud's heterosexist bias in "Compulsory Heterosexuality and Lesbian Existence."

2. For Freud, power, aggression, and the exercise of authority are all phallic traits. Hence, his essays on femininity assume that the active disposition of little girls can only be understood as "phallic." I have chosen to use Freud's terminology in my analysis of these essays not because I agree with it but in order to expose the internal inconsistency of his argument. From my point of view, power is clearly separable from the gender position of the male and compatible with that of the female.

3. Luce Irigaray argues in *Speculum of the Other Woman* that for Freud there is really only *one* sex and it is male, so that he conceives of the girl as either a "little man" or a deficient boy. I discuss Irigaray's views at greater length in Part II, "Femininity as Subversion."

as well as herself. Her desire for a penis causes her to turn away from her mother, whom she blames for her own anatomical deficiency at the same time that she abandons her habit of masturbation out of disappointment with the inferiority of her clitoris. This repression of the girl's active libido, accompanied by the destruction of her early love for her mother, is necessary, in Freud's view, for her later adoption of the social roles of wife and mother. "Normal" femininity leaves no room for phallic activity. Freud's evocation of the concept of female castration seems intended to divorce his ideal of feminine (and maternal) behavior from the disturbing element of aggression.

Freud's affirmation of bisexuality does not fully accord with his appeal to sexual difference in his invocation of female castration.[4] Thus, for instance, a girl *should* give up her desire for a penis on the grounds that she can never have one. The repression of her bisexual tendencies rests on a biological imperative. As the following passage indicates, the persistence of masculine behavior in girls assumes a pathological character due to its basis in unreality.

> The hope of some day obtaining a penis in spite of everything and so of becoming like a man may persist to an incredibly late age and may become a motive for strange and otherwise unaccountable actions. Or again, a process may set in which I should like to call a 'disavowal', a process which in the mental life of children seems neither uncommon nor very dangerous but which in an adult would mean the beginning of a psychosis. Thus a girl may refuse to accept the fact of being castrated, may harden herself in the conviction that she *does* possess a penis, and may subsequently be compelled to behave as though she were a man. [SE 19:253]

Whereas a boy may adopt a "feminine" position in relation to his father as a result of the castration complex without incurring the

---

4. I disagree with Juliet Mitchell here, who maintains that Freud does not abandon his adherence to the notion of bisexuality. She reads his essays on femininity as documenting the cultural inscription of gender within a patriarchal social construct (*Psychoanalysis and Feminism* 42–52). My interpretation is more in tune with that of Sarah Kofman, who sees Freud as backing away from the implications of female self-sufficiency and of bisexuality contained in his emphasis on the little girl's early "phallic" activity. I agree with her that Freud appeals to a form of biological determinism in order to enforce his concept of femininity (*Enigma of Woman*).

charge of psychosis, a girl who does not repress her masculinity is not only unfeminine but also flies in the face of biological reality. There is an essential queasiness in Freud's argument for bisexuality, an argument that founders on the issue of sexual difference when it attempts to prescribe norms for female behavior. The result is a curious sort of vacillation between the image of woman as both castrated and as potentially (albeit pathologically) phallic.

Freud's description of the scene of female castration reveals his perspective as essentially masculine. The penis observed is "strikingly visible and of large proportions" despite the fact that it belongs to a child, a brother, or a playmate rather than to an adult. Having noted that the little girl immediately recognizes its superiority to her own "small and inconspicuous organ," Freud shifts his attention to the boy's reaction to the sight of female genitals. When coupled with the threat of castration, such an experience is traumatic. "It arouses a terrible storm of emotion in him and forces him to believe in the reality of the threat which he has hitherto laughed at." This reaction in turn gives rise to one of the following attitudes toward women: "horror of the mutilated creature or triumphant contempt for her." The latter becomes enshrined in the concept of penis envy, whereby the little girl internalizes the boy's response. "She makes her judgement and her decision in a flash. She has seen it and knows that she is without it and wants to have it" (*SE* 19:252). As many readers have noted, Freud's insistence on female castration seems to stem from his own perception that a body without a penis must be deficient.[5] Such a perception, of course, must also include the body of the mother. Freud's concept of bisexuality, however, poses problems for this scenario. While the girl's phallic sexuality undergoes repression as a consequence of her castration complex, it is always in danger of returning. Although Freud

5. Karen Horney expresses this point of view succinctly. In a paper that appeared in print not long after Freud's first essay on femininity, she states: "The present analytical picture of feminine development differs in no case by a hair's breadth from the typical ideas that the boy has of the girl" ("Flight from Womanhood" 174). For a useful survey of responses to Freud's three essays, see Jean Strouse, ed., *Women and Analysis*. That the concepts of penis envy and female castration are still at issue in the psychoanalytic community is evidenced by Elizabeth Mayer's article " 'Everybody Must Be Just Like Me': Observations on Female Castration Anxiety." Mayer strives, however, to reverse Freud's emphasis on maleness as the sexual norm for girls.

characterizes such willful masculinity as deviant, he clearly sees it as problematic. The development toward "normal femininity" is tortuous and subject to many mishaps. Thus the woman who fails to achieve femininity, despite the fact of her castration, will display the attributes of phallic aggression. Freud's account of feminine development paradoxically enhances the image of female power which he struggles theoretically to subdue. In his two subsequent essays on femininity he continues to wrestle with this problem.

"Female Sexuality" (1931)

In "Female Sexuality" Freud returns to the question of the girl's preoedipal attachment to her mother and the means by which it is attenuated. The significance of the preoedipal stage grows in this essay at the same time that Freud insists even more strongly that it must pass in order to insure the development of heterosexual femininity. The essay begins with a description of the strength of the mother-daughter bond.

> I was struck, above all, by two facts. The first was that where the woman's attachment to her father was particularly intense, analysis showed that it had been preceded by a phase of exclusive attachment to her mother which had been equally intense and passionate. . . . Her primary relation to her mother had been built up in a very rich and many-sided manner. The second fact taught me that the *duration* of this attachment had also been greatly underestimated. . . . Indeed, we had to reckon with the possibility that a number of women remain arrested in their original attachment to their mother and never achieve a true change-over towards men. This being so, the pre-Oedipus phase in women gains an importance which we have not attributed to it hitherto. [*SE* 21:225–26]

Freud remarks, almost in passing, that "our insight into this early, pre-Oedipus, phase in girls comes to us as a surprise, like the discovery, in another field, of the Minoan-Mycenean civilization behind the civilization of Greece" (*SE* 21:226). This archeological reference, touching as it does on the issue of mother-goddess worship and its displacement in Greece by the emergence of patriarchal religion, highlights an issue Freud elsewhere evades in his consideration of mother-right: the absence or irrelevance of the father to the early stages of individual and cultural development. That this feature of the mother-daughter relationship gives rise to anxiety is evidenced by the discussion that follows, in which Freud gradually reopens the question of maternal aggression.

After affirming his own inadequacy to deal with the issues at hand, given his unsuitability as an object of mother transference for his female patients, Freud claims that attachment to the mother plays a role in the etiology of hysteria. "Both the phase and the neurosis," he reminds us, "are characteristically feminine," and this condition of dependence on the mother helps to explain "the germ of later paranoia in women." Already Freud imagines the child in a passive and more or less helpless relationship to a powerful maternal figure. The next observation, although it refers specifically only to the girl child, adds to this impression.

> For this germ appears to be the surprising, yet regular, fear of being killed (?devoured) by the mother. It is plausible to assume that this fear corresponds to a hostility which develops in the child towards her mother in consequence of the manifold restrictions imposed by the latter in the course of training and bodily care and that the mechanism of projection is favoured by the early age of the child's psychical organization. [*SE* 21:227]

What begins in fantasy (the fear of being killed by the mother) is shown to have a basis in reality (the restrictions imposed in the process of training). As Freud continues to discuss the origins of the girl's hostility toward her mother, he brings up more examples of the mother's power. She not only prohibits the girl's masturbation but she also emerges as the original source of castration threat. Although the girl may construe the "fact" of her castration as a punishment for masturbation and regard her father as its agent, it is the mother, Freud claims, who first articulates this threat. The same is true for boys, who "regularly fear castration from their father, although in their case, too, the threat most usually comes from their mother" (*SE* 21:233).

In addition to threatening castration, the mother may act as a seducer. The girl learns to masturbate, for instance, as a result of routine nursery care. "The part played in starting it [masturbation] by nursery hygiene is reflected in the very common phantasy which makes the mother or nurse into a seducer. . . . Actual seduction, too, is common enough; it is initiated either by other children or by someone in charge of the child who wants to soothe it, or send it to sleep or make it dependent on them" (*SE* 21:232).

"Someone in charge of the child" may refer to the mother or to that other figure reminiscent of Freud's own childhood, the nurse. The distinction between nursery hygiene and seduction which Freud introduces into this passage, moreover, is not so clear in other instances. In attempting to explain the evolution of the daughter's hostility to her mother, for example, Freud states that the girl resents the fact that her mother "first aroused her sexual activity and then forbade it" (*SE* 21:234), as though the child's state of sexual excitement were intentionally induced. In the following passage, Freud's affirmation of a basis in reality of the girl's fantasies of seduction renders the discrimination between ordinary maternal care and seduction equally problematic.

> In regard to the passive impulses of the phallic phase, it is noteworthy that girls regularly accuse their mother of seducing them. This is because they necessarily received their first, or at any rate their strongest, genital sensations when they were being cleaned and having their toilet attended to by their mother (or by someone such as a nurse who took her place). Mothers have often told me, as a matter of observation, that their little daughters of two and three years old enjoy these sensations and try to get their mothers to make them more intense by repeated touching and rubbing. The fact that the mother thus unavoidably initiates the child into the phallic phase is, I think, the reason why, in phantasies of later years, the father so regularly appears as the sexual seducer. When the girl turns away from her mother, she also makes over to her father her introduction into sexual life. [*SE* 21:238]

Despite Freud's attempt to focus the discussion of infantile sexuality on the child, he cannot avoid representing the mother as initiator, as someone who actively arouses desire. This emphasis tends to reverse that of the Oedipus complex, in which the mother appears as the passive object of her son's phallic love. It is significant, in this light, that Freud fails to consider the implications of his argument concerning the preoedipal phase in boys. This area of obvious avoidance is most evident in his discussion of infantile ambivalence.

Freud's characterization of the mother-daughter relationship is marked by hostility on both sides, a condition that helps him explain the girl's acquiescence to her "feminine" role in heterosexual relations. He offers a superabundance of reasons for the daughter's turning away from her mother, including quite a few that range beyond the notion of female castration with its emphasis on the matter of sexual difference. He considers, for instance, the possibility that the daughter reproaches her mother for not having given her enough milk. This statement gives rise, in turn, to a more general observation about early weaning practices among civilized peoples. "It is as though our children had remained for ever unsated," Freud exclaims, "as though they had never sucked long enough at their mother's breast." Backing away from the implications of this remark in terms of the mother's refusal to nurture her young, he offers the sober afterthought: "But I am not sure whether, if one analysed children who had been suckled as long as the children of primitive peoples, one would not come upon the same complaint." Freud concludes by diverting the issue of blame from mother to infant. "Such is the greed of a child's libido!" (*SE* 21:234). His subsequent arguments, however, raise as many questions as they answer.

Evidently unsatisfied with his efforts to elucidate the sources of the daughter's hostility toward her mother, Freud begins anew. The reasons he has brought forth, including the withdrawal of the breast, castration, maternal seduction, and the prohibition of masturbation, "seem nevertheless insufficient to justify the girl's final hostility," he states categorically. "Perhaps the real fact," he goes on to suggest, "is that the attachment to the mother is bound to perish, precisely because it was the first and was so intense." Drawing an analogy between the fate of love in first marriages and a girl's passion for her mother, Freud argues that "in both situations the attitude of love probably comes to grief from the disappointments that are unavoidable and from the accumulation of occasions for aggression." It is not clear, in this context, that disappointment and aggression are not mutual, an ambiguity that Freud's final statement does nothing to dispel. "As a rule, second marriages," he offers sagely if somewhat cryptically, "turn out much better" (*SE* 21:234). The problems Freud sidesteps in this discussion concern the specter of maternal aggression, as well as the possibility that boys experience hostility equal to that of girls to their mothers. The latter consideration is nearly taboo in Freud's work.

Both the issue of premature weaning and that of ambivalence in the mother-infant relationship obviate questions of sexual difference. Thus when Freud asserts the strongly ambivalent nature of the daughter's early attachment to her mother, he cannot avoid the implication that the same is true for boys. Yet he clearly does not want to pursue this line of thought. Having persuaded himself of the significance of the girl's ambivalence toward her mother due to the inherent structure of the relationship, he pauses to ask himself a loaded question: "How is it, then, that boys are able to keep intact their attachment to their mother, which is certainly no less strong than that of girls?" Freud's explanation of this phenomenon reveals his need to preserve the Oedipal construct. Instead of entertaining the possibility that sons do, in fact, experience hostility to their mother, causing them to lessen their attachment, he asserts that they "are able to deal with their ambivalent feelings towards their mother by directing all their hostility on to their father." Closing off further inquiry, Freud then refers to the incompleteness of his psychoanalytic insight into the preoedipal phase. "But, in the first place, we ought not to make this reply until we have made a close study of the pre-Oedipus phase in boys, and, in the second place, it is probably more prudent in general to admit that we have as yet no clear understanding of these processes, with which we have only just become acquainted" (*SE* 21:235).

In his zeal to explain the inevitability of the daughter's disillusionment with her mother and the destruction of her infantile love, Freud stumbles into issues that threaten his idealization of the Oedipal bond between mother and son. The questions of maternal seduction and aggression which he labors to banish from his construction of masculine development have a way of resurfacing in his arguments concerning feminine development, at the same time that his discussion of ambivalence raises doubts about the mutual gratification he ascribes to the mother-son relationship.

"Femininity" (1933)

In "Femininity," an essay published only six years before his death, Freud returns to the question of feminine aggression, rearranging the structure of his earlier argument in order to focus on the crucial significance of castration, the feature that enforces the development of "normal" womanhood, which he considers "biologically destined" (*SE* 22:119). Once again, his insistence on an original bisexual disposition causes him to emphasize the phallic and aggressive activity of the little girl. "It might have been expected," he claims, "that in girls there would already have been some lag in aggressiveness in the sadistic-anal phase, but such is not the case" (*SE* 22:117–18). Instead, "analysis of children's play has shown our women analysts that the aggressive impulses of little girls leave nothing to be desired in the way of abundance and violence. With their entry into the phallic phase the differences between the sexes are completely eclipsed by their agreements." "The little girl," he concludes resoundingly, "is a little man" (*SE* 22:118).

Having thus endowed the girl child with the masculine trait of activity, Freud then labors to take it away from her. Early in the essay, he makes known his intentions by referring in no uncertain terms to the "suppression of women's aggressiveness which is prescribed for them constitutionally and imposed on them socially" (*SE* 22:116). Later, in describing the effects of the girl's abandonment of masturbation, he explains how "a wave of development like this, which clears the phallic activity out of the way, smooths the ground for femininity" (*SE* 22:128). Both statements contribute to the sense of struggle that characterizes the essay as a whole. The tendency toward aggression must, it seems, be eliminated from the girl's personality structure, at the cost of her love for her mother, her early expression of clitoral sexuality, her self-esteem, and to judge from Freud's final pessimistic statement about her prospects as a mature woman, even her zest for life.

The explanations Freud offers for removing the girl's phallic activity are by now familiar. She fears aggression from her mother, regards her as a seducer, resents her prohibition of masturbation, and cannot get over the pain of losing her breast. As if this were not enough to ensure that the "attachment to the mother ends in hate"

(*SE* 22:121), Freud expands on his earlier discussion of the constitutional ambivalence of the love relationship between mother and child. He begins with a general statement about the coexistence of opposing emotions.

> It might be thought indeed that this first love-relation of the child's is doomed to dissolution for the very reason that it is the first, for these early object-cathexes are regularly ambivalent to a high degree. A powerful tendency to aggressiveness is always present beside a powerful love, and the more passionately a child loves its object the more sensitive does it become to disappointments and frustrations from that object; and in the end the love must succumb to the accumulated hostility.

Although Freud focuses in this statement on the hostility born of frustration experienced by the child, he goes on to discuss the mother's role in eliciting this reaction.

> Or the idea that there is an original ambivalence such as this in erotic cathexes may be rejected, and it may be pointed out that it is the special nature of the mother-child relation that leads, with equal inevitability, to the destruction of the child's love; for even the mildest upbringing cannot avoid using compulsion and introducing restrictions, and any such intervention in the child's liberty must provoke as a reaction an inclination to rebelliousness and aggressiveness. [*SE* 22:124]

Two subjects emerge here, both equally capable of disrupting Freud's argument. The first concerns the possibility that the mother herself may experience an ambivalence that alienates the child's affections, or that she may behave in an aggressive fashion to discourage it. Freud does not discuss this topic, which raises the specter of phallic activity on the part of the mother. The second issue, which Freud does address, involves the question of the son's hostility. "All these factors," he admits, "are, after all, also in operation in the relation of a *boy* to his mother and are yet unable to alienate him from the maternal object" (*SE* 22:124). At this point Freud invokes the concept of castration to distinguish, once and for all, between the girl's course of development away from her mother and that of the boy, who must retain his mother (or her surrogate) as a love object. That Freud saves this distinction for the point in his argument which poses the most serious threat to his conception of the mother-son relationship suggests how much he needs to preserve it in idealized form. Ultimately, of course, he will maintain that it is the "most perfect, the most free from ambivalence of all human relationships" [SE 22:133]. In order to arrive at this conclusion, however, he must excise the element of aggression from the girl's phallic self-expression. The concept of female castration neatly accomplishes this, ensuring that the daughter suppresses her own "masculinity" at the same time that it destroys her image of a phallic mother. Mothers and daughters both, if they conform to the social ideal of womanhood, lose the threatening aspect of power which derives from their inherent bisexuality. The result of this work of repression is a state of psychic passivity and inflexibility which signals the death of the personality. In contrast to a thirty-year-old man, who appears youthful and forward looking, a woman of the same age, Freud maintains,

> often frightens us by her psychical rigidity and unchangeability. Her libido has taken up final positions and seems incapable of exchanging them for others. There are no paths open to further development; it is as though the whole process had already run its course and remains thenceforward insusceptible to influence—as though, indeed, the difficult development to femininity had exhausted the possibilities of the person concerned. [SE 22:134–35]

Stepping back from Freud's three essays on femininity, and setting aside the controversy over penis envy which they sparked among many of his contemporaries, one can see a similarity of structure that suggests a level of unconscious participation on the part of the author. Girls, Freud insists, have a bisexual disposition, which gives rise to the "phallic" masturbation of childhood, in addition to other forms of aggressive behavior. But they are also castrated, a condition that mandates the suppression of the masculine side of their temperament in favor of the development of heterosexual femininity. The original bisexual impulses, however, may reassert themselves in ways that are considered neurotic or socially undesirable. Thus a woman who persists in phallic self-assertion presents a not unfamiliar phenomenon, but one that is considered "sick." Maternal seduction and aggression, examples of which Freud cites himself, appear as real threats, yet as instances of phallic behavior they must be considered deviant. Although Freud banishes the element of aggression to the margins of his conception of "normal" femininity, he does not dismiss it entirely. As a result, the underlying image of woman which emerges from these essays is one that represents her as simultaneously phallic and castrated. While Freud's emphasis falls on castration, the force of his own argument supports the double image.

The essays on femininity, which appear designed to dissociate the figure of woman from power, work paradoxically against their ostensible aim. Freud's evasion of the implications of *Beyond the Pleasure Principle* and *Inhibitions, Symptoms and Anxiety* in regard to maternal power, as evidenced by his insulation of the mother-son relationship from the discussion of preoedipal issues and his insistence on the girl's submission to his Oedipal paradigm, only partly succeeds. The flaws and gaps in his argument, which he himself describes as "incomplete and fragmentary," highlight the very issues that he struggles theoretically to contain.

The importance Freud ascribes to female castration in "Femininity" serves at least two functions. It severs phallic activity from his ideal of feminine behavior at the same time that it safeguards his concept of aggressive masculinity. The result of this theoretical labor points in the direction of *Moses and Monotheism*, where Freud reaffirms his faith in the Oedipal basis of masculine development and its role in the construction of culture. The more disturbing and subversive representations of femininity that emerge from *Beyond the Pleasure Principle* and *Inhibitions, Symptoms and Anxiety* thus appear to undergo repression. If we look at what was happening in Freud's life during the period in which he was writing his three essays on femininity, we may arrive at a better understanding of this process.

Freud's paper prepared for the Ninth International Psychoanalytic Congress at Bad-Homburg, "Some Psychical Consequences of the Anatomical Distinction between the Sexes," was read not by himself but by his daughter Anna, who had assumed the role of representing him in public.[6] Freud had already undergone the first

6. Elizabeth Young-Bruehl thinks that this essay may have incorporated insights Freud derived from the analysis he undertook with Anna, in which case one might

of his many operations for cancer and had begun to rely heavily on Anna, not only for personal nursing care but also for professional assistance. It was she who was entrusted with the painful job of helping him insert his mouthpiece, the ill-fitting prosthesis designed to separate his oral and nasal cavities, just as she herself became his voice in the world, appearing on his behalf at psychoanalytic meetings, reading his papers, taking dictation, and transcribing manuscripts. If we look once again at the Emma Eckstein incident, this time in terms of Freud's naming of his daughter Anna and his dependence on her late in his life, we may begin to see some of the factors that contributed to the direction of his thinking at this time.

The circumstances of Anna Freud's birth were already overdetermined. She was not only the youngest of his three daughters and the last of his six children but she was also conceived shortly before the episode of Emma Eckstein's bleeding and was born during the period of Freud's rationalization of his friend's culpability.[7] Writing to Fliess a few days before her birth, Freud describes his impatience for her delivery at the same time that he mentions his own nasal problem in addition to his continuing faith in Fliess as a physician. "I have, by the way, never doubted the success of your minor surgical interventions," he states, with confidence, "and thus have earned my well-being" (Masson, *Letters* 152). Four days later, Freud writes again to announce Anna's birth, claiming that had she been born a boy he would have named her Wilhelm. Anna Freud was ostensibly named for Anna Hammerschlag Lichtheim, a patient and friend of the family, as well as one of the subjects of Freud's Irma dream.[8] This dream, which Freud records as occurring in July

---

expect his personal involvement to have affected his interpretations (*Anna Freud* 125). Had Freud drawn his observations from one of his other daughters—Sophie, for instance, who was her mother's favorite—he might have created a different (and more positive) portrayal of the mother-daughter relationship

7. According to Young-Bruehl, Anna Freud saw her birth as inseparably intertwined with that of psychoanalysis, though not with her father's relationship with Fliess, as I argue here. "To Anna Freud's reckoning," Young-Bruehl states, "she and psychoanalysis were twins who started out competing for their father's attention" (15).

8. See Young-Bruehl (46). Uwe Peters includes Freud's sister Anna and Anna O. among Freud's possible associations to his daughter's name (*Anna Freud* 4). For Wayne Koestenbaum, the association between Anna O. and Anna Freud is crucial. He argues that "if Anna is his daughter, then Anna O., the origin of psychoanalysis,

1895, during the height of the Eckstein episode, has obvious parallels with Emma's situation. Marianne Krüll regards the figures of Emma and Anna as fused in Irma (*Freud and His Father* 21).[9] If we add to this list of primary associations that of Anna O., the subject of Breuer's study on hysteria, it becomes apparent that Freud's daughter entered the world already deeply entangled in the web of her father's early relationship to psychoanalysis.

Freud's naming of Anna enmeshes her specifically in the complexity of his relationship to Fliess and the process whereby he came to renounce the seduction theory. One might even say that he memorializes this period of his life in her. Because of the associations that accrued to her name, Anna's relationship with her father may well have been charged with suppressed conflict.[10] Such a possibility becomes even more evident if one compares the relationship that evolved between Freud and Anna as a result of his illness with the structure of his relation to Emma/Irma. If one takes into account a reversal of roles, the two display an uncanny resemblance.

Freud's traumatic encounter with Emma Eckstein takes place as the result of her bleeding profusely from the nose. Because of his own experience of surgery at the hands of Fliess, as I have argued earlier, he must have been concerned about his own fate. His mirror reaction suggests such a response. Such feelings, however, appear to

---

is no longer that mother to whom he owes intellectual fealty. Creating Anna O. in his own bloody anus makes his body the origin of psychoanalysis and protects him from acknowledging that Anna O. herself is its immaculately conceiving mother. . . . By placing Anna O. and birth within the domain of male friendship and scientific partnership, Freud privileges the comrade and collaborator over the woman" ("Privileging the Anus" 76).

9. Young-Bruehl is more cautious about this identification, but she admits that Irma "may well have had an element of the troubling Emma Eckstein in her" (28). Both Peter Gay and Max Schur, on the other hand, regard Irma as a screen for Emma (*Freud: A Life for Our Time* 84; "Some Additional 'Day Residues' of the 'Specimen Dream of Psychoanalysis'" 55–85).

10. Young-Bruehl points to another source of conflict—Freud's rapidly increasing family. She notes that Anna Freud in adulthood offered the opinion that if "any acceptable, safe means of contraception had been available to her parents she would not have been born" (27). We know, of course, from Freud's correspondence with Fliess concerning the etiology of the "actual neuroses," that he considered anything short of full unprotected intercourse harmful to men's (and by extension women's) health. The conventional view is that the Freuds stopped having children only when they ceased having sexual relations, that is to say, after Anna's birth.

have been unacceptable to Freud, who hastened to dissociate himself from Eckstein. To bleed like her would amount, symbolically at least, to an admission of castration, pointing on the one hand to an underlying feminine identification, or on the other to a perception of having been physically violated by Fliess. Late in his life, Freud took his turn in Eckstein's place, bleeding from the mouth due to the surgical interventions necessitated by his oral cancer. On the first of these occasions, his daughter assumed the role that she was to play until his death. Jones describes the incident:

> After a few days of reflection Freud quietly turned up at Hajek's clinic without saying a word to anyone at home; it should be said that the clinic was part of a general teaching hospital that had no private wards. Presently the family were surprised by getting a telephone message from the clinic requesting them to bring a few necessities for him to stay the night. Wife and daughter hurried there to find Freud sitting on a kitchen chair in the out-patient department with blood all over his clothes. The operation had not gone as had been expected, and the loss of blood had been so considerable that it was not advisable for the patient to return home. There was no free room or even a bed in the clinic, but a bed was rigged up in a small room already occupied by a cretinous dwarf who was under treatment. The ward sister sent the two ladies home at lunch time, when visitors were not allowed, and assured them the patient would be all right. When they returned an hour or two later they learned that he had had an attack of profuse bleeding, and to get help had rung the bell, which was, however, out of order; he himself could neither speak nor call out. The friendly dwarf, however, had rushed for help, and after some difficulty the bleeding was stopped; perhaps his action saved Freud's life. Anna then refused to leave again and spent the night sitting by her father's side. [*Life* 3:90]

Anna Freud was with her father on another alarming occasion. The summer following Freud's first operation, she accompanied him on his last trip to Rome. Once again, Freud hemorrhaged. "They spent a night and the following day in Verona, taking the night express from there to Rome. . . . A grim episode in the train, however, took place during breakfast. Suddenly a stream of blood spurted from Freud's mouth, a hard crust having evidently loosened a piece of tissue. There was no doubt of its significance in either of their minds" (3:93–94). Despite the terrible nature of this scene,

Jones offers the opinion that the visit to Rome was "highly enjoyable," quoting in evidence Freud's praise of Anna: "Rome was very lovely, especially the first two weeks before the sirocco came and increased my pain. Anna was splendid. She understood and enjoyed everything, and I was very proud of her" (3:94). It is not clear from this statement whether Freud refers primarily to Anna's appreciation of Rome or to her comprehension of his condition, including his pain. The bleeding, moreover, was not to end, given that Freud faced a radical operation on his mouth and jaw on his return to Vienna in September. It was this second extensive surgery that necessitated the use of a prosthesis to separate Freud's nasal cavity from his mouth. This mouthpiece, according to Jones, "was a horror; it was labeled 'the monster.'" Describing the task of insertion and removal, he states: "In the first place it was very difficult to take out or replace because it was impossible for him to open his mouth at all widely. On one occasion, for instance, the combined efforts of Freud and his daughter failed to insert it after struggling for half an hour, and the surgeon had to be fetched for the purpose" (3:95). On the whole, however, it was Anna who assisted Freud in these most intimate circumstances. Jones states categorically that "from the onset of this illness to the end of his life Freud refused to have any other nurse than his daughter Anna." Moreover, "he made a pact with her at the beginning that no sentiment was to be displayed; all that was necessary had to be performed in a cool matter-of-fact fashion with the absence of emotion characteristic of a surgeon" (3:96).

Having found himself in the role formerly occupied by the unfortunate Emma Eckstein, Freud now seems to place his daughter in the position vacated by Fliess. In any event, the demeanor he wishes her to adopt is one he regards as masculine rather than feminine. Indeed, Jones claims that Anna Freud's dispassionate manner, "her courage and firmness, enabled her to adhere to the pact even in the most agonizing situations" (3:96). Unlike her father, who once nearly fainted at the sight of blood, Anna evidently displays the sangfroid of a physician.

There is yet another dimension of this father-daughter relationship which recalls the Emma Eckstein incident. The dream of Irma's injection, as more than one observer has noted, appears to encode certain elements of Freud's relationship to Eckstein.[11] If it is true that Freud named his daughter for her godmother, Anna Hammerschlag Lichtheim, the ostensible subject of the dream, then he had already formed an association, albeit unconscious, between her and Eckstein. Anna's role as the inspector and caretaker of her father's mouth late in his life reevokes this line of association in reverse. It is she who now plays the part of physician, searching his oral cavity for signs of unusual development, while Freud takes the place of Irma/Emma as patient. An examination of the dream in question reveals the complexity of response that such a role reversal might be expected to elicit.

The dream of Irma's injection stands in a unique relationship to Freud's development of psychoanalytic theory. Writing to Fliess, he subsequently credited it with the force of revelation in his understanding of dream interpretation. "Do you suppose," he muses to his friend, "that someday one will read on a marble tablet on this house:

> Here, on July 24, 1895,
> the secret of the dream
> revealed itself to Dr. Sigm. Freud.
> [Masson, *Letters* 417]

The secrets that Freud discloses in his interpretation of this dream, however, are less telling than the ones he manages to conceal. Behind his readily confessed self-reproaches for the ill treatment of his patient Irma lie implicit accusations against Fliess for his bungling of Eckstein's surgery. Freud also dissociates himself from Irma as a victim of physical violation in order to confirm himself instead in the less threatening, if professionally problematic, role of her physician.

---

11. Schur was the first to draw this parallel, I believe ("Some Additional 'Day Residues' "). Gay, who gives a less detailed reading of the dream, nevertheless sees it as "a carefully constructed, highly intricate scenario designed at least in part to rescue Freud's idealized image of Fliess" (82). See also Alexander Grinstein (*Sigmund Freud's Dreams* 21–46). None of these interpreters pursues the implications of Freud's identification with Irma/Emma, however. See Erik Erikson for a reading of Freud's "feminine" identification as a sign of his creativity ("The Dream Specimen of Psychoanalysis").

Freud reports the dream as follows:

A large hall—numerous guests, whom we were receiving.—Among them was Irma. I at once took her on one side, as though to answer her letter and to reproach her for not having accepted my 'solution' yet. I said to her: 'If you still get pains, it's really only your fault.' She replied: 'If you only knew what pains I've got now in my throat and stomach and abdomen—it's choking me'—I was alarmed and looked at her. She looked pale and puffy. I thought to myself that after all I must be missing some organic trouble. I took her to the window and looked down her throat, and she showed signs of recalcitrance, like women with artificial dentures. I thought to myself that there was really no need for her to do that.—She then opened her mouth properly and on the right I found a big white patch; at another place I saw extensive whitish grey scabs upon some remarkable curly structures which were evidently modelled on the turbinal bones of the nose.—I at once called in Dr. M., and he repeated the examination and con-firmed it. . . . Dr. M. looked quite different from usual; he was very pale, he walked with a limp and his chin was clean-shaven. . . . My friend Otto was now standing beside her as well, and my friend Leo-pold was percussing her through her bodice and saying: 'She has a dull area low down on the left.' He also indicated that a portion of the skin on the left shoulder was infiltrated. (I noticed this, just as he did, in spite of her dress.) . . . M. said: 'There's no doubt it's an infection, but no matter; dysentery will supervene and the toxin will be elimi-nated.' . . . We were directly aware too, of the origin of the infection. Not long before, when she was feeling unwell, my friend Otto had given her an injection of a preparation of propyl, propyls . . . propionic acid . . . trimethylamin (and I saw before me the formula for this printed in heavy type). . . . Injections of that sort ought not to be made so thoughtlessly. . . . And probably the syringe had not been clean. [*SE* 4:107]

Even a casual reading of this dream reveals a number of probable allusions to Emma Eckstein's situation. The patient complains of pains her physician has been unable to cure. When Freud examines her oral cavity, which has features that resemble those of the nose, he finds an infection. Her shoulder too is affected as a result of a careless medical intervention. Neither Freud's friend Otto nor his friend Dr. M. seems particularly concerned. In its main outline, this dream seems to validate Freud's first conclusion regarding Eckstein's trauma as reported to Fliess: "So we had done her an injustice" (March 8, 1855; 117). Yet Freud's interpretation stresses his feelings of self-doubt in relation to everything but Eckstein, and his explicit references to Fliess are favorable. His associations with the figure of Irma (his daughter, a patient named Mathilde, and his wife) similarly fail to include the most obvious one. As a result, Freud appears to use the process of dream interpretation to divert his conscious attention from a matter of grave concern to him at this time—his complicity with Fliess in inducing Eckstein's suffering.

There is evidence, moreover, that on some levels Freud identifies with his patient. In his discussion of the significance of the turbinal bones, Freud recalls "a worry about my own state of health" (*SE* 4:111) due to nasal swellings and the use of cocaine. Later, he explains the reference to rheumatism in the dream as an allusion to "the rheumatism in my own shoulder, which I invariably notice if I sit up late into the night." Even more explicitly, he states: "Moreover the wording in the dream was most ambiguous: '*I noticed this, just as he did. . . .*' I noticed it in my own body, that is" (*SE* 4:113). Freud does not pursue this line of thought, but if one considers it in the light of his later discussion of trimethylamin, another dream picture begins to emerge which links Freud with Eckstein in a scene of sexual violation.

Freud's associations with the formula for trimethylamin lead him directly to Fliess, whom he credits with the idea that trimethylamin is a product of sexual metabolism. He has no difficulty integrating this new factor into the fabric of his dream. Trimethylamin, he explains, alludes to the importance of sexuality in his theory of neurosis, as well as to Irma's status as a young widow whom her friends wished to see married. As if unsatisfied with these explanations, however, Freud describes the influence of Fliess in even greater detail, making a specific connection between his friend's nasal theory and the reference to Irma's turbinal bones.

> Trimethylamin was an allusion not only to the immensely powerful factor of sexuality, but also to a person whose agreement I recalled with satisfaction whenever I felt isolated in my opinions. Surely this friend who played so large a part in my life must appear again elsewhere in these trains of thought. Yes. For he had a special knowledge of the consequences of affections of the nose and its accessory cavities;

and he had drawn scientific attention to some very remarkable con-
nections between the turbinal bones and the female organs of sex. (Cf.
the three curly structures in Irma's throat.) I had had Irma examined
by him to see whether her gastric pains might be of nasal origin.   [*SE*
4:117]

Freud all but identifies Irma with Eckstein in this passage, though
he himself fails to see the point. If we follow his train of thought one
step further, moreover, we come upon the dream phrase *"Injections
of that sort ought not to be made so thoughtlessly,"* an apparent
indictment of Fliess himself. If one reconstructs Freud's associations according to this alignment, one arrives at the following account of the dream: Fliess is guilty of malpractice for having violated Eckstein. The distortions of the dream bring out the theme of
sexual violation (the injection of a sexual substance with a dirty
instrument) in addition to Freud's split identification with Fliess
and with his female patient. Freud seems to have found it easier,
however, to blame himself for other professional lapses than for his
complicity with Fliess in their joint treatment of Eckstein. He
evidently also found the role of the self-critical physician more
congenial than that of the abused woman.

When Freud developed cancer of the mouth, he suddenly found
himself in a situation parallel to that of Emma Eckstein, subject to
surgical interventions on his oral and nasal cavities which led to
hemorrhage. Anna herself, through the circumstances of her naming in addition to her role as nurse or medical assistant to her father,
would have reminded Freud on some level of his own earlier stance
in relation to the dream figure Irma and the woman she represented,
Emma Eckstein. I suggest that the state of Freud's health at this
point reevoked his underlying identification with Eckstein as well
as his reaction of flight. The other associations Freud is likely to
have made between Anna and Dora, and even more explicitly between her and Cordelia, lend support to such an interpretation.[12]

In his relationship with Anna, Freud seems to have enacted something he was able to imagine but could not theorize. In his case
study of Dora, for instance, he produces the fantasy of an impotent

12. Both Peter Rudnytsky and Jeffrey Masson have drawn parallels between
Dora's and Emma's situations, though neither makes the connection with Anna that
I suggest here (*Freud and Oedipus* 38; *Assault on Truth* 122).

father, whose daughter not only nurses him in a conventional sense but who also wishes to "nurse," or suck at his penis. Superimposed on this fantasy of ambiguous sexual identification, however, in which the father plays a passive, quasi-maternal role, Freud offers a more stereotyped image, that of a virile, phallic male who pursues a young girl in spite of her resistance. Gradually, his fascination with the fortunes of Herr K. appears to overtake his interest in the more threatening and volatile scene of father-daughter incest. Although Dora, like Irma, refuses his "solution," Freud nevertheless persuades himself of the correctness of his Oedipal interpretation. He leaves unexamined the question of the father's position of vulnerability, as one who is both physically ill and sexually disabled. Freud's essays on femininity, which emphasize female disability (castration) while attempting to reserve the role of phallic masculinity for the male, adopt a strategy resembling the one that insists on an Oedipal construction of Dora's desire. The subject Freud avoids in this instance is his own vulnerability, his implicitly feminine role in relation to his daughter. This issue virtually escapes representation, appearing only on the margins of his late work.

A very explicit analogue to the special nature of Freud's relationship with Anna does exist, however, in one of his earlier essays: "The Theme of the Three Caskets." If not the best loved of Freud's three daughters (Sophie would have that honor), Anna, like Cordelia in *King Lear*, is the youngest.[13] Freud himself made this connection. Writing to Ferenczi in July 1913, he describes Anna as his "closest companion" in his travels. She "is developing very well at the moment," he continues, adding in parentheses, "You will long ago have guessed the subjective condition for the 'Choice of the Three Caskets'" (July 9, 1913; E. Freud, *Letters* 301). What Lear wishes for and briefly obtains, moreover, Freud enjoys until the end of his life: his daughter's "kind nursery." Assuming that Freud was sensitive to the overtones of incest in Lear's demand for the exclusive love of his daughters, one might see in this parallel another

13. Marjorie Garber reads Freud's transposition of the "Theme of the Three Caskets" from Shakespeare's *The Merchant of Venice* onto *King Lear* as an evasion of the issue of women's power to choose. She also sees Freud's discussion of Cordelia as alluding to his own choice of Anna as caretaker in his illness and old age (*Shakespeare's Ghost Writers*).

evocation of the father-daughter relationship, as Freud perceives it, in the Dora case history.[14] But King Lear wants his daughters not only to respond like lovers but also to look after his needs as though he were an infant. He confuses daughter with mother.[15] That Freud understood this level of meaning in the play is evident in his interpretation of the triple goddess of antiquity as a representative of the three most important relationships a man has to woman: "the mother herself, the beloved one who is chosen after her pattern, and lastly the Mother Earth who receives him once more" (*SE* 12:301). Anna Freud, in this light, not only assumes the role of mother but also plays the role of the Goddess of Death.

In his illness Freud reproduced the relationship with the preoedipal mother which he strove to repress from his theory. The condition of infantile helplessness which he began to investigate through the redefinition of castration as separation appears to have been too threatening for him to pursue in the context of his increasing reliance on his daughter, who played the role of nurse as well as mother to him. Unable to examine the implications of his position of dependence on his daughter, as he had earlier been unwilling to explore his sympathetic identification with his female patients, Freud theorizes instead the suppression of women's aggression through the concept of female castration and returns in his last major work to his Oedipal paradigm of civilized development. It is as though he uses theory to deny his likeness to the bleeding and violated Irma/Emma, as well as to perform an imaginative disjunction between the figure of caretaker, mother or nurse, and the exercise of power.

Freud's explicit and repeated identification of Anna with Antigone, the offspring of Oedipus and his mother, Jocasta, speaks to both conscious and unconscious sides of this negotiation. Writing to Ferenczi in October 1928, five years after the discovery of his cancer, Freud conveys his greetings "to you as to Frau Gisella, also from

14. For a discussion of the intensely close relationship between Freud and his daughter Anna which developed in part as a consequence of his illness, see Gay (428–46) and Young-Bruehl (23–139). Young-Bruehl sees Anna Freud as arriving at a positive solution to her father complex, whereas Gay very nearly describes it as a form of emotional incest.

15. Coppélia Kahn argues this point convincingly in "The Absent Mother in *King Lear*." See also my essay "I Wooed Thee with My Sword."

my faithful Antigone-Anna" (October 12, 1928; 382). In corresponding with Arnold Zweig at a much later date, he expresses his disinclination to travel with a reference to himself as the blinded Oedipus, guided by his daughter: "Even supported by my devoted Anna-Antigone I could not undertake any journey" (May 2, 1935; E. Freud, *Letters of Sigmund Freud and Arnold Zweig* 106). Uwe Henrik Peters, an early biographer of Anna Freud, regards this designation as honorific, pointing to Antigone's heroism as her father's defender (*Anna Freud* 16). Freud, moreover, evidently wished to praise his daughter for her supportive role by comparing her with Antigone, the self-sacrificing daughter of the suffering Oedipus. If, however, one considers more clearly the fate of the outcast king, whose self-inflicted blindness Freud understood in terms of castration, the identification of Anna with Antigone becomes more problematic.

The reference to Antigone not only returns Freud to the subject of his disability, figured metaphorically as castration and hence a reminder of Eckstein's condition, but it also introduces the issue of incest into the father-daughter relationship. Antigone, as the product of incestuous union, forms an attachment to her father which supersedes all others until his death. If Freud's allusion to Anna as Antigone appears to praise her, on the one hand, as capable of heroic effort, it seems, on the other, to bind her to him with unusual force.[16] Lear's outrageous and implicitly incestuous demand that his daughters provide him with their exclusive love appears to find expression here through the overdetermination of Freud's analogy. It is not hard to regard Freud's choice in this matter as a representation of his unacknowledged desire.[17]

16. Gay, after first cautioning his readers not "to press this affectionate name too far," goes on to say: "It is a truism that Oedipus's children were all exceptionally close to him; having been fathered with his mother, they were his siblings as much as his offspring. But Antigone was preeminent among Oedipus's children. She was his gallant and loyal companion, just as Anna became her father's chosen comrade over the years. It is Antigone who, in *Oedipus at Colonnus*, leads her blind father by the hand, and by 1923, it was Anna Freud who was firmly installed as her wounded father's secretary, confidante, representative, colleague, and nurse. She became his most precious claim on life, his ally against death" (442).

17. Freud's letters about Anna give evidence of divided feelings. On the one hand, he appears to have wanted her to develop along conventional feminine lines and to marry, but he also seems to have dreaded this possibility. His actions, moreover, belied his words. He not only accepted but relied on her ministrations. When it

On a conscious level, Freud's reference to Anna as Antigone affirms her role as her father's devoted daughter and the defender of his life's work. Unconsciously, however, it points to the problematically incestuous father-daughter relationship that haunts the Dora case history as well as Shakespeare's portrayal of King Lear. The daughter's role in both instances, moreover, has a tendency to fuse with that of mother, while the relationship with mother evokes associations with death. Thus Antigone, like Dora and Cordelia, returns Freud to the specter of maternal power which he represents through the triple goddess in his essay on the three caskets. Freud's last request of his physician, Max Schur, that he inform Anna of his readiness to die, reads uncannily like a final admission of this underlying structure of relationship. On September 21, 1939, according to Schur, Freud asked him to fulfill his earlier promise that when the time came, he would help him die. Schur writes: "I indicated that I had not forgotten my promise. He sighed with relief, held my hand for a moment longer, and said: 'Ich danke Ihnen' ('I thank you'), and after a moment of hesitation he added: 'Sagen Sie es der Anna' ('Tell Anna about this'). All this was said without a trace of emotionality or self-pity, and with full consciousness of reality" (Schur, *Freud Living and Dying* 529). Freud's laconic statement "Sagen Sie es der Anna" may be subject to more than one interpretation. At the very least, however, it would seem to indicate that Freud was asking his daughter's consent.[18] Though Schur does not report his conversation with Anna Freud, he does indicate that he informed her of her father's wish before administering the lethal doses of morphine. It is as though Freud endowed her, at this crucial moment of decision, with the attributes of the "silent Goddess of Death," who was ready now to "take him into her arms."

---

became apparent that Anna Freud was developing a close relationship with Dorothy Burlingham, who had come to Vienna with her four children to be analyzed and who took an apartment in the same building as the Freud household, Freud took steps to treat Dorothy himself, thus keeping watch over her growing intimacy with his daughter. It is well known, moreover, that Anna underwent an analysis with her father, so that most (though not all) of her inner life was revealed to him. For details of these circumstances, see in particular Young-Bruehl (65–139).

18. Young-Bruehl, who as official biographer has had access to much unpublished information, including Anna Freud's private papers, maintains that "what Schur did was to ask Anna Freud to agree to her father's decision, which she did, reluctantly" (239).

PART II

Femininity as Subversion:
Freud and Post-Freud

The relationship that Freud strove to repress from his theory appears to have found expression in terms that he himself would have regarded as hysterical, his body giving voice to a truth that his late theoretical work could not. Freud's illness returned him, bleeding, orally violated, and barely capable of speech, to the scene of his confrontation with Emma Eckstein. Only this time the roles were reversed. His daughter Anna, linked by name and association with his former patient, now played the part of physician, while he took Eckstein's place. The uncanny nature of this circumstance tempts one to speculate about its unconscious content. One might regard it, for instance, as pantomimic of a fantasy of the mother-son relationship which circulates through Freud's texts without his acknowledgment. This fantasy draws together isolated strands in his writing which deal with issues of infantile helplessness (or castration) in relation to maternal power (seduction, aggression, and "phallic" self-sufficiency). In its most threatening aspect it assumes the form of "phallic" mother/"castrated" son. If this fantasy has any validity, then the reactive character of Freud's writing becomes apparent on a large scale. Looking at his theoretical activity from this perspective, moreover, the suppressions and displacements that typify his attempts to deal with the preoedipal period begin to make another kind of sense.

When Freud looked at Eckstein what he saw was castration, a condition that he might have originally attributed to her position as victim, but that he theorized as the sign of femininity itself. Sympathetic identification with her, in this light, could have only one meaning—his own loss of potency, both physical and social. At the same time that Eckstein's bleeding caused him to recoil in horror, moreover, Freud backed away from the implications of maternal seduction, evidence of which he nonetheless continued to cite. The power of the mother or the nurse to arouse, as well as to prohibit and to shame, slipped to the margins of his consideration of childhood sexuality as he focused instead on the vicissitudes of the boy's aggressive Oedipal desire. To have explored the mother's desire would have brought the concept of female castration into conjunction with that of "phallic" motherhood, an evidently unthinkable prospect. By keeping these two notions separate, Freud manages for the most part to avoid articulating the fantasy they jointly elicit, that of the emasculated and emasculating mother. He does not succeed, however, in banishing this spectral figure. She appears briefly in his treatise on Leonardo and in the case histories and the essays on the psychology of love. Freud struggles to subdue her in his various attempts to account for the phenomenon of mother-goddess worship, and finally he imagines her as an avatar of death.

Freud's attempts to theorize the preoedipal period, if not the role of the preoedipal mother herself, in *Beyond the Pleasure Principle* and *Inhibitions, Symptoms and Anxiety* reveal both his fascination with this subject and his ultimate inability to integrate it smoothly into his Oedipal construct. If anything, the dyadic mother-child relationship threatens to subvert the triangular Oedipal structure. The concepts of repetition compulsion and the death instinct appear to give the lie to the progressive model of development based on the paternal threat of castration and the male child's renunciation of desire for his mother. Instead they memorialize a prior sense of loss, instituting a form of mastery that seeks its own undoing. In his reformulation of castration as separation from the mother, Freud carries the implications of this line of argument one step further. This concept obliterates the phallic mark of distinction between the sexes at the same time that it focuses attention on the infant's initial state of helplessness and dependence. The effect of such a theoretical shift, as Freud himself seems to have divined, is devastating to his Oedipal model of masculine identity and, in a larger sense, of patriarchal culture. Yet Freud maintained his allegiance to his earlier developmental scheme, which clearly subordinates the preoedipal to the Oedipal period, thus formalizing the conflict of interpretation regarding the figure of the preoedipal mother which runs through his work. The meaning that attaches to femininity, as a result, is subversion.

If Freud consciously represented femininity in his late essays on the subject as taking its meaning from the "fact" of female castration, his work as a whole conveys a different message. In his portrayals of the preoedipal mother and the preoedipal period generally, Freud suggests that the infant's relation to the feminine threatens the structure of masculine development, yet he cannot accept systems of explanation, such as those of Jung, Bachofen, or Rank, which rest on assumptions of female priority. As a result he locks femininity into a position of subordination and disruption. This structure, in turn, has had a significant impact on subsequent developments of psychoanalytic theory. Neither object relations theory nor Lacanian psychoanalysis, to take two prominent examples thereof, succeeds in transforming the implicit meaning of femininity as subversion.

The schools of object relations theory and Lacanian psychoanalysis, each of which encodes a different aspect of Freud's ambivalence toward the preoedipal mother, both fail to question her subordination within the Oedipal-preoedipal hierarchy. It is important to examine the assumptions of these schools in order to understand their inherent structures of limitation, especially in light of their appeal to psychoanalytic feminists. Taken together what they reveal most clearly, perhaps, is the figuration of femininity as subversion within patriarchy.

There is, at the same time, a major difference between these two approaches in their conceptualization of the preoedipal mother. Whereas object relations theory stresses maternal presence (and plenitude) through the concept of mother-infant fusion, Lacan downplays the role of the biological mother to the point where she barely seems to exist in a corporeal sense. A brief comparison between Lacan's formulation of the mirror stage and D. W. Winnicott's adaptation of it reveals their very different emphases in regard to the mother's function, on the one hand, and her physical presence, on the other.

Lacan's concept of the mirror stage, first presented in an address to the Sixteenth International Congress of Psychoanalysis at Zurich in 1949, is central to the later development of his theory. In it, he constructs a fable of the formation of the "I" which sets his endeavor apart from that of the future ego psychology and object relations schools. Lacan describes the infant's moment of recognition of his own image and hence his perception of a coherent self: "Unable as yet to walk, or even to stand up, and held tightly as he is by some support, human or artificial (what, in France, we call a *trotte-bébé*), he nevertheless overcomes, in a flutter of jubilant activity, the obstructions of his support and, fixing his attitude in a slightly leaning-forward position, in order to hold it in his gaze, brings back an instantaneous aspect of the image" (*Écrits* 1–2). At the same time that the mirror image gives the infant a perception of itself as a unified subject, however, it lies. The image is external, inverted, alienated, giving rise to a false comprehension of the self as integrated and whole. Prior to the mirror stage, the infant experiences its body as fragmented, its movements as discrete and uncoordinated. The inception of the "I" displaces and suppresses this condition, while introducing a gap between the subject's understanding of itself (always based on the illusion of integrity) and its underlying state of fluid disintegration. The ego, a product of misrecognition, is thus founded on a split in being that can never be healed. The very structure of the "I" incorporates an absence. Its emergence, moreover, is remarkably independent of human interaction. While the mother's gaze, in the absence of a mirror, might perform the same function, she is in no way indispensable to the process.

Although Winnicott invokes Lacan's concept of the mirror stage in the opening of his essay on the "Mirror-Role of Mother and Family in Child Development," his very choice of a title signals the difference of his approach. Winnicott subordinates the function of the mirror to that of the mother's face, a shift of focus that also sets the parameters for his understanding of subjectivity. The process of ego development, in his view, begins with a condition of dual unity, in which the infant does not yet perceive its mother as a separate person.

The bare statement is this: in the early stages of the emotional development of the human infant a vital part is played by the environment which is in fact not yet separated off from the infant by the infant. Gradually the separating-off of the not-me from the me takes place, and the pace varies according to the infant and according to the environment. The major changes take place in the separating-out of the mother as an objectively perceived environmental feature. [111]

An important stage in this process of separating out involves the reflection that the infant receives of itself from its mother's face. Winnicott includes here the mother's entire manner of relating to her infant as expressed in her gaze. "What does the baby see when he or she looks at the mother's face? I am suggesting that, ordinarily, what the baby sees is himself or herself. In other words the mother is looking at the baby and *what she looks like is related to what she sees there*" (112). The mother's role as an agent in the process of reflection means that her responsiveness to her infant has a profound influence on its subsequent development. The more she resembles a mirror, in fact—passive, distracted, or withdrawn—the less her infant is able to use the image she provides. Such a circumstance, according to Winnicott, fosters the emergence of pathology. In an optimal situation, the infant perceives itself as organized through its mother's attentive gaze, an essential step toward the condition of autonomy and the feeling of being in possession of one's own reality.

Winnicott's disarmingly simple statement that "the precursor of the mirror is the mother's face" (111) performs a significant transformation on the concept of the mirror stage. He not only inserts the process of ego development into the field of object relations but he also sees the mother's role as virtually omnipotent. The mother is as essential to Winnicott's account as she is irrelevant to Lacan's.

Because object relations theory develops the implications of the mother's physical presence (as well as her loss) within the preoedipal period, it also directs our attention to questions of sexual difference. Lacan, in contrast, is less concerned with the preoedipal period itself than with its structural relation to the Oedipal phase that supersedes it. His interest in structural linguistics, moreover, further removes his consideration from the material realm. By fusing the concepts of cultural and linguistic development, both of which he inserts into Freud's Oedipal construct, Lacan lifts the question of sexual difference out of the field of anatomy and into that of language. Although these two approaches are different enough to make them appear mutually exclusive, they have one thing in common. They both locate femininity, as a category of sexual difference or as a function of language, in the position of subversion. This construction, in turn, has some serious drawbacks for feminists who have adopted one or the other version of it, depending on their allegiance to Anglo-American or French theory.[1] The Freudian substratum of these latter-day theoretical developments remains stubbornly resistant.

Object Relations Theory

Object relations theory posits an initial condition of dual unity between mother and infant, from which the infant gradually differentiates a separate self. In Margaret Mahler's words, " 'Growing up' entails a gradual growing away from the normal state of human symbiosis, of 'one-ness' with the mother" ("On the First Three Subphases of the Separation-Individuation Process" 333). This basic assumption of object relations theory both draws on and extends the implications of Freud's fleeting and fragmentary observations concerning the preoedipal period. It emphasizes the mother's presence and influence at the same time that it desubjectivizes her, substituting stereotypes of "good" mother and "bad" mother for the complexity of a fully developed adult personality. Object relations theory appears to accept Freud's idealized portrait of the mother-son relationship as its model for "good enough" mothering, a condition in which the mother subordinates her interests to those of her infant. Winnicott's advice to prospective mothers makes clear what he considers normal behavior in this regard.

> A woman's life changes in many ways when she conceives a child. Up to this point she may have been a person of wide interests, perhaps in business, or a keen politician, or an enthusiastic tennis player, or one who has always been ready for a dance or a 'do'. . . . Experience shows,

1. The editors of the *Yale French Studies* issue titled *Feminist Readings: French Texts/American Contexts* identify the subversive possibilities of focusing on the preoedipal period in both Anglo-American and Lacanian theory, but they do not critique the Oedipal/preoedipal hierarchy per se. This stance, I believe, is typical of psychoanalytic feminism to date.

however, that a change gradually takes place in the feelings as well as in the body of the girl who has conceived. Shall I say her interest gradually narrows down? . . . As you become more and more sure that you will soon become a mother you begin to put all your eggs into one basket, as the saying is. You begin to take the risk of allowing yourself to be concerned with one object, the little boy or girl human being that will be born. [*The Child, the Family, and the Outside World* 19–20][2]

Because of this nearly exclusive emphasis on the mother's role in early child rearing, disturbances in development are easily attributable to maternal dysfunction. Mahler explains one child's difficulty in managing the process of separation, for instance, as a response to his mother's ambivalence.

Mark was one of those children who had the greatest difficulty in establishing a workable distance between himself and mother. His mother was ambivalent as soon as Mark ceased to be part of herself, her symbiotic child. At times she seemed to avoid close body contact; at other times she might interrupt Mark in his autonomous activities to pick him up, hug him and hold him. She did this, of course, when *she* needed it, not when *he* did. This ambivalence on mother's part may have been what made it difficult for Mark to function at a distance from his mother. [335–36]

Object relations theory, true to its Freudian base, appears most comfortable with the figure of the preoedipal mother when she expresses no needs of her own. Her greatest fault in this schema proceeds from a failure to provide the optimum environment in which the infant can differentiate itself from her. When she ceases to be self-sacrificing, her power manifests itself in harmful ways.

Object relations theory reproduces Freud's split conception of the preoedipal mother—as ideally loving and fulfilled by her maternity, on the one hand, and as intrusive, overwhelming, or aggressive, on the other. It also brings out an assumption implicit in Freud's theory that the mother's authority precedes and thus threatens to undermine that of the father. The concept of mother-infant fusion, which focuses specifically on the newborn's perception of continuity with its mother's body, reinforces this idea at the same time

2. While some prospective mothers may recognize themselves in this description, it seems to be addressed to a narrow audience of bourgeois married women who are expecting their first child.

that it challenges Freud's Oedipally organized representation of sex and gender difference.

In Freud's account the primacy of the phallus is unquestioned. Its presence or absence, in the context of the castration complex, determines the future course of masculinity and femininity. For the boy, it is the little girl's lack that gives meaning to the threat of castration from his father, which in turn dissolves his Oedipus complex. The little girl's perception of lack also precipitates her castration complex, causing her to reject her mother as a love object. The anatomical distinction between the sexes, which becomes significant at the point of intersection between the Oedipus and castration complexes, thus strengthens Freud's concept of phallic masculinity at the expense of feminine development. Object relations theory effectively reverses this emphasis.

By positing an initial state in which the infant does not perceive itself as separate from the body of its mother, object relations theory contains the suggestion at least that the infant's first physical identification is also female. Robert Stoller pursues this line of thought to its logical conclusions. Primary identity, he maintains, for boys and girls alike, is both feminine and female. Stoller regards this condition as unproblematic for girls.

> And females? Not only are they probably the stronger, not to say the primary sex, but their very "homosexuality" may give them an advantage. Once again we recall that the anatomical "homosexuality," looked at from the mother-infant relationship in the first months, need not threaten the girl. Developing indissoluble links with mother's femaleness and femininity in the normal mother-infant symbiosis can only augment a girl's identity. If a mother can lay down *that* foundation in her daughter, then a strength—a permanence, a part of identity—is well situated and can serve the child even in the face of later gender adversities, as in the oedipal situation.   ["Facts and Fancies" 359]

The more difficult, if not tortuous, path of development awaits the little boy, whose achievement of masculinity depends on a process of disidentification from the femaleness of his mother.

> While it is true the boy's first love is heterosexual, he must perform a great deed to make this so: he must first separate his identity from hers. Thus the whole process of becoming masculine is at risk in the

little boy from the day of birth on; his still-to-be-created masculinity is endangered by the primary, profound, primeval oneness with mother, a blissful experience that serves, buried but active in the core of one's identity, as a focus which, throughout life, can attract one to regress back to that primitive oneness. That is the threat lying latent in masculinity, and I suggest that the need to fight it off is what energizes some of what we are familiar with when we call a piece of behavior "masculine." [358]

Stoller's characterization of the urge to regress to a state of oneness with mother is reminiscent of Freud's portrayal of the death instinct in *Beyond the Pleasure Principle*. Common to both accounts is an emphasis on the male child's struggle for mastery over his desire for his mother's presence. For Freud, the fort/da game memorializes the loss that it is meant to control. Little Ernst, in the very act of overcoming his regressive urges, pays tribute to their strength. His achievement of mastery is thus founded on a continuous suppression of his desire to return to a state of nondifferentiation which Stoller equates with mother-infant union and Freud finally associates with death. The threat to masculine development which remains implicit in Freud's text, however, is quite explicit in Stoller's: "So—something I never quite articulated before—in one sense, the process of the development of core gender identity is not the same in males as in females. There is a conflict built into the sense of maleness that females are spared; core gender identity in males is not, as I have mistakenly said . . . quite so immutable. It always carries in it the urge to regress to an original oneness with mother" (358). Stoller's interpretation of the theory of mother-infant fusion highlights the conflict latent in Freud's conception of the relationship of the preoedipal to the Oedipal period. For the boy at least, preoedipal identification with (or attachment to) his mother poses a continual risk to his sense of maleness.

While object relations theory gives priority to femininity over masculinity, it does not seriously challenge the stereotypes on which the cultural understanding of these gender categories is based. It also tends to confuse or to equate matters of sex and gender difference.[3] These problems carry over into the feminist uses of the

3. Feminist discourse achieved a major advance by distinguishing between sex as a biological category (male or female) and gender as a matter of cultural ascription (masculinity or femininity). Nevertheless these terms are often confused or used

theory, as an examination of Nancy Chodorow's *Reproduction of Mothering* and its impact on psychoanalytic feminists reveals.

Chodorow looks to object relations theory for an answer to the question of why women mother. Her aim is to alleviate women's oppression by altering the social structure in which the mothering role is performed almost exclusively by females. To do so, however, she believes it is necessary to understand the psychological processes that induce women not only to accept this role but also to desire it in an active way. As she states in her introduction, "The contemporary reproduction of mothering occurs through social structurally induced psychological processes" (7). Her argument assumes that new social arrangements will transform the psychological bases of masculinity and femininity in ways that will permit women a fuller participation in the creation of culture.

Chodorow considers herself a "cultural school" feminist, that is, one who does not subscribe to the notion that masculinity and femininity are tied to the categories of sexual difference. The essentialist bias of object relations theory, which gives priority to femininity on the basis of the mother's femaleness, however, tends to subvert her argument for the psychosocial construction of femininity. Her representation of femininity, moreover, is so positive on the whole that it has persuaded many feminists to regard it as an inherent and desirable aspect of female identity.[4] In this way, Chodorow's account of the formation of gender identity which is characteristic of the psychosocial structure of patriarchy takes on an essentialist cast that defeats her main objective. The problem lies in

---

interchangeably. Freud himself cannot seem to make up his mind whether or not femininity properly belongs to the female sex.

4. I believe that this is a common misunderstanding. Evelyn Fox Keller, whose gender analysis of science is indebted to Chodorow's interpretation of object relations theory, often finds that she is being misread in this way. Regarding the reception of her book on Barbara McClintock, for instance, she says: "Many feminists have continued to read the McClintock story as a manifesto of a 'feminist science' (in the sense, i.e., of a specifically female science)—in the process either celebrating me as its proponent, or, if they respond at all to my disclaimers, implying that I lack the courage of my convictions—sometimes even suggesting that I lack the courage of McClintock's convictions" ("Gender/Science System" 43). Janet Sayers documents the ways in which Chodorow's work has been understood as essentialist in *Sexual Contradictions* (72–77). I also find that students encountering Chodorow for the first time tend to miss her insistence on the *cultural* production of the feminine personality.

object relations theory itself, which Chodorow only partially succeeds in bending to her own uses.

Chodorow's account of the basic tenets of object relations theory
reveals the difficulty of discriminating between questions of sex
and gender difference. "At birth," she explains, "the infant is not
only totally dependent but does not differentiate itself cognitively
from its environment" (61). What begins as a statement about the
infant's surround, however, quickly turns into one about its primary caretakers and concludes with an observation about a single
person from whom it does not yet distinguish itself, presumably its
mother: "The infant experiences itself as merged or continuous
with the world generally, and with its mother or caretakers in
particular. Its demands and expectations (not expressed as conscious wants but unconscious and preverbal) flow from this feeling
of merging. Analysts call this aspect of the earliest period of life
primary identification, aptly emphasizing the infant's object cathexis of someone it does not yet differentiate from its self" (61).
Although Chodorow later argues that the infant identifies with the
gender of its mother, rather than her anatomical femaleness, this
distinction is hard to keep in mind in the context of her descriptions
of mother-infant fusion. During the symbiotic phase, for instance,
she states that "the infant oscillates between perceptions of its
mother as separate and as not separate. For the most part, in spite of
cognitive perception of separateness, it experiences itself as within
a common boundary and fused, physically and psychologically,
with its mother" (62). The infant's sense of physical fusion with its
mother would logically seem to include an identification with her
anatomical femaleness.[5]

Chodorow's interpretation of the preoedipal period, as viewed
through object relations theory, leads her to articulate a distinctly
feminine form of personality structure. The mother's perception of
gender difference, she argues, affects the way in which both boys
and girls respond to issues of separation and autonomy. Whereas
mothers propel their sons toward differentiation, the development
of firm ego boundaries, and an Oedipally organized relationship to

5. Janet Sayers, for instance, assumes that this is what Chodorow means. Describing Chodorow's position, she writes: "Mothers . . . tend to experience their
daughters, on account of their being the same sex as themselves, as more merged and
identified with them than are their sons" (70).

them, they tend to prolong the periods of symbiosis and relaxed ego boundaries with their daughters, whom they do not perceive as clearly Other. Here again, however, there is some slippage in Chodorow's representation of gender difference.

> Because they are the same gender as their daughters and have been girls, mothers of daughters tend not to experience these infant daughters as separate from them in the same way as do mothers of infant sons. In both cases, a mother is likely to experience a sense of oneness and continuity with her infant. However, this sense is stronger, and lasts longer, vis-à-vis daughters. Primary identification and symbiosis with daughters tend to be stronger and cathexis of daughters is more likely to retain and emphasize narcissistic elements, that is, to be based on experiencing a daughter as an extension or double of a mother herself, with cathexis of the daughter as a sexual other usually remaining a weaker, less significant theme. [109]

Surely the fact that mothers perceive their daughters as doubles of themselves has something to do with their perceptions of sexual difference. Chodorow admits as much in her allusion to the mother's awareness of having been a girl, and in her invocation of sexual likeness as a basis for mothers' narcissistic identification with their daughters. This area of unclarity or instability in Chodorow's argument has led to some confusion about her characterization of femininity among feminists who have been attracted to her work. While "cultural school" feminists take her description of masculine and feminine personality structures as typical of patriarchal social organization and thus subject to change, others have accepted it as true in an essential way.[6] There is a secondary reason for the latter phenomenon.

Chodorow's portrait of feminine personality, while agreeing with

---

6. I would include Evelyn Fox Keller (*Reflections on Gender and Science* and *A Feeling for the Organism*) and Carol Gilligan (*In a Different Voice*) among the cultural school feminists who are indebted to Chodorow. See Marianne Hirsch ("Mothers and Daughters," "A Mother's Discourse"), Jane Flax ("Mother-Daughter Relationships"), Claire Kahane ("Gothic Mirror"), and Coppélia Kahn (*Man's Estate*) for some examples of the essentialist uses of Chodorow. Some of these critics in their more recent work have moved away from object relations theory and toward French theory as represented by Cixous, Irigaray, and Kristeva. One does not escape the problem of essentialism so easily, however, as the practice of *l'écriture féminine* has come under attack for this as well.

that of Freud in certain respects, reverses his negative evaluation in a way that appeals to some feminists. Her emphases, in particular, on women's sense of connectedness to the world, their capacity for empathic identification, and their lifelong allegiances to other women have an imaginative appeal that for many feminists offsets her argument in favor of alternative gender arrangements. It becomes seductive, from this point of view, to read Chodorow's description of the mother-daughter relationship as one that is inherent and positive, rather than an undesirable outcome of the condition of exclusive female mothering. The attractiveness of Chodorow's portrayal of the mother-daughter bond offers an inducement for many readers to valorize, rather than to critique, this relationship. The feminist transformation of an old misogynist construction of woman as Other and inferior would then consist in a reversal of evaluative categories toward an affirmation of that which is female.

Even cultural school feminists are affected by Chodorow's appealing account of feminine development. While these interpreters tend to emphasize the difficulty for women of fully separating from their mothers and thus achieving autonomy as boys more typically do, they do not reject the positive aspects of feminine personality structure which also derive from the condition of mother-infant symbiosis and female child rearing. Despite their recommendations for social transformation they do not anticipate that women will thereby resemble men in their anxious relation to maternity and corresponding repudiation of "femininity." Rather, they argue in favor of more flexible ego boundaries in men and firmer ego boundaries in women.[7] While pointing to problem areas in female development, they view women's capacities for empathic identification, for forming close bonds with one another, and for nurturance with approval. It is difficult under these circumstances to dispense with the idea of core masculine and feminine identities, which the essentialist reading of Chodorow openly affirms.[8]

---

7. See, for instance, Carol Gilligan's recommendations for a mature morality as founded on both an "ethic of justice" (characteristic of men) and an "ethic of care" (characteristic of women). She does not argue in favor of a wholesale transposition of typically masculine and feminine concerns, but a closer integration of them within individual personalities and, by extension, society at large (151–74).

8. Although Chodorow has recently taken Lacan to task for sexualizing his

The object relations concept of mother-infant fusion, by focusing on the physical as well as the emotional bond between mother and child, introduces an instability into Chodorow's argument for the predominance of social factors in the psychological construction of gender. The result is a drift toward essentialism, which threatens to reinscribe (albeit in a more positive way) the existing stereotypes of masculinity and femininity.[9] The real liability of Chodorow's argument is its very success. The lucidity of her exposition is such that change in the psychological structure of masculinity and femininity appears either impossible to achieve on the one hand or undesirable on the other. Yet she herself regards the reproduction of mothering as fundamental to women's oppression and the developmental sequences she describes as characteristic of men and women *in patriarchy*. From her own perspective, object relations theory offers a means of analyzing the reproduction of this social order. She does not critique object relations theory itself as problematically inscribed within patriarchy.

While Stoller's notion of primary femininity brings out the buried logic of object relations theory in regard to the precariousness of masculine identity, it does not alter the position of the preoedipal mother as object rather than subject, whose participation in biological reproduction excludes her from cultural creation. Her role may be subversive in regard to the structure of masculine development, but it is not revolutionary. Instead she remains firmly fixed within the Oedipal/preoedipal hierarchy established by Freud. Even the feminist uses of object relations theory cannot help but reproduce this basic dilemma.

------

theory through his choice of the phallus as signifier, she does not appear to have fundamentally altered her stance toward object relations theory. Noting that the academic and psychoanalytic communities remain isolated from each other, however, she calls for a greater interchange of ideas among clinicians and literary theorists of whatever persuasion (lecture on the University of California, Berkeley campus, fall 1986).

9. Jacqueline Rose, who cherishes Lacan for what she considers his nonbiological description of the acquisition of sexual identity, takes Chodorow to task, along with Ernest Jones and Karen Horney, for attempting to "resolve the difficulties of Freud's account of femininity by aiming to resolve the difficulty of femininity itself" (Mitchell and Rose, eds., *Feminine Sexuality* 29). Chodorow's failure to problematize female sexual identity, according to Rose, makes her argument essentialist.

Jacques Lacan

Although Lacan transforms Freud's theory in many ways, he retains his hierarchical ordering of the Oedipal and preoedipal periods, which ultimately locates femininity, as a function of language (rather than sexual difference), in the position of subversion. Because his theory is generally construed as a rejection of biologism, it appeals to feminists who are leery of essentialist formulations. Its appeal to them consists in part in the elegance of his explanation of the phallocentrism of culture, and in part in his own playful investment in exposing the element of sham in its construction.[10] While Lacan himself maintains the inevitability of phallocentrism in language and hence cultural production, he appears to take sides with those who seek its disruption. This double stance, which renders the signification of the phallus at once incontrovertible and arbitrary, valorizes the position of subversion, while fixing it within a larger structure of containment. Feminists who pursue the implications of Lacan's work regarding the possibility of a feminine form of writing that would oppose the strictures of patriarchal discourse find themselves similarly boxed into the paradox of subversion. The position of disruption does not permit transformation. What this situation does allow is a certain argument for discursive androgyny, in which male writers for the most part, somewhat on the order of Lacan himself, can become exponents of *l'écriture féminine*. The drawback of this stance is that it tends to subordinate the interests and writing of actual women.[11]

The Imaginary phase in Lacan's system of thought corresponds

10. See, for instance, Rose's Introduction to *Feminine Sexuality*, which concludes: "In these texts Lacan gives an account of how the status of the phallus in human sexuality enjoins on the woman a definition in which she is simultaneously symptom and myth. As long as we continue to feel the effects of that definition we cannot afford to ignore this description of the fundamental imposture which sustains it" (57).

11. Ann Rosalind Jones points out, for instance, that "Franco-feminist deconstruction has so far been aimed largely at male-authored texts" ("Inscribing Femininity" 96). She also provides a lucid critique of the politics of marginality for women (107). I would add only that it is difficult to give up privilege once you have it, so that middle- (and upper-) class white males are not risking much by adopting a discourse of subversion, particularly if their political activity consists chiefly in the practice of a certain style of writing.

roughly with that of the preoedipal period.[12] During this phase, there is neither language nor differentiation for the infant, who does not perceive a separate selfhood. Where object relations theory builds a rich drama of separation and individuation, however, Lacan posits a single moment of division instigated by the father, whose prohibition of incest introduces the child into the circuits of language and desire, both of which are governed by the law of the Symbolic. It is the father's phallus, as the mark of (sexual) difference, that at once separates the infant from its experience of maternal plenitude and reveals the differential basis of signification in language. From this point the history of desire, fueled by the perception of absence, is subsumed into that of language, which is similarly founded on a lack. Because the father is almost the accidental agent, the impersonal but necessary third term that intervenes in the incestuous mother-infant relationship, the phallus also appears as an arbitrary signifier of difference. In any event it serves as a reminder of absence—of the mother and the preoedipal experience of plenitude, on the one hand, and of the elusive signified in language, on the other. What desire and the signifier have in common is their endless pursuit of the unattainable. Because they have both been set in motion by the differential stroke of the phallus, moreover, they are both subject to the law of the father. Language and society, for Lacan, can only have meaning within patriarchy. The father's prohibition of incest, his *non*, thus becomes synonymous with his *nom*, the order of naming by which the child takes its place in society.

Sexual difference in Lacan's system appears to be a by-product of the child's entry into language, which in turn distinguishes the Symbolic from the Imaginary stage. Both the boy and the girl must suffer the division from the mother which gives them access to language and to social exchange, and in this sense both are "castrated." The ego, which reveals its construction around a lack in the

12. My summary of Lacan is based on my reading of his *Ecrits* in conjunction with various explications of his thought. I am chiefly indebted to Terry Eagleton, *Literary Theory* 163–74; Catherine Clément, *Lives and Legends of Jacques Lacan*; Juliet Mitchell and Jacqueline Rose, Introduction to *Feminine Sexuality*; John P. Muller and William J. Richardson, "Toward Reading Lacan"; Ellie Ragland-Sullivan, *Jacques Lacan and the Philosophy of Psychoanalysis*; and Stuart Schneiderman, *Jacques Lacan: The Death of an Intellectual Hero*. Among these, I found Mitchell, Rose, and Ragland-Sullivan the most useful.

mirror stage, now assumes the consequences of this split. Neither sex possesses the self-identity or fullness of being that the phallus elusively promises. Yet because the phallus serves as the signifier of difference par excellence, it organizes the sexes (hitherto undifferentiated) around the terms "masculine" and "feminine." The boy and girl thus take up positions as male and female in a system of language and society that privileges the phallus as signifier. The term "woman" in this economy will appear to represent lack itself—the lack within being associated with the mirror stage and the subsequent recognition of division from the mother, as well as the lack of the phallus, which Freud refers to as the "fact" of female castration. Lacan, however, in contradistinction to Freud, finds this condition of lack the most interesting matter for investigation at the same time that it is virtually impossible to speak of.

A series of analogies structures Lacan's paradoxical stance in regard to the feminine. What desire, language, and subjectivity share is a particular relationship to lack. Each is informed by an absence that undermines the dream of plenitude. Desire can never attain its object; the signifier cannot capture or contain the signified; the subject must remain forever unknown to him or herself. The phallus itself, from this standpoint, represents an illusion of wholeness and self-sufficiency. Yet its status as belonging to the father, whose intervention in the mother-infant dyad Lacan, like Freud, considers crucial to human development, determines the phallic (and patriarchal) organization of language and culture. It should not be surprising from this standpoint that Lacan would valorize the position of woman within this system, since she represents the term of "lack" within the (admittedly arbitrary) system of sexual difference. In his Seminar "Encore," Lacan reveals his fascination with and allegiance to the position that takes the side of that which is missing in the phallic economy. Although he identifies this position with "woman," his own account of sexual difference allows him to speak in her place, provided of course that his utterance contains enough gaps or holes to be subversive.

In "Encore," Lacan theorizes a position beyond the phallic economy through the concept of *jouissance*, a word that refers specifically to the pleasure of sexual orgasm but also to an ineffable state of enjoyment that Lacan relates to the mystical transports of the saints. Because woman enters the Symbolic order on the side of lack, she has a privileged relationship to this condition. She thereby also escapes language and categorization. "There is no such thing as *The* woman," Lacan states somewhat provocatively. "There is no such thing as *The* woman since of her essence—having already risked the term, why think twice about it?—of her essence, she is not all" (144). Being "not all" means that woman exceeds all systems of representation. It also means that she herself, "as excluded by the nature of things, which is the nature of words," cannot speak of her own *jouissance*. "There is a *jouissance* proper to her, to this 'her' which does not exist and which signifies nothing. There is a *jouissance* proper to her and of which she herself may know nothing, except that she experiences it—that much she does know" (145).

It is the unspeakable, unrepresentable, and excessive nature of *jouissance* that calls forth the analogy with mystical experience. "As for Saint Theresa—you have only to go and look at Bernini's statue in Rome to understand immediately that she's coming, there is no doubt about it. And what is her *jouissance*, her *coming* from? It is clear that the essential testimony of the mystics is that they are experiencing it but know nothing about it" (147). *Jouissance*, the property of woman and her sexuality, achieves the status of something that escapes and transcends the Symbolic order with its dependence on the phallus as signifier. "Might not this *jouissance* which one experiences and knows nothing of," Lacan speculates, "be that which puts us on the path of ex-istence? And why not interpret one face of the Other, the God face, as supported by feminine *jouissance*?" (147). In his invocation of the "Other, the God face," Lacan draws woman into conjunction with his understanding of the unconscious, the truth of which the subject habitually avoids, and which in some absolute sense must always be deferred.

At the same time that Lacan insists on the law of the father as constitutive of language and society, he hankers after the possibility of its disruption or displacement. Woman in "Encore" stands for this possibility, though she herself, as represented in an actual woman for instance, knows nothing of it. Lacan, on the other hand, displacing himself from the Symbolic order through his elliptical and hermetic prose style, seems to regard himself as the medium by which *jouissance* can articulate itself, however imperfectly. Speaking of the writings of the mystics, Lacan states that they "are neither idle gossip nor mere verbiage, in fact they are the best thing you can read—note right at the bottom of the page. *Add the* Écrits *of Jacques Lacan,* which is of the same order" (147). The complexity of Lacan's stance here, which appears to valorize woman at the expense of women, whom he seems to silence in his many protestations that he alone can speak the truth of *jouissance,* has contributed to the development of a highly controversial phenomenon among feminists: *l'écriture féminine.*

L'Ecriture Féminine

Lacan wants to distinguish the term "woman" from women, just as he wants to discriminate between the phallus (as privileged signifier) and the penis in order to sustain his argument that the category of sexual difference is a product of language and culture rather than biology.[13] Such a stance has an obvious appeal to feminists who feel trapped by the dictum "anatomy is destiny." Further-

13. Jane Gallop comments on the difficulty of sustaining the distinction between penis and phallus: "Even though Lacan might intend the word 'phallus' to mean a 'neutral,' 'differential function,' because he uses a word that is already in the language, already in use, in the lexicon—*Le Petit Robert,* for example, defines it as 'virile member'—the confusion is inevitable" (*Reading Lacan* 136). This confusion has led many to regard Lacan's theory as sexualized, that is, biologized. Ragland-Sullivan does as well as anyone can to oppose such an interpretation. She writes: "As we have seen, Lacan treats the penis as privileged because of a confusion of the virile member with a phallic signifying function. The Phallus introduces the alienating effect of difference into the pleasurable and natural mother-infant dyad, and this Oedipalizing, dividing effect gradually becomes substantivized around the Name-of-the-Father. Lacan points out, however, that the purely signifying and thus arbitrary nature of the Name-of-the-Father is nowhere more obvious than in the fact that paternity is not provable, in some cultures, indeed, is not necessarily associated with copulation and birth" (290). But if the phallus is *not* based on the function of the penis in copulation, for instance, and hence paternity, then it is not clear why culture must be androcentric. Either the phallus collapses into the penis or it becomes completely arbitrary as a sign of difference and thus uncoupled from any necessary connection with patriarchy. Despite the vehement, and often eloquent, protestations of Lacanian theorists to the contrary, I see no way out of this dilemma. For a very lucid discussion of the slippage between "phallus" and "penis" in Lacan's work, see David Macey's chapter "The Dark Continent" in his *Lacan in Contexts* (177–209). He comments succinctly: "Just as the symbolic Name-of-the-Father tends to regress to being little more than an invocation of the name or imago of the real father, so the symbolic phallus tends to become the biological penis" (190).

more, in his essay "Encore," Lacan seems to promote a form of writing that has the power to disrupt the rigid constructions of the Symbolic order. Taken together, these two concepts have contributed to the development of *l'écriture féminine*, a practice of writing on the side of woman and of the Imaginary against the phallogocentrism of Western culture.

In its strict philosophical form, *l'écriture féminine* is antiessentialist, emphasizing the deconstruction of the linguistic categories on which our assumptions about masculinity and femininity are based.[14] As such, it can be invoked by both men and women, and indeed the writing most often cited in evidence of this practice is male authored. At the same time, there is an area of slippage in the theory of *l'écriture féminine*, which is perhaps related to the difficulty of consistently dissociating the phallus from the penis. Despite Lacan's apparent dismissal of the preoedipal mother from a position of prominence or authority in his system of thought, she tends to surface in the writings of Cixous, Irigaray, and Kristeva in ways that suggest a fascination with female anatomy as well. The evocation of the Imaginary itself invites a focus on the figure of the preoedipal mother, which in turn elicits speculation about the signifying ground of the female body. This strain, though sometimes subdued in the literature that constitutes the main body of theory concerning feminine writing, is nevertheless strong enough to have generated serious controversy about its essentialist tendencies.[15] Feminine writing appears, in one of its guises at least, to reinscribe the very problem it attempts to redress. Finally, moreover, Lacan's allegiance to Freud's progressive scheme in his insistence on the

14. This is the position taken by Alice Jardine in *Gynesis* and Toril Moi in *Sexual/Textual Politics*. Moi, however, points to the inconsistencies in the work of Cixous and Irigaray, which cause them to be understood as essentialist.

15. Ann Rosalind Jones takes this view of *l'écriture féminine* in "Writing the Body." "Briefly, French feminists in general believe that Western thought has been based on a systematic repression of women's experience. Thus their assertion of a bedrock female nature makes sense as a point from which to deconstruct language, philosophy, psychoanalysis, the social practices, and the direction of patriarchal culture as we live in and resist it" (361). She criticizes this stance on the grounds that it universalizes female experience, ignoring women's material and political differences. She argues, in contrast, that "only through an analysis of the power relationships between men and women, and practices based on that analysis, will we put an end to our oppression—and only then will we discover what women are or can be" (369).

dissolution of the preoedipal phase through the triumph of the Oedipus complex and the inception of the Symbolic order fixes feminine writing, along with any possible theorizing about the signifying aspects of the mother-infant relation, firmly within a position of subordination, subversive perhaps but not transformative.

Hélène Cixous

Hélène Cixous and Catherine Clément, in *La Jeune Née* (recently translated as *The Newly Born Woman*), provide a theoretical basis for *l'écriture féminine*. In the opening essay, "The Guilty One," Clément examines the sorceress and the hysteric as figures of excess and subversion who in a historic sense have posed challenges to the Symbolic order. These women, through their mad or indecipherable speech, induce a state of carnival or suspension of the normal order of things.

> The mythology of the celebration contains the inversion of daily life in its development: feast, binge, drunkenness, dissolute ingestion of food, and regurgitation all demonstrate that it is not simply a matter of getting unusual pleasures but of pushing them to their very limit. Exchanges, undersides: partners cross-breeding, borrowing the forbidden other's clothes—transvestites, masks, and music at a different tempo signifying the break with the tempo of work. . . . The sorceress and the hysteric manifest the festival in their bodies, do impossible flips, making it possible to see what cannot be represented, figures of inversion. [22–23]

Woman as sorceress or hysteric is an outlaw, a renegade, who mocks the Symbolic order by turning it on its head.[16] Like Kundry

16. Peter Swales traces another line of association regarding witchcraft and hysteria. Noting Freud's references to witchcraft in describing the fantasies of his female patients, Swales argues that this path of association played a role in Freud's abandonment of the seduction theory. "In extending the analogy between witches and his own patients, then, Freud implied that all of them—witches and patients—were experiencing *fantasies*" ("A Fascination with Witches" 24). Whereas Freud uses the comparison between hysterics and witches to undermine the credibility of women patients (concerning the reality of seduction), Clément uses it to valorize their disruptive energy.

in Wagner's *Parsifal*, "she laughs, and it's frightening" (32). Or like Dora in Freud's case history, she gives the lie to the sordid exchange of women which sustains patriarchy. Together the hysteric and the sorceress provide models for the specifically linguistic activity that Cixous advocates in the second half of the book, where she develops her concept of *l'écriture féminine* as a program to disrupt the phallogocentrism that suppresses women and the realm of the Imaginary alike.

In the binary system of opposition and hierarchical pairing which organizes language (matter/spirit, nature/culture, passivity/activity), Cixous also reads the oppression of women, who are inevitably associated with the rejected or despised Other. Because the order of language is equivalent to the Symbolic order, which in turn depends on the signification of the phallus, the strategy for disruption must appeal to the Imaginary, a stage that is prelinguistic or protolinguistic at the same time that it revolves around the figure of the mother. While the appeal to the Imaginary does not necessarily involve a valorization of the female body, it does open possibilities for speculation along those lines. Thus Cixous can claim that she affirms a principle of bisexuality at the same time that she makes an impassioned plea for women to write from their physical and sexual experience. These two strains tend to alternate in "Sorties" without confronting each other directly. Readers of this text, depending on which passages they emphasize, may then also arrive at conflicting conclusions regarding the subject of sexual difference.[17]

When Cixous focuses on woman as a category in language created by the inception of the Symbolic order, she affirms a principle of bisexuality. She envisions an ego structure, for instance, which is fluid, playful, inventive—apparently unmarked by anatomical distinctions.

Men or women: beings who are complex, mobile, open. Accepting the other sex as a component makes them much richer, more various,

17. Thus, for instance, Alice Jardine describes Cixous as anti- or postfeminist due to the Derridean cast of her thought, while Ann Rosalind Jones regards her as obviously essentialist (*Gynesis* 20; "Writing the Body" 366). Moi sees both strains at work in *La Jeune Née*. "Fundamentally contradictory," she writes, "Cixous' theory of writing and femininity shifts back and forth from a Derridean emphasis on textuality as difference to a full-blown metaphysical account of writing as voice, presence and origin" (*Sexual/Textual Politics* 119).

stronger, and—to the extent that they are mobile—very fragile. It is
only in this condition that we invent. Thinkers, artists, those who
create new values, "philosophers" in the mad Nietzschean manner,
inventors and wreckers of concepts and forms, those who change life
cannot help but be stirred by anomalies—complementary or contradictory. That doesn't mean that you have to be homosexual to create.
But it does mean that there is no *invention* possible, whether it be
philosophical or poetic, without there being in the inventing subject
an abundance of the other, of variety: separate-people, thought-/
people, whole populations issuing from the unconscious, and in each
suddenly animated desert, the springing up of selves one didn't
know—our women, our monsters, our jackals, our Arabs, our aliases,
our frights. That there is no invention of any other I, no poetry, no
fiction without a certain homosexuality (the I/play of bisexuality)
acting as a crystallization of my ultrasubjectivities. I is this exuberant,
gay, personal matter, masculine, feminine or other where I enchants, I
agonizes me. [84]

As a principle of identity, bisexuality undermines the "Phallocentric Performing Theatre" (85), exploding the cultural categories
of masculine and feminine. In evidence of the capacity of male
authors to participate in this phenomemon, Cixous celebrates the
writing of Genet, Kleist, and Shakespeare. Like Lacan, who claims
to speak for "woman" and her *jouissance*, these authors "do not
repress their femininity" (81). At the same time, however, Cixous
claims that "today, writing is woman's," because "it is much
harder for man to let the other through him" (85). As she develops
the view that women are in effect less repressed than men in regard
to their bisexuality, she begins to blur the previously drawn distinction between language and anatomy.

Women, Cixous affirms, are less threatened than most men are by
the presence of an otherness within. As she elaborates this concept,
it gradually takes on the character of a biological predisposition,
rooted in the nature of maternity as well as the expression of female
desire. In the following passage, for instance, women's special writing talents appear to derive from the fluid organization of female
sexuality.

Let masculine sexuality gravitate around the penis, engendering this
centralized body (political economy) under the party dictatorship.
Woman does not perform on herself this regionalization that profits

the couple head-sex, that only inscribes itself within frontiers. Her libido is cosmic, just as her unconscious is worldwide: her writing also can only go on and on, without ever inscribing or distinguishing contours, daring these dizzying passages in other, fleeting and passionate dwellings within him, within the hims and hers whom she inhabits just long enough to watch them, as close as possible to the unconscious from the moment they arise; to love them, as close as possible to instinctual drives, and then, further, all filled with these brief identifying hugs and kisses, she goes and goes on infinitely. [87–88]

It is not just woman's position in relation to the Symbolic order that dictates this capacity (the way in which she acquires language in the phallocentric system described by Lacan) but also her relationship to the fact of maternity and ultimately to the physiological properties of her own body. Attempting to reimagine the "relation borne to the child," Cixous offers a lyrical meditation on the signification of pregnancy in terms of the capacity of the female body to contain otherness without violence. It is this ability to accept the "nonselfsame" within that, in turn, characterizes the form of writing she advocates.

Really experiencing metamorphosis. Several, other, and unforeseeable. That cannot but inscribe in the body the good possibility of an alteration. It is not only a question of the feminine body's extra resource, this specific power to produce some thing living of which her flesh is the locus, not only a question of a transformation of rhythms, exchanges, of relationship to space, of the whole perceptive system, but also of the irreplaceable experience of those moments of stress, of the body's crises, of that work that goes on peacefully for a long time only to burst out in that surpassing moment, the time of childbirth. In which she lives as if she were larger or stronger than herself. It is also the experience of a "bond" with the other, all that comes through in the metaphor of bringing into the world. How could the woman, who has experienced the not-me within me, not have a particular relationship to the written? To writing as giving itself away (cutting itself off) from the source? [90]

The body of the mother, traversed by the desire of an other, becomes a model for the kind of writing that allows itself to be possessed by the voice of the ultimate Other, the unconscious. The lack of enclosure that characterizes the woman's body in child-birth, moreover, provides an image for writing as a form of infinite letting go. "Voice! That, too, is launching forth and effusion with-out return. Exclamation, cry, breathlessness, yell, cough, vomit, music. Voice leaves. Voice loses. She leaves. She loses. And that is how she writes, as one throws a voice—forward, into the void" (94).

Finally, Cixous concludes that "woman must write her body." Moreover, because "woman is body more than man is," she is capable of "more writing" (95). At this point, it is no longer possible to distinguish between the term "woman" as a linguistic category created in culture and the individual human beings we recognize as women. However antiessentialist in theory or intention, *l'écriture féminine* in this moment of characterization grounds its appeal in the facts of sexual difference. That this appeal reverses the tradi-tional psychoanalytic devaluation of female anatomy does not alter its biologism.

The distinction between woman and women, at best a slippery one, is nearly always in danger of collapse within the context of psychoanalytic theory. Lacan's overlay of structural linguistics on Freud's own internally inconsistent body of work has the virtue for feminists of exposing the arbitrariness of the phallus as signifier and thus seeming to open up possibilities for feminist intervention in the system of language that governs culture. By claiming the phal-lus as signifier at all, however, in his effort to bind the process of language acquisition to the Oedipus complex, Lacan cannot help to some extent sexualizing his project as a whole. His transposition of Freud's preoedipal and Oedipal stages into his own terminology of the Imaginary and the Symbolic, moreover, does not entirely suc-ceed in dispelling the aura of actual maternal and paternal presence which accrues to these developmental phases in Freud's texts. Lacan's insistence on the *non du père* as a prohibition inherent in the structure of language and culture, detached from any particular action or person, is hard to sustain in light of Freud's vivid narrative practice. So too, it is difficult to exclude the body of the mother along with the entire context of the mother-infant relationship from consideration of the Imaginary. It is almost as though Lacan's deliberate disregard of the figure of the mother, his relegation of her function to a precultural stage, calls forth a specific effort on the part of feminists to imagine her presence and influence. Thus *l'écriture féminine*, despite its stated allegiance to a principle of bisexuality and cultural transformation, tends to focus with particular intensity on the female body in its sexual and maternal functions. The preoedipal mother, effectively erased from Lacan's elegant theoretical formulations, returns in the interstices of Cixous's text. Luce Irigaray, on the other hand, sees the mother's absence from representation as the driving force behind Western systems of discourse.

Luce Irigaray

In *Speculum of the Other Woman* Irigaray interprets Freud's texts on femininity as a radical denial of sexual difference, which she attributes to his repression of the preoedipal mother. Tracing this repression back to its Platonic source, she then theorizes its impact on the development of Western philosophy. In maintaining that the dominant discourses of the West repress sexual otherness, Irigaray also allies the prospect of feminine writing with her own concept of sexual difference, so that it becomes difficult to separate out essentialist from antiessentialist strains. Whereas her desire to deconstruct the monolithic phallocentrism of Western philosophic discourse (including that of Freud) would seem to be consonant with the bisexual aspect of feminine writing affirmed by Cixous, her lyric evocations of female eroticism appear to validate such writing by specific reference to the female body.

Irigaray argues that Freud's concept of femininity does not in fact allow for the existence of two sexes. Instead, he regards the phallus as the only sexual organ of significance and male desire as the norm. He treats the clitoris as an atrophied penis and describes the little girl's masturbatory activity as "phallic." "Sexual difference," she maintains, "is a derivation of the problematics of sameness, it is, now and forever, determined within the project, the projection, the sphere of representation, of the same" (26–27).

So we must admit that THE LITTLE GIRL IS THEREFORE A LITTLE MAN. A little man who will suffer a more painful and complicated evolution than the little boy in order to become a normal woman! A little man with a smaller penis. A disadvantaged little man. A little man whose libido will suffer a greater repression, and yet whose faculty for sublimating instincts will remain weaker. Whose needs are less catered to by nature and who will yet have a lesser share of culture. A more narcissistic little man because of the mediocrity of her genital organs (?). More modest because ashamed of that unfavorable comparison. More envious and jealous because less well endowed. Unattracted to the social interests shared by men. A little man who would have no other desire than to be, or remain, a man.   [26]

The threat of a possible otherness in the figure of the mother is contained through the concept of female castration and the definition of her desire for a child as a displacement of penis envy. The mother's role in this scheme is purely and simply reproductive. She offers "the challenge of an indefinite regeneration, of a reproduction of the *same* that defies death, in the procreation of the *son* this same of the procreating father" (27). As a result the particular configuration of the girl's relationship to her mother remains untheorized. "Woman's symbolization of her beginning, of the specificity of her relationship to the origin, has always already been erased, or is it repressed? by the economy that man seeks to put in place in order to resolve the problem of his primary cause. A problem to be solved by putting the Phallus at the beginning, and at the end" (60). Because Freud cannot imagine desire as other than phallic, moreover, he is unable to conceive of female homosexuality in other than masculine terms. "That a woman might desire a woman 'like' herself, someone of the 'same' sex, that she might also have auto- and homo-sexual appetites," Irigaray states, "is simply incomprehensible to Freud" (101).[18]

In the middle sections of *Speculum* Irigaray expands on her ideas concerning the suppression of sexual difference from Freud's theory. Here she connects this problem to the more general phenomenon in Western culture of the repression of the Imaginary, including all the possible ways of conceiving the mother-child relationship. In the last section of the book, she interprets Plato's parable of the cave as a paradigmatic example of the project of Western philoso-

18. For a discussion of the heterosexism that pervades Freudian as well as post-Freudian psychoanalytic theory, see Shirley Nelson Garner, "Feminism, Psychoanalysis, and the Heterosexual Imperative."

phy, which seeks to transcend the conditions of birth and death through the contemplation of timeless essences. The cave itself, she argues, represents the womb, the organ responsible for the production of forms. By seeking to efface knowledge of the womb, Plato sets the stage for a system of philosophy that establishes the law of the father.

> Eclipse of the mother, of the place (of) becoming, whose non-represen-
> tation or even disavowal upholds the absolute being attributed to the
> father. He no longer has any foundation, he is beyond all beginnings.
> Between these two abysses—nothing/being—language makes its
> way, morphology takes shape, once the mother has been emptied out.
> Enumerating all the "beings" formed in her, and their properties, in
> order to relate them to the father. In conformity with his desire and his
> law. [307]

Freud's phallic economy, with its emphasis on the authority of the father, who enforces the prohibition against incest, shares the principle of self-identity that governs Western philosophy. Irigaray's preoccupation with Freud's repression of sexual difference thus dovetails with her interest in deconstructing the codes that establish the terms "masculine" and "feminine" in Western culture. These two concerns are effectively intertwined in her descriptions of the Imaginary and the kind of writing that it might produce.

For Irigaray any discussion of the Imaginary involves first and foremost a consideration of the body of the mother. "Although the mother represents only a mute soil, a mystery beyond metaphor, at least she is still *pregnant*. Obviously, you will find opaqueness and resistance in the mother, even the repulsiveness of matter, the horror of blood, the ambivalence of milk, the threatening traces of the father's phallus, and even that hole that you left behind when you came into the world. But she—at least—is not nothing." In the place of this "void of representation" (228), Irigaray offers her own conception of the body of the mother/woman as fluid in form and multiple in its pleasures. *"The/a woman never closes up into a volume.* The dominant representation of the maternal figure as volume may lead us to forget that woman's ability to enclose is enhanced by her fluidity, and vice versa. Only when coopted by phallic values does the womb preclude the separation of the lips"

(239). Because "woman is neither open nor closed" and because her body contains a principle of otherness within, she figures a condition of indifferentiation which disrupts the entire phallic economy. "She is indefinite, in-finite, *form is never complete in her*. She is not infinite but neither is she *a* unit(y), such as letter, number, figure in a series, proper noun, unique object (in a) world of the senses, simple ideality in an intelligible whole, entity of a foundation, etc. This incompleteness in her form, her morphology, allows her to continually become something else, though this is not to say that she is ever univocally nothing" (229).

In the first part of *Speculum* Irigaray suggests a strategy for undermining the phallocentrism of discourse through a specific linguistic practice of disrupting the order of the sentence.

> Turn everything upside down, inside out, back to front. . . . *Overthrow syntax* by suspending its eternally teleological order, by snipping the wires, cutting the current, breaking the circuits, switching the connections, by modifying continuity, alternation, frequency, intensity. . . . Not by means of a growing complexity of the same, of course, but by the irruption of other circuits, by the intervention at times of short-circuits that will disperse, diffract, deflect endlessly, making energy explode sometimes, with no possibility of returning to one single origin. [142]

As Irigaray develops her argument concerning the repression of the Imaginary, this kind of exhortation, which appears to be sex neutral, begins to attach itself to her descriptions of female morphology, so that her linguistic and philosophic projects finally coincide with her aim to articulate a principle of sexual difference. Certain passages in Irigaray's *This Sex Which Is Not One* make this conjunction explicit.

Female speech, Irigaray affirms, reflects the conditions of female sexuality and desire. Because women's sex organs and hence sources of pleasure are plural, their language is multivocal, impossible to focus on a single object or set of meanings.

> But *woman has sex organs more or less everywhere*. She finds pleasure almost anywhere. . . . "She" is indefinitely other in herself. This is doubtless why she is said to be whimsical, incomprehensible, agitated, capricious . . . not to mention her language, in which "she" sets

off in all directions leaving "him" unable to discern the coherence of any meaning. Hers are contradictory words, somewhat mad from the standpoint of reason, inaudible for whoever listens to them with ready-made grids, with a fully elaborated code in hand. For in what she says, too, at least when she dares, woman is constantly touching herself. [28–29]

In this last image, Irigaray evokes a concept that underlies all of her theorizing on the subject of sexual difference. If woman's sex is "not one," it is in part because of the two lips of the vulva, continually touching each other without ever resolving themselves into a unity—like the phallus. Irigaray moves easily between the image of the two-lipped vulva to that of the woman's lips opening and closing in speech. The title of her concluding essay in *This Sex Which Is Not One*, "When Our Lips Speak Together," thus effaces the distinction between language and sexuality. In this lyrical prose poem, Irigaray describes an ethos of feminine writing while demonstrating it in her own practice. "Open your lips; don't open them simply. I don't open them simply. We—you/I—are neither open nor closed. We never separate simply: *a single word* cannot be pronounced, produced, uttered by our mouths. Between our lips, yours and mine, several voices, several ways of speaking resound endlessly, back and forth. One is never separable from the other. You/I: we are always several at once" (209). The open eroticism of this essay (which may be understood either as an address to a lover or to the self) makes it impossible to separate the issue of sexuality from that of speech. Irigaray gives the distinct impression here of attempting to "write the body."

> Kiss me. Two lips kissing two lips: openness is ours again. Our "world." And the passage from the inside out, from the outside in, the passage between us, is limitless. Without end. No knot or loop, no mouth ever stops our exchanges. Between us the house has no wall, the clearing no enclosure, language no circularity. When you kiss me, the world grows so large that the horizon itself disappears. Are we unsatisfied? Yes, if that means we are never finished. If our pleasure consists in moving, being moved, endlessly. Always in motion: openness is never spent nor sated. [210]

Irigaray's interest in the notion of fluid exchange finds expression in another brief essay written in the same lyrical mode, "And the

One Doesn't Stir without the Other." This essay, as if to answer Irigaray's own question about "what might become of psychoanalytic notions in a culture that did not repress the feminine" (73), sets forth the dynamics of the mother-daughter relationship, viewed from the perspective of the Imaginary. The daughter-speaker sees herself entangled with her mother's body and image, unable to draw clear lines of demarcation between them. "I look like you, you look like me. I look at myself in you, you look at yourself in me. You're already big, I'm still little. But I came out of you, and here, in front of your very eyes, I am another living you" (61). Rather than celebrating this condition, however, the speaker sees it as problematic. She is entrapped in her mother's reflection. "So that your body would move to the rhythm of your desire to see yourself alive, you imprisoned me in your blindness to yourself. In the absence of love that provoked or accompanied the mobility of your features, your gestures. You desired me, such is this love of yours. Imprisoned by your desire for a reflection, I became a statue, an image of your mobility" (64). At the heart of this dilemma lie the conditions of pregnancy and birth themselves, the fact that human consciousness derives from a state of division in fusion which has no analogue outside of reproduction.

> Of the two of us, who was the one, who the other? What shadow or what light grew inside you while you carried me? And did you not grow radiant with light while I lived, a thing held in the horizon of your body? And did you not grow dim when I took root in your soil? A flower left to its own growth. To contemplate itself without necessarily seeking to see itself. A blossoming not subject to any mold. An efflorescence obeying no already known contours. A design that changed itself endlessly according to the hour of the day. Open to the flux of its own becoming. [65–66]

Although the speaker mourns her mother's apparent inability to fashion a life that does not use her daughter as a projection of her own thwarted desires, she conceives of a more egalitarian relationship in which both might prosper.

> Haven't you let yourself be touched by me? Haven't I held your face between my hands? Haven't I learned your body? Living its fullness. Feeling the place of its passage—and of the passage between you and me. Making from your gaze an airy substance to inhabit me and

shelter me from our resemblance. From your/my mouth, an unending horizon. In you/me and out of you/me, clothed or not, because of our sex. In proportion to our skin. Neither too large nor too small. Neither wide open nor sutured. Not rent, but slightly parted. [66–67]

The concluding image in this passage recalls Irigaray's reference earlier to the speech circulated between two women whose lips are never simply open or closed. Indeed the speaker imagines the possibility of such a relationship with her mother. "Didn't I already have my/your lips? And this body open on what we would never have stopped giving each other, saying to each other?" (67) Feminine writing here is almost synonymous with mother-daughter discourse. For Irigaray, it is impossible to undo the repression of the Imaginary and hence to disrupt the phallogocentrism of culture without confronting some specter of the mother and her difference.

Julia Kristeva

Whereas Lacan believes that he can speak in the place of "woman" without being one, women themselves seem to have greater difficulty in discriminating between the position of cultural disruption signified by the Imaginary and the fact of being female. The woman theorist who strives most consistently to maintain this distinction is Julia Kristeva, who finds her own ideas concerning the subversive properties of "semiotic" writing best exemplified by male authors.[19] On occasion, however, even she intimates that the maternal body might be capable of producing a unique form of discourse.

Kristeva's assault on phallogocentrism draws her, like Cixous

---

19. Moi sees Kristeva as rejecting "any idea of an *écriture féminine* or a *parler femme* that would be inherently feminine or female" (*Sexual/Textual Politics* 163) and thus regards any approximation of the "semiotic" to the "feminine" as a misreading. This distinction is in danger of collapse, however, in Kristeva's "Stabat Mater," where her attempt at maternal discourse does seem to presuppose a female body. Moi, in her Introduction to *Kristeva Reader*, acknowledges that there is some slippage in Kristeva's thought on this ground (11). See also Domna Stanton, "Difference on Trial," which examines Kristeva's use of the maternal metaphor. Stanton cautions against the appeal to female difference because of the ease with which it may be made to serve conservative ends.

and Clément, to the Bakhtinian concept of carnival. "Carnival-esque discourse," she claims, "breaks through the laws of a language censored by grammar and semantics and, at the same time, is a social and political protest. There is no equivalence, but rather, identity between challenging official linguistic codes and challenging official law" ("Word, Dialogue, and Novel" 36). Kristeva's semiotic theory provides an expanded context for understanding the dynamic heterogeneity of such writing. Here, moreover, Kristeva's Lacanianism reveals its structural significance in her thought.

Like the Imaginary, the semiotic precedes the Symbolic, subsisting within it as the possibility of disruption. The character of the semiotic as a signifying process is thus prelinguistic, containing the energy of the preoedipal drives, as yet unorganized by the symbolic system instigated by the prohibition of the father.

> Discrete quantities of energy move through the body of the subject who is not yet constituted as such and, in the course of his development, they are arranged according to the various constraints imposed on this body—always already involved in a semiotic process—by family and social structures. In this way the drives, which are 'energy' charges as well as 'psychical' marks, articulate what we call a *chora*: a non-expressive totality formed by the drives and their stases in a motility that is as full of movement as it is regulated. ["Revolution in Poetic Language" 93]

The chora is a locus of rhythms, pressures, and pulsions that "connect and orient the body to the mother" (95). This loose association of drives must give way, however, to the advent of the Symbolic stage, which acts to repress it. Transgressive in nature, the semiotic fights back, making its presence felt through ruptures in discourse. The semiotic gives expression to a sort of lawlessness within the structures of language and society.

Kristeva makes it clear that she does not imagine the possibility of a "pure" semiotic discourse—one that exists somewhere outside of or apart from the Symbolic.

> Although originally a precondition of the symbolic, the semiotic functions within signifying practices as the result of a transgression of the symbolic. Therefore the semiotic that 'precedes' symbolization is only a *theoretical supposition* justified by the need for description. It

exists in practice only within the symbolic and requires the symbolic break to obtain the complex articulation we associate with it in musical and poetic practices.   ["Revolution" 118]

There is no access either to the Imaginary or to the semiotic except through the route of the Symbolic. In this respect, Kristeva follows Lacan's two-tiered system of development, carefully aligning his structural model with her linguistic concerns. The mirror stage, for instance, in her view "permit[s] the constitution of objects detached from the semiotic *chora*" (100), a necessary precondition for the process of signification. Castration completes this process by detaching the subject from dependence on the mother. "This is a decisive moment fraught with consequences: the subject, finding his identity in the symbolic, *separates* from his fusion with the mother, *confines* his *jouissance* to the genital and transfers semiotic motility on to the symbolic order" (101). Because "castration" functions as a recognition of lack, which in turn structures the relationship between signifier and signified, it inaugurates the Symbolic stage in which language formation is possible. Not to experience "castration" condemns the subject to the state of linguistic incoherence perceived as psychosis. Kristeva's adherence to Lacan's (and Freud's) developmental scheme, in which the Symbolic (or Oedipal phase) must supersede the Imaginary, means that she cannot endorse Irigaray's project for the recovery of a language unique to the Imaginary or to the mother-daughter relationship in its earliest form. In this respect her linguistic project is consistent with Lacan's stance in "Encore." *Jouissance* can only find expression through a speaking subject already constituted by his or her passage into the Symbolic and as an effect of resistance or disruption. *L'écriture féminine* does not derive from the privilege of female anatomy but rather from a position one takes in relation to the Symbolic.

Kristeva's insistence on the androgynous nature of semiotic writing has allied her with the "anti-feminism" of French women theorists who oppose any form of essentialism.[20] When she discusses men's writing, her position is consistent in this regard. When she describes the relationship of women to language, due to their spe-

20. Alice Jardine explains the use of the term "anti-feminist" to describe the position of theorists like Kristeva in "Gynesis."

cial inheritance of the Oedipus complex, however, her stance appears to be more conflicted.

In *About Chinese Women*, Kristeva addresses the question of woman's place in phallocentric culture. Here she discusses the way in which patriarchal monotheistic religion posits a sexual division that excludes the mother from knowledge and power by locating her in a position marginal to language. "Monotheistic unity," she maintains, "is sustained by a radical separation of the sexes: indeed, this separation is its prerequisite. For without this gap between the sexes, without this localization of the polymorphic, orgasmic body, laughing and desiring, in the other sex, it would have been impossible, in the symbolic sphere, to isolate the principle of One Law— One, Purifying, Transcendent, Guarantor of the ideal interest of the community" (19). The relegation of the mother to the realm of reproduction and her corresponding exclusion from the Symbolic create a double-bind situation for the daughter, who, in the process of her own development, must choose between maternal and paternal identification.

In arriving at the Symbolic stage, the girl takes the side of her father against her mother. She is rewarded by this move with access to language and power; what she loses is participation in the mother's *jouissance*. While the man can momentarily flee the paternal order and hence return to this state of pleasurable lawlessness, the woman in doing so risks her fragile hold on the Symbolic. In identifying with her mother, the woman becomes "ecstatic, nostalgic, or mad." Hence, she "has nothing to laugh about when the paternal order falls" (30). Kristeva provides an extremely lucid account of this dilemma. On the one hand, "we cannot gain access to the temporal scene, i.e. to political affairs, except by identifying with the values considered to be masculine (dominance, superego, the endorsed communicative word that institutes stable social exchange)." To refuse this role, sullenly holding back, on the other hand, means "neither speaking nor writing," and places one "in a permanent state of expectation, punctuated now and then by some kind of outburst: a cry, a refusal, an 'hysterical symptom'" (37). Ultimately, "if no paternal 'legitimization' comes along to dam up the inexhaustible non-symbolized impulse," a woman will collapse "into psychosis or suicide" (41). Although Kristeva attempts to articulate a median path between these equally undesirable extremes, her recommendation for taking sides with the "unspoken in speech" (38), with the new, the eccentric, and the incomprehensible, does not seem adequate to the magnitude of the problem she has described.

Lacan's insistence on the phallocentrism of language and culture makes it impossible to locate a position from which to speak which is not already governed by the Symbolic order. This problem is compounded for the woman speaker, who must also deny her primary identification with the body of her mother. In Kristeva's depiction of this dilemma it appears that a woman must do violence to her very femaleness in order to grow up.

Kristeva's distinction between woman as a creation of culture and women as sexually differentiated human beings threatens finally to collapse when she addresses the subject of motherhood. Here she begins to sound more essentialist. There are several instances in which Kristeva maintains that pregnancy offers a unique set of paradoxes. In "Women's Time," for example, she describes pregnancy as "the radical ordeal of the splitting of the subject: redoubling up of the body, separation and coexistence of the self and of an other, of nature and consciousness, of physiology and speech" (206). Later, in "A New Type of Intellectual: The Dissident," she sees pregnancy as "an identity that splits, turns in on itself and changes without becoming other: the threshold between nature and culture, biology and language." Each of these depictions negates the dichotomized relationship between the Imaginary and the Symbolic which characterizes Lacan's developmental scheme. The splitting of the subject, which he posits as a product of the mirror stage and the subsequent recognition of castration, here seems specific to the body of the mother and to the process of human gestation. The mother's experience of the changes taking place in her own body would seem to offer her a privileged rather than a marginal relationship to language—itself based on the splitting of the subject and its corollary, the gap between signifier and signified. In any event, Kristeva seems to suggest, as Cixous and Irigaray do in their own ways, that there is something special about a mother's discourse, hitherto repressed from culture. "After the Virgin," Kristeva asks somewhat poignantly, "what do we know of a mother's (introspective) speech?" (297). In at least one essay, "Stabat Mater," she attempts to answer this question.

"Stabat Mater" contains two kinds of discourse. One, rational and analytical, examines the evolution within Christianity of the cult of the Virgin Mary. The other, lyrical and autobiographical, gives voice to the experience of motherhood, attesting to the intricacy of the mother-infant relationship. The mother's discourse appears shortly after the beginning of the essay and often takes up half of a page divided down the middle. Because the two types of writing do not interact in an obvious way, it is up to the reader to make sense of their juxtaposition.

Kristeva argues that the focus on Mary's virginity, and later on her "immaculate conception," originates in a fantasy of circumventing death. Since sexuality and death "are mutually implicated with each other," she explains, "one cannot avoid the one without fleeing the other" (165). Such a construction permits the elevation of Mary to a position of power (as the mother of God) at the same time that it divorces her from the ordinary lot of childbearing women. It also helps to exclude such women, mired in the exigencies of the flesh, from access to the divine Word, the sublimated Symbolic order upheld by paternal authority. "A woman will only have the choice to live her life either *hyper-abstractly* ('immediately universal', Hegel said) in order thus to earn divine grace and homologation with symbolic order; or merely *different*, other, fallen ('immediately particular', Hegel said). But she will not be able to accede to the complexity of being divided, of heterogeneity, of the catastrophic-fold-of-'being' ('never singular', Hegel said)" (173). Kristeva's argument recapitulates her position in *About Chinese Women* concerning the status of woman in the Symbolic order. Either she accepts a paternal identification, ruthlessly excising from her consciousness those aspects of her experience which are irreducibly female, or she accedes to her position as "fallen," identified with her flesh, and thus mute, removed from the signifying process. A third possibility emerges, however, in Kristeva's reference to the condition of being divided, and the complexity of the "catastrophic-fold-of-'being.'" Although Kristeva remains hesitant about proclaiming this option as one that would revolutionize woman's place in respect to language, her maternal discourse provides a point of departure for theorizing along these lines.

The mother's discourse in "Stabat Mater" supplements that of the Virgin by giving utterance to the heterogeneity of the experience of pregnancy and birth. Using a stream-of-consciousness style, Kristeva attempts to find a language for a state of radical paradox, in which subjectivity is both single and plural. "A mother," she states, "is a continuous separation, a division of the very flesh. And consequently a division of language—and it has always been so" (178). Sometimes it appears that maternity is beyond language, that it can only achieve expression through the necessary reduction of the Symbolic. At other times it seems that Kristeva wants to propose the maternal as its own standard for articulation. Her description of conception hovers in between these two possibilities.

> Flash—instant of time or of dream without time; inordinately swollen atoms of a bond, a vision, a shiver, a yet formless, unnameable embryo. Epiphanies. Photos of what is not yet visible and that language necessarily skims over from afar, allusively. Words that are always too distant, too abstract for this underground swarming of seconds, folding in unimaginable spaces. Writing them down is an ordeal of discourse, like love. What is loving, for a woman, the same thing as writing. Laugh. Impossible. Flash on the unnameable, weavings of abstractions to be torn. Let a body venture at last out of its shelter, take a chance with meaning under a veil of words. WORD FLESH. From one to the other, eternally, broken up visions, metaphors of the invisible. [162]

For Kristeva the challenge to identity posed by maternity offers a challenge to writing. In the following passage in which she defines the mother's union-in-separation with her newborn child, she pushes her own language to its limits of comprehensibility.

> Then there is this other abyss that opens up between the body and what had been its inside: there is the abyss between the mother and the child. What connection is there between myself, or even more unassumingly between my body and this internal graft and fold, which, once the umbilical cord has been severed, is an inaccessible other? . . . To say that there are no sexual relationships constitutes a skimpy assertion when confronting the flash that bedazzles me when I confront the abyss between what was mine and is henceforth but irreparably alien. Trying to think through that abyss: staggering vertigo. No identity holds up. [178–79]

If Kristeva seems doubtful on the whole about the possibility of recovering in language the fullness of the experience of maternity, she permits herself to imagine a cultural moment in which such a project might have had meaning.

> The languages of the great formerly matriarchal civilizations must avoid, do avoid, personal pronouns: they leave to the context the burden of distinguishing protagonists and take refuge in tones to recover an underwater, trans-verbal communication between bodies. It is a music from which so-called oriental civility tears away suddenly through violence, murder, blood baths. A woman's discourse would that be it? [182]

For an instant at least, Kristeva allows herself to think a way out of the double-bind situation for women in Western culture. That she arrives at this speculation through a meditation on her own experience of motherhood and a reference to ancient societies devoted to worship of a mother goddess allies her thinking here with that of Irigaray on the repression of the mother and with that of Cixous on the signifying aspects of the female body. However briefly, Kristeva entertains the notion that the heterogeneity of the mother's body provides a ground for heterogeneity in discourse. To this extent, she flirts with essentialism.

Conclusions

Freud's response to Emma Eckstein is emblematic of his difficulty in recognizing the importance of the preoedipal mother in his accounts of individual case histories as well as his inability to theorize her significance generally. Furthermore, in his construction of the Oedipus complex, Freud proposes a heroic model of masculine development which acts as a safeguard against the threat of maternal seduction and aggression. His conception of the boy's renunciation of his desire for his mother acquires a different kind of resonance, however, in his elaboration of the death instinct. Here, the regressive urge encoded in the fort/da game implies the existence of a continuous struggle against its own undoing within the process of development. Because the desire to return to an inorganic state is first associated with the body of the mother, she, in turn, becomes identified with death. As such, she stands outside of the progressive structure of patriarchal culture and the development of masculine personality on which it rests. In this way the preoedipal mother becomes a figure of subversion. She acts within the Oedipus complex to undermine it, creating an undertow toward death which may be diverted though not deflected from its aim. To the extent that women are identified with their reproductive functions they also come to represent this threat. Renegades to culture, creatures of the flesh, they appear hostile to masculinity and to phallic civilization alike. Neither object relations theory nor Lacanian psychoanalysis succeeds in altering this picture much. Their nearly opposite points of departure, however, cause them to stress different aspects of it.

Taking advantage of Freud's relative disregard of the preoedipal phase, object relations theorists focus on the figure of the mother, positing an initial state of mother-infant fusion, which, as Robert Stoller has pointed out, implies the concept of primary femininity. While such a discourse allows a revaluation of Freud's negative characterization of the feminine, it also suggests that gender differences are rooted in a biological given. Chodorow's arguments for the psychocultural determinants of femininity are thus in part undermined by the logical consequences of the theory she is using. The essentialism of Stoller's position, which in turn derives from the basic tenets of object relations theory, renders her position unstable and contributes to a reading of her text which contradicts her stated aim. Many feminists, as a result, have taken her description of the feminine personality structure within patriarchy as a celebration of the female character per se. Ironically such a reading participates in the very phenomenon that Chodorow is trying to change—the reproduction of socially structured psychological processes that lead to the condition of exclusive female mothering.

Where Freud evokes fleeting images of the preoedipal mother, object relations theory constructs a presence, but one that is devoid of the complexity usually attributed to an adult personality. Instead, the mother is described almost exclusively from the child's point of view, as either gratifying or frustrating, sensitive or insensitive, to her infant's needs. Such a manner of characterization reproduces Freud's own split conception of the preoedipal mother as either self-effacingly absorbed in the contemplation of her (male) offspring or disturbingly seductive and aggressive. Object relations theory thus inscribes the ambivalence that structures Freud's avoidance of the preoedipal mother at the same time that it places her in the spotlight of our attention. The result is a figure of contradictions who appears to be good or "good enough" when she is suitably responsive to her child, bad or even pathological when she is not. One can argue that the idealized image of maternal plenitude which characterizes both Freud's conception of the mother-son relationship and the "good enough" mother of object relations theory creates its own ugly opposite and hence the ease with which mothers are blamed for failures in development. Such a view of maternal responsibility and culpability is hardly conducive to feminist theorizing. As if to acknowledge this, Chodorow focuses on the mother as a figure of gratification.

In contrast to the object relations theorists who emphasize maternal presence, Lacan seems on the whole indifferent to the figure of the mother apart from her general function as representative of the Imaginary. This feature of his thought corresponds to Freud's repression of the mother. The abstractness of Lacan's own discourse contributes, moreover, to the effect of her disappearance or erasure. His linguistic concerns further discourage speculation along biological lines, so that his celebration of woman and her *jouissance* finally refers not to women themselves but to a position in language. While this stance has the advantage of offering a non-gender-based description of writing that has the seeming capacity to undermine the phallocentrism of culture, it has at least two disadvantages for women. First, by denying the relevance of sexual difference, this form of writing makes it difficult for women as women to create a presence in discourse. The effects of sexual difference—in the historical, material, and physiological terms that form the bases of feminist inquiry and concern—seem to have no place in such writing. To date, moreover, the antiessentialist view of feminine writing has tended to promote the reputations and careers of male writers almost exclusively. Second, Lacan's adherence to Freud's hierarchical ordering of the Oedipal and preoedipal stages and his conflation of the Oedipus complex with language acquisition makes it impossible to conceive of feminine writing as anything other than subversive, able to disrupt but not to overthrow. Once again such a position inhibits the feminist project of cultural transformation. As if responding to these limitations in Lacan's system of thought, the female proponents of *l'écriture fémi-*

nine have tended to reinscribe the figure of the mother and to focus on female anatomy as offering a new set of metaphors for writing.

Cixous, Irigaray, and Kristeva all begin with Lacan's assumption regarding the ascendance of the Symbolic over the Imaginary. They each pit themselves against the Symbolic, constructing various strategies for mitigating, if not destroying, its power and influence. Nominally they ascribe to an antiessentialist position, affirming feminine writing as a stance taken in relation to language which aims to deconstruct its phallocentrism. In different ways, however, they each display a fascination with the female body as a locus for this kind of discourse and suggest at times that women may have privileged access to such writing based on their experience as mothers or their relationship to the Imaginary.

Cixous valorizes women in her portrayal of the female libido as cosmic and the maternal body as having the extra resource of containing an otherness within. Both properties, she claims, contribute to women's special talent for writing. For Irigaray, a linguistic economy based on a true understanding of sexual difference, as opposed to the reproduction of the same that characterizes the project of Western philosophy, would admit a form of writing modeled on the openness of the female body and the fluidity of female desire. Even Kristeva, whose antiessentialist stance remains for the most part consistent, indulges the speculation that the mother's unique relationship to subjectivity offers a position from which to theorize about writing. From a position that proclaims itself as antibiologistic, each of these writers veers toward essentialism.

More or less banished from Lacan's theory, the preoedipal mother surfaces in the texts of Cixous, Irigaray, and Kristeva, as if in response to the conviction that something vital has been missing. Almost too present in object relations theory, the preoedipal mother in Lacanian theory is not quite present enough. Both options (maternal presence and maternal absence) lead to conceptual difficulties for feminists. Whereas one position inscribes a drift toward essentialism, the other makes it hard to focus on the concerns of women as women. Neither seems adequate to the demands of contemporary feminists. A further irony proceeds from the fact that while Chodorow tries to move object relations theory in the direction of a cultural interpretation, the female Lacanians shift his nonbiological account of the acquisition of language and culture in the direction of primary femininity. What this situation suggests is that psychoanalytic feminism needs a way to account for femininity in both biological and cultural terms.[21] At present, such a manner of theorizing does not appear to exist. Instead, psychoanalytic feminists tend to polarize around these issues, unable to reconcile their differences or to perceive what they have in common.[22]

21. Paul Smith has another way of understanding this problem. He writes: "It seems to me that the actual 'subject' that feminism is in a position now to discern is very much akin to what I have been calling the agent. At the junctures of feminism's variously posed and differently constructed propositions, a properly feminist agent can be discerned. At the interstices between a humanistically identified 'subject' and some more radical or utopian and dispersed 'subject,' both notions operate in a mutually enabling dialectic, bound together by their very contradictions or by the negativity that underpins their heterogeneity. Understood in this context, contemporary feminist theory could perhaps be regarded as a project which recognizes that its aims would scarcely be met by either the positing of a fixed identity or the conjuring of some new and dispersed 'subject.' And in this respect it is almost unique—and thus salutary—among the various discourses of resistance" (*Discerning the Subject* 150). I am interested to see how this approach might be put into practice.

22. The same can be said about the deep division between the practice of Anglo-American literary criticism and French feminist theory. Janet Todd in *Feminist Literary History* has attempted a survey of both types of writing without invoking the usual oppositional rhetoric. I look forward to more studies in this vein.

PART III

Alienating Grace

If it is true, as Juliet Mitchell in *Psychoanalysis and Feminism* and Nancy Chodorow in *The Reproduction of Mothering* maintain, that the unconscious of any given social order is culture specific, then we may be genuinely indebted to Freud for illuminating the psychological underpinnings of Western patriarchal society. In this system, it appears that the subordination of women manifests itself in the inability adequately to theorize the position of the preoedipal mother and hence in the psychocultural understanding of femininity as subversion. While this configuration allows of a certain romanticization of the position of subversion, it does not permit an alteration of the structure as a whole. In psychoanalytic terms, it thus becomes difficult to imagine any significant change of attitude toward the mother as, on the one hand, providing the ground for subjectivity and, on the other, lacking in subjectivity herself. As long as the Oedipus complex remains identified with the stage of mastery in masculine development which acts as a prerequisite for civilization, moreover, the mother will continue to represent a threat to both.

The question for psychoanalytic feminism is whether the theories and techniques of investigation developed by Freud and amplified by his followers are capable of yielding a paradigm for psychological development which does not simply reproduce this dilemma. It is my own view that some movement in this direction, beginning from a consideration of the mother which does not automatically posit her exclusion from culture, is possible. To do so, however, one must set aside for a moment the bias in favor of the Oedipal stage which predetermines her role and status. It becomes useful, from this perspective, to reexamine Freud's redefinition of castration as separation from the mother and to consider the full implications of such a transposition of theory.

The Ego and the Id (1923)

Freud begins to muse in *The Ego and the Id* about the relationship between mourning and the construction of the ego in a way that intersects with his redefinition of castration as separation from the mother. The linkage between these two lines of thought has the potential, in turn, for revolutionizing his understanding of the pre-oedipal period.

Freud reminds us of the mechanism by which melancholia works, enshrining the object that has been lost within the ego. He goes on to speculate about the resemblance between this process and the construction of the ego itself.

> When it happens that a person has to give up a sexual object, there quite often ensues an alteration of his ego which can only be described as a setting up of the object inside the ego, as it occurs in melancholia; the exact nature of this substitution is as yet unknown to us. . . . At any rate the process, especially in the early phases of development, is a very frequent one, and it makes it possible to suppose that the character of the ego is a precipitate of abandoned object-cathexes and that it contains the history of those object-choices. [SE 19:29]

Although Freud develops this notion in conventional terms, attributing the boy's masculine character, for instance, to his identification with his father, which includes the incorporation of his image, he opens a space for a more radical interpretation.

If one adopts the model of mourning rather than that of melancholia to describe the construction of the ego, then the phrase "precipitate of abandoned object-cathexes" takes on another resonance. The ego, in this reading, owes its existence to an originary loss, its very structure predicated on an absence. This view of the ego, as an elegiac formation, corresponds in some ways to Lacan's insistence on the fundamental alienation of the self as represented in the mirror stage. Like the plaster casts of the victims of Pompeii, the ego bodies forth an image of wholeness while attesting to an inner absence. In this sense the ego acts as a memorial, a continual reminder of the loss that has brought it into being. As such, it recalls Freud's description of the fort/da game, in which the child's achievement of mastery encodes the very trauma of helplessness it seeks to control.

Toward the end of *The Ego and the Id*, Freud associates the fear of death with that of castration, relating both to the "first great anxiety-state of birth and the infantile anxiety of longing—the anxiety due to separation from the protecting mother" (*SE* 19:58). In *Inhibitions, Symptoms and Anxiety*, he moves closer to an identification of castration with separation per se, the prototype of which is the child's first awareness of disunion from its mother. "Castration," he maintains, "can be pictured on the basis of the daily experience of the faeces being separated from the body or on the basis of losing the mother's breast at weaning" (*SE* 20:129–30). Furthermore, "the first experience of anxiety which an individual goes through . . . is birth, and, objectively speaking, birth is a separation from the mother" (*SE* 20:130). Even if the child does not have the developmental capacity to experience birth as separation, subsequent losses will glance back at this first great dislocation and derive meaning therefrom. In this sense, the loss (or separation) that precipitates the organization of a self is always implicitly the loss of the mother. Freud as much as acknowledges this in his paradigmatic example of the fort/da game.

To take this line of reasoning a few steps further: assuming that the structure of the ego internalizes an absence through a process somewhat analogous to that of mourning and that the originary loss is felt as the loss of the mother, then the Oedipus complex begins to recede in importance while the drama of mother-infant separation emerges into the foreground. Freud's reformulation of castration as separation diminishes the role of the father at the same time that it highlights the preoedipal mother, a hitherto spectral figure in his work. Both object relations theory with its focus on issues of mother-infant separation and Lacanian psychoanalysis in its fascination with the Imaginary attest to this strain in Freud's thinking.

Neither, however, has succeeded in pursuing the full theoretical implications of this shift. Rather, as I have argued, the mother remains an unrealized figure, subsumed, on the one hand, into her role as the object of infantile fantasy and nearly effaced, on the other, by the function of the phallus. In her reproductive capacity the mother is deprived of subjectivity and denied access to signification.

Yet if one looks more closely at the concept of castration as separation from the mother, another set of possibilities begins to emerge. If the ego from its inception internalizes an absence understood as "castration," or a state of incompleteness that derives from an awareness of separation from the body of the mother, then the mother herself can no longer represent a simple state of plenitude. The state of division experienced as consciousness is mirrored in her body as the site of division itself. Rather than representing a condition of blissful nondifferentiation (as indicated by the object relations view of the preoedipal period as well as the Lacanian concept of the Imaginary) the body of the mother would seem to signal the process of mourning. Because the very existence of the ego is coincident with the awareness of loss, there is no time at which mother has not been Other. As the carnal origin of every human subject, the body of the mother represents at once the dream of plenitude and the recognition of its impossibility. When confronted with such a divided image of maternity, psychoanalytic theory generally acts to suppress one half of it, but on one occasion at least Freud pursues this line of thought toward some startling conclusions.

"The 'Uncanny'" (1919)

Parts of "The 'Uncanny'" seem to develop out of Freud's essay "The Theme of the Three Caskets," where he proposes that the figure of the triple goddess represents the three relations man has with woman: with "the mother herself, the beloved one who is chosen after her pattern, and lastly the Mother Earth who receives him once more" (SE 12:301).[1] One thread of speculation that runs

1. Neil Hertz, in "Freud and the Sandman," proposes another genealogy for this essay. Noting that Freud undertook it at a time when he had put aside his first draft

through "The 'Uncanny'" relates it not only to this perception but also to Freud's later elaboration of the concepts of repetition compulsion and the death instinct—all of which posit the mother as a focus of longing as well as dread.

What excites Freud's investigation into the uncanny is its dual affect. The uncanny, he states, "is that class of the frightening which leads back to what is known of old and long familiar" (*SE* 17:220). The uncanny exercises its eerie influence precisely because of this contradictory state, which Freud begins by locating in the etymology of the word *heimlich*. Like other primal words that contain antithetical meanings, *heimlich* designates not only what is familiar and known but also that which is secret or concealed. *Unheimlich* thus appears as a split off meaning of *heimlich*.

> In general we are reminded that the word '*heimlich*' is not unambiguous, but belongs to two sets of ideas, which, without being contradictory, are yet very different: on the one hand it means what is familiar and agreeable, and on the other, what is concealed and kept out of sight. '*Unheimlich*' is customarily used, we are told, as the contrary only of the first signification of '*heimlich*', and not of the second. [*SE* 17:224–25]

Toward the end of "The 'Uncanny'" Freud offers an example of the uncanny that establishes the mother's body as its prototype.[2]

---

of *Beyond the Pleasure Principle* for later revision, he reads "The 'Uncanny'" as a manifestation of the mechanism of repetition compulsion, the effects of which Freud felt in his life through the repetition of two triangular sets of relationship: first with Lou Andreas-Salomé and Victor Tausk and then with Tausk and Helene Deutsch. Hertz relates these issues to Freud's preoccupation with his own originality and with his fear of being plagiarized by Tausk. Repetition compulsion, Hertz maintains, in contrast, offers a *mise en abîme* perspective in which an originating moment cannot be established with certainty. My own reading traces Freud's interest in origins to the figure of the uncanny (m)other.

2. Jane Marie Todd also sees Freud's concept of the *unheimlich* as fundamentally associated with women, although her emphasis is somewhat different from mine. She writes: "It is women who are *unheimlich*, either because the sight of their genitals provokes the male's fear of castration, or because women's gaze reminds men of the 'valuable and fragile thing' they fear to lose, or because the desire to be female resurfaces as a fear of death" ("Veiled Woman in Freud's '*Das Unheimliche*'" 527). She argues that Freud's own castration fear caused him to disguise or to veil his meaning from himself.

It often happens that neurotic men declare that they feel there is something uncanny about the female genital organs. This *unheimlich* place, however, is the entrance to the former *Heim* [home] of all human beings, to the place where each one of us lived once upon a time and in the beginning. There is a joking saying that 'Love is homesickness'; and whenever a man dreams of a place or a country and says to himself, while he is still dreaming: 'this place is familiar to me, I've been here before', we may interpret the place as being his mother's genitals or her body. In this case too, then, the *unheimlich* is what was once *heimisch*, familiar; the prefix *'un'* ['un-'] is the token of repression. [*SE* 17:245]

Although Freud maintains that women's genitals appear uncanny or unhomelike because of repression, his earlier investigation into the antithetical meanings of *heimlich* suggests otherwise. What Freud refers to as the process of repression seems rather to involve the removal of ambiguity from the word *heimlich*, a failure to acknowledge its inherent double nature. The estrangement Freud speaks of in relation to the female genitals is thus not a secondary condition (as in the adding of a prefix) but an originary one. The body of the (m)other represents both home and not home, presence and absence, the promise of plenitude and the certainty of loss. That Freud also relates the phenomenon of involuntary repetition (his anecdote of returning to the red-light district in Rome) and that of the doppelgänger to the uncanny further associates the figure of the mother with the fear and longing he attaches to the death instinct. The body of the (m)other is the very site of the uncanny.

In "The 'Uncanny'" Freud comes close to acknowledging a condition of estrangement at the heart of being. Had he committed himself to such a vision, instead of vacillating between an image of mother as source of terror and of ultimate gratification, he might have conceived the process of individual development in less phallocentric terms. Had he meditated further on the condition of separation as a given of ego formation, recognizing in the body of the (m)other the indwelling of the uncanny which characterizes both memory and desire, he might have offered a model of preoedipal relations which would include the possibility of maternal discourse. Instead, psychoanalytic theory has remained predominantly a discourse of childhood, fixated on issues of male subjectivity, and the elaboration of patriarchal culture from which the mother is effectively excluded as an agent.

The Body of the (M)other

But let us follow such clues as we have in imagining the body of the (m)other as a locus of difference and estrangement, instead of the privileged place of unity and fulfillment she has appeared to represent in aspects of Freud's writing and in that of his successors. Rather than indulge the nostalgia for lost origins, let us consider that such a condition of plenitude does not exist, can never exist, except at the cost of the subjectivity of the mother herself. When mothers write, moreover, they unravel the fiction of mother-infant symbiosis which underlies the object relations view of development, not to mention Lacan's conception of the Imaginary.[3] Whatever feelings of tenderness, physical attachment, and pleasure a mother may feel in caring for her newborn, she does not experience a total fusion of self with Other, an absolute identity with her infant. Or if she believes that she does, such feelings can only be fleeting at best and a testimonial to the desire that love elicits to efface the distinctions between self and Other. To say that a mother feels one with her child is primarily a poetic statement about her passionate involvement in its physical well-being as well as her hopes for its future. It is not a description of the inner workings of a mother's consciousness, of the variety of her needs and interests, nor can it express the multiple trajectories of her desire. The concept of *mother*-infant symbiosis is an obvious absurdity, for a mother can only act as a mother if she perceives herself as such, as separate and different from her infant. A mother who felt in every way like an infant would be worse than useless as a caretaker.

Symbiosis ceases to be a meaningful concept when it applies to only one-half of a partnership. Freud's understanding of the uncanny, on the other hand, allows for difference and familiarity on both sides of the mother-infant relationship. If the mother's body in its otherness represents estrangement as well as origin, it also provides a paradigm for the construction of the ego, itself a form of

---

3. See, for instance, the autobiographical parts of Adrienne Rich's *Of Woman Born*, or Jane Lazarre's *Mother Knot*. Susan Suleiman also deconstructs this fiction in her analysis of works by Rosellen Brown ("Writing and Motherhood"). Tillie Olsen, in *Silences*, provides a particularly eloquent description of the conflicts experienced by a mother of young children who also writes, while Toni Morrison's brilliant portrayal of the character Sethe, in her novel *Beloved*, should serve as a caution to anyone who seeks to sentimentalize the mother-child relationship.

memorial, or a presence that enfolds absence. By revealing the otherness within mother, the uncanny simultaneously unveils the otherness that stimulates the elaboration of the ego, or in Lacan's terms the lack that fuels desire. To return this discussion once more to the context of Freud's description of the fort/da game, it is the mother's desire that leads her away from her infant, and her absence in turn that elicits the child's creativity, its primitive gestures toward selfhood and mastery. Founded on lack, however, the restless games of the ego reaffirm what they seek to control, the otherness within that prevents fullness of being, just as it occludes the possiblity of mother-infant fusion. It is not necessary to invoke the function or signification of the phallus to arrive at such a representation of development. The body of the (m)other provides its own sources of signification and ultimately a ground for reconciliation between the preoedipal (m)other and culture, between the (m)other and the Symbolic order.

Tracing clues in Kristeva's writing concerning the heterogeneity of the mother's desire, Mary Jacobus states:

> To what does the mother give birth? Surely (to vary a feminist catchphrase of the seventies) at once to herself and to an other, in a movement of differentiation imaging the movement which gives birth to meaning. To figure maternity as division is to acknowledge the process of separation which gives rise both to the subject and to language. If to imagine maternity as unity is to fantasize the possibility of wholeness, making the Madonna the guarantee of a masculine representational and sexual economy, her role in an alternative, feminist economy might be to provide an emblem of the subject's difference from itself and its division by, and in, both language and the unconscious. . . . In Kristevan terms, the discourse of maternity is another name for the movement of parturition which (re)produces the subject in, and of, representation. [*Reading Woman* 147]

This characterization of maternity as a condition not of fullness or plenitude but of internal splitting offers a model for the development of language (and hence culture) as represented by Lacan, without, however, invoking the phallus as the agent by which difference becomes felt or known. Does Jacobus, then, believe that the (m)other can signify? At one point in her Kristevan reading of the Dora case history it appears that she does: "For Kristeva, division is the condition of all signifying processes. No pre-oedipal language, no maternal discourse, can be free of this split. We live (Kristeva writes) on the frontier, in a permanent parting, a division of the flesh which is also a division of language. The biological processes of conception and parturition are at once metaphor, analogue, and foundation for this originating difference" (169–70). Elsewhere in her argument, Jacobus takes the more orthodox view that the phallus intervenes between mother and child so as to shatter the kind of primary identification that obliterates the possibility of language. Thus: "Dora constitutes herself as a representing (fantasizing and desiring) subject by identifying herself with the imaginary phallic object instead of the mother. The consequence is the casting out or abjecting of the mother, the radical exclusion of what threatens to collapse all distinctions between self and other, and with them, meaning" (181). Jacobus reproduces the strain of ambivalence, and hence irresolution, in Kristeva's writing concerning the Oedipal/ preoedipal hierarchy. Because Kristeva herself does not finally break faith with Lacan, nor with his authority, Freud, it is difficult to use her work as a whole in the service of such a transformation. This should not prevent us, however, from choosing among her more radical insights to further our own aims.

For Kristeva, pregnancy creates a condition of nonidentity. She describes a state of being that is vertiginous, abyssal, one that has no official status in Western discourse and yet one that is incontrovertibly real and evident to the senses. In "Stabat Mater" she seeks a language for a division that is both physiological and metaphysical, a product of the body registered in consciousness. "A mother," she says, "is a continuous separation, a division of the very flesh. And consequently a division of language—and it has always been so" (178). The condition of pregnancy creates a radical paradox in terms of subjectivity. The mother is neither one nor two but two-in-one, her body the ground of an otherness that is nevertheless experienced as an aspect of self.[4] It doesn't take much imagination to

4. Recently, Martha Noel Evans has stated a similar position, although she does not appear to make use of Kristeva. "When reproduction is seen not as the antinomy of discourse but rather as a process of desire," she writes, "the mythologized oneness of mother and child yields to other forms. Although the baby is literally a part of the mother during pregnancy, she may very well think of it as different from her, as an other—protégé or parasite; it does not merge with her. . . . From a biological as well as a social point of view, women function as the trace of difference, the origin of the symbolic" (*Masks of Tradition* 34–35). My own conclusions parallel and support these.

transpose this description onto Freud's understanding of the unconscious as Other, or onto Lacan's account of the ego as constituted by the mirror stage. Yet neither cared much to investigate the nature of maternal subjectivity, preferring to focus their fascinated gaze on that emblem of male virility and authority, the phallus. The function of the father, however, to divide the mother from her infant seems hardly necessary if division has already taken place, if division is somehow embedded in the process by which each individual consciousness emerges into being. "WORD FLESH" (162), Kristeva says, attempting to conjure into meaning something of the enigma of incarnation.

Lacan's account of the movement from the Imaginary to the Symbolic, which he bases on Freud's progressive Oedipal model of development, separates Word from Flesh. It follows, then, that the mother's body as the fleshly origin of human subjectivity is excluded from signification in the complex process by which children acquire language—this despite the fact that it is primarily mothers (and female caretakers) who teach children their first words. But the importance Lacan attributes to the phallus as a representation of difference, in terms of language as well as division from the mother's body, seems misplaced in light of Kristeva's emphasis on the ontological status of division, on the "catastrophic fold-of-being" (178), as she puts it, of the (m)other's body. Her point is essentially Derridean, although she does not altogether abandon a Lacanian framework. Derrida, on the other hand, who labors to deconstruct what he calls the phallogocentrism of Lacan's system, does not himself speculate about the signifying ground of the (m)other's body.[5] It would not be difficult, however, to pursue such a project, by juxtaposing his theory of supplementation with that of Kristeva's maternal discourse.

Using Rousseau as his example in *Of Grammatology*, Derrida deconstructs the division between nature and culture which characterizes Romantic literature and philosophy. Where Rousseau wants to distinguish between speech and writing on the basis of the self-presence of speech as opposed to the substitute or supplemen-

---

5. Derrida deconstructs the transcendental status of the phallus as signifier through his interpretation of Lacan's commentary on Poe's story "The Purloined Letter." See "The Purveyor of Truth."

tary status of writing, for instance, Derrida claims that speech itself is supplementary, that there is no point at which the process of substitution (creating a presence in the place of an absence) does not take place. Each supplement, moreover, calls attention to the very condition of lack it seeks to obliterate, thus participating in the ironic structure of Freud's fort/da game. Derrida's discussion of the supplement is fundamental to his project of deconstructing the terms of presence, plenitude, and identity which underpin Western metaphysics. Whereas Rousseau's argument assumes a moment of violent rupture from a condition of oneness with nature, which he equates with the "true mother," and a fall into endless substitute gratifications, which he considers dangerous or perverse, Derrida regards supplementation as originary, equating it with what he calls *différance,* the differential and deferring gesture that renders Being accessible to language and hence consciousness. Supplementation, for all intents and purposes, *is* Being, for it exists from the moment we attempt to represent ourselves to ourselves.

> There have never been anything but supplements, substitutive significations which could only come forth in a chain of differential references, the "real" supervening, and being added only while taking on meaning from a trace and from an invocation of the supplement, etc. And thus to infinity, for we have read, *in the text* that the absolute present, Nature, that which words like "real mother" name, have always already escaped, have never existed; that what opens meaning and language is writing as the disappearance of natural presence. [*Of Grammatology* 159]

Making this point more succinctly, Derrida later states that "one wishes to go back *from the supplement to the source:* one must recognize that there is *a supplement at the source"* (304).

Derrida's understanding of the supplement resembles Freud's conception of the ego as a product of mourning, if one assumes that mourning (or castration as separation) is originary. Describing the operation of language as supplement, for instance, Derrida might also be offering a gloss on the phrase "the precipitate of abandoned object cathexes," as well as the mechanism of repetition compulsion which underlies the death instinct. "We are dispossessed of the longed-for presence in the gesture of language by which we attempt to seize it. . . . The speculary dispossession which at the same time institutes and deconstitutes me is also a law of language. It operates as a power of death in the heart of living speech: a power all the more redoubtable because it opens as much as it threatens the possibility of the spoken word" (141).

Although Derrida's treatment of the supplement verges on psychoanalytic myth, he is anxious to dissociate his reading from psychobiography, which he terms "most banal, most academic, most naive" (159). His antipathy for this type of interpretation accounts perhaps for his lack of interest in Rousseau's biological mother, apart from her status as absent. Yet her very absence, due to her death in giving birth to Jean Jacques, supports his philosophical point concerning the lack that is constitutive of Being. Curiously, Derrida manages to remove the figure of the mother from signification at the same time that he requires her presence as absent in what amounts to a revised version of Freud's account of ego development. While this strategy avoids the problem of essentialism that inheres in the concept of mother-infant symbiosis, it runs the risk of altogther excluding the preoedipal mother from the drama of infantile subjectivity.

From a feminist and psychoanalytic standpoint, poststructuralist theory suffers from a tendency to render the condition of biological motherhood either meaningless or irrelevant, thus repeating the repression of motherhood that Irigaray perceives at the heart of Western culture. Derrida's analysis of the supplement lies open, however, to another line of interpretation. Not all mothers, after all, die in childbirth, nor is it necessary to make this claim in the figurative way that Derrida does when he describes "birth in general [as] written as Rousseau describes his own: 'I cost my mother her life; and my birth was the first of my misfortunes.'" Birth as understood from the mother's point of view may be seen as the completion of a process of internal division that begins with conception. The mother's body itself in the state of pregnancy figures a condition of absent presence or fullness which derives from an indwelling of otherness. From a woman's perspective, the "breaching of plenitude" (309) which Derrida attributes to the moment of birth actually begins in the womb. Kristeva refers to this condition as a "catastrophic fold-of-being."

More recently, the novelist Marilynne Robinson has attempted another form of description of the alienation of Being that is shared simultaneously by mother and fetus. This novel deconstructs the myth of maternal plenitude, which sentimentalizes the mother-daughter relationship while desubjectifying the mother herself. Although written from the daughter's point of view, *Housekeeping* is obsessively concerned with mothering, including its onset at the moment of conception. The narrative moves toward a dazzling vision of origins, which acts as a commentary both on Derrida's removal of the mother and on Kristeva's attempts to include her in their respective accounts of coming into being.

Housekeeping (1981)

A prose poem in the form of a novel, *Housekeeping* traces the development of two sisters, orphaned by their mother's suicide and raised first by their grandmother Sylvia and subsequently by their aunt Sylvie in a remote town in Idaho called Fingerbone. The tone established from the beginning of this novel emphasizes alterity, as though the entire fiction were narrated from the other side of a looking glass. Ruth describes her grandmother, for instance, as someone who

> had never really wished to feel married to anyone. She sometimes imagined a rather dark man with crude stripes painted on his face and sunken belly, and a hide fastened around his loins, and bones dangling from his ears, and clay and claws and fangs and bones and feathers and sinews and hide ornamenting his arms and waist and throat and ankles, his whole body a boast that he was more alarming than all the death whose trophies he wore. Edmund was like that, a little.

What Sylvia appreciates about her husband is his "otherness," his self-possession. When they would search the woods together for wildflowers, for instance, "he was as forgetful of her as he was of his suspenders and his Methodism, but all the same it was then that she loved him best, as a soul all unaccompanied, like her own" (17). If Sylvia seems strange, it is because she acknowledges an unbridgeable gap between self and Other, self and the world. Early in her marriage, she had already concluded "that love was half a longing of a kind that possession did nothing to mitigate" (12).

When their grandmother dies, the two girls, Ruth and Lucille, find themselves in the care of two great-aunts, who summon in turn their mother's sister, Sylvie. Sylvie's distraction and unworldliness are even more remarkable than her mother's, and her manner of housekeeping decidedly unusual. "Sylvie in a house was more or less like a mermaid in a ship's cabin. She preferred it sunk in the very element it was meant to exclude. We had crickets in the pantry, squirrels in the eaves, sparrows in the attic. Lucille and I stepped through the door from sheer night to sheer night" (99).

Gradually, the two sisters move apart, divided by their adolescent development and their conflicting responses to their aunt. While Lucille mounts an aggressive campaign to conventionalize herself, learning to look and behave like other teenage girls, Ruth adopts Sylvie's unworldly habits and manners. Observing their likeness, Sylvie begins to include Ruth in her hitherto solitary wanderings. One day she takes her across the lake to a remote clearing in the woods and leaves her among the ancient ruins of a house to contemplate her wild surroundings. As the frost on the grass and trees begins to melt, Ruth imagines herself in a garden to which ghost children from the woods are attracted. This fantasy develops into a meditation on motherhood and mourning.

> Lot's wife was salt and barren, because she was full of loss and mourning, and looked back. But here rare flowers would gleam in her hair, and on her breast, and in her hands, and there would be children all around her, to love and marvel at her for her beauty, and to laugh at her extravagant ornaments, as if they had set the flowers in her hair and thrown down all the flowers at her feet, and they would forgive her, eagerly and lavishly, for turning away, though she never asked to be forgiven. Though her hands were ice and did not touch them, she would be more than mother to them, she so calm, so still, and they such wild and orphan things. [153]

This passage seems to recast Ruth's relationship to her own absent mother, as though the fact of loss itself were responsible for its special beauty. For Ruth, desire is born of mourning, and all the pleasure of having, conditional on not having.[6] "To crave and to

---

6. Juliet Mitchell formulates this process (which she derives from Lacan) in the following way: "The object that is longed for only comes into existence *as an object* when it is lost to the baby or infant. Thus any satisfaction that might subsequently

have are as like as a thing and its shadow. For when does a berry break upon the tongue as sweetly as when one longs to taste it, and when is the taste refracted into so many hues and savors of ripeness and earth, and when do our senses know any thing so utterly as when we lack it?" (152).

Lucille's attempts to be like other girls, which finally precipitate her break with her sister when she leaves to take up residence with a sympathetic schoolteacher in town, appear in Ruth's eyes as evasions of an essential reality. For Ruth, Sylvie's stance as exile expresses her own understanding of the world. Not to confront one's originary loss, in her view, is to condemn oneself to the deeper exile of what the world considers familiar and ordinary. In the wild solitude that Sylvie cultivates, on the other hand, there is another kind of consolation. In this state, Ruth recovers the sense of her lost mother, as she nearly catches sight of the ghost children.

> It is better to have nothing. . . . If I could see my mother, it would not have to be her eyes, her hair. I would not need to touch her sleeve. There was no more the stoop of her high shoulders. The lake had taken that, I knew. It was so very long since the dark had swum her hair, and there was nothing more to dream of, but often she almost slipped through any door I saw from the side of my eye, and it was she, and not changed, and not perished. She was a music I no longer heard, that rang in my mind, itself and nothing else, lost to all sense, but not perished, not perished. [159–60]

The development of Ruth's and Sylvie's points of view in the second half of the novel is responsible for its radical alterity. As they move toward their decision to put "an end to housekeeping" (209), by setting fire to the house where they had lived, in favor of an openly transient existence, Ruth begins to give shape to her perception of life as necessarily haunted. Casting her meditation within the biblical framework of the expulsion from Eden and the final promised reunion, Ruth imagines the passage of human time as motivated by loss: "The force behind the movement of time is a

---

be attained will always contain this loss within it. . . . Desire persists as an effect of a primordial absence and it therefore indicates that, in this area, there is something fundamentally impossible about satisfaction itself" (*Feminine Sexuality* 6).

mourning that will not be comforted. That is why the first event is known to have been an expulsion, and the last is hoped to be a reconciliation and return. So memory pulls us forward, so prophecy is only brilliant memory—there will be a garden where all of us as one child will sleep in our mother Eve, hooped in her ribs and staved by her spine" (192).

Housekeeping, as it deconstructs its title, deconstructs "mother." It is absence, the novel insists, which creates the dream of presence, a dream that must never be taken literally, since its fulfillment lies beyond the limits of human life. The Fall, in this light, is that which is responsible for memory and desire, a moment of separation (like the death of Ruth and Lucille's mother) which precedes the beginning of narrative. "Memory is the sense of loss, and loss pulls us after it. God Himself was pulled after us into the vortex we made when we fell, or so the story goes" (194).

Robinson's use of biblical allusion and analogy expands the context of the novel in such a way as to depersonalize the dilemma of the two orphan sisters. Toward the end, in particular, Ruth becomes the voice of the uncanny. Adopting the perspective attributed by Freud to the triple goddess, Ruth surveys her origin and destiny, both of which derive their special character from the fact of her mother's absence. Ruth's otherness, what makes her side with the wild ghost children of the forest, is inherent in the human condition, a separateness that reaches back into the womb, to the beginning of life itself.

> Of my conception I know only what you know of yours. It occurred in darkness and I was unconsenting. I (and that slenderest word is too gross for the rare thing I was then) walked forever through reachless oblivion, in the mood of one smelling night-blooming flowers, and suddenly—My ravishers left their traces in me, male and female, and over the months I rounded, grew heavy, until the scandal could no longer be concealed and oblivion expelled me. But this I have in common with all my kind. By some bleak alchemy what had been mere unbeing becomes death when life is mingled with it. So they seal the door against our returning.   [214–15]

Conception itself is responsible for the loss of oblivion which constitutes exile. Being, in this little allegory, is a product of time and memory, both of which weave their substance around absence. The state of plenitude, in turn, can only be imagined or dreamed by one who has already suffered a fall into human existence. In Robinson's words, "By some bleak alchemy what had been mere unbeing becomes death when life is mingled with it." This statement, which insists on the coexistence of life and death, bears a curious resemblance to Derrida's assertion that "from the moment that presence, holding or announcing itself to itself, breaches its plenitude and starts the chain of its history, death's work has begun" (*Of Grammatology* 309). The difference lies in Robinson's evocation of a maternal body as a space that offers not a haven from this condition but a locus for its inception. To quote Kristeva again, "A mother is a continuous separation, a division of the very flesh. And consequently a division of language—and It has always been so" ("Stabat Mater" 178).

What difference does it make to psychoanalytic theory if the process of supplementation begins in the mother's body, if, in its capacity to enfold otherness, the maternal body images this very condition? At the very least it would appear that Freud's equation between the achievement of Oedipal masculinity and the emergence of culture no longer makes sense. Only if one assumes that the father as the bearer of the threat of castration must intervene between mother and son to prevent incest does this model work. If, as Freud sometimes hints, and Derrida everywhere insists, the condition of castration (or separation from the mother as representative of the dream of plenitude) is both originary and universal, then the process of enculturation begins with the onset of life itself. To perceive the body of the (m)other as a carnal metaphor for the fundamental estrangement of Being also collapses the hierarchical relationship between the Oedipal and preoedipal periods, or in Lacan's terms between the Imaginary and Symbolic stages. From a psychoanalytic point of view, there ceases to be any justification for the phallogocentrism of culture.

The Oedipus complex, like Lacan's choice of the phallus as signifier, both explains and sustains patriarchy. From this point of view, one can analyze the institution of psychoanalysis as politically informed and motivated, as inscribed within a particular set of social constraints that Freud understood as essential to civilized behavior and universal. Taking Freud's own work as an example, one can examine the aura of fear that surrounds the figure of the mother as a cultural as well as a personal phenomenon. From this standpoint, it appears that patriarchy itself is founded on a continual repression that takes its toll in terms of an anxiety about mastery, which Freud refers to, appropriately, as the death instinct.[7] At the heart of phallogocentrism lies the terror as well as the certainty of its own undoing. And this undoing is associated with the body of a woman, who must be controlled, who must be prevented from achieving a condition of power from which she can exercise this threat. Like all systems of oppression, moreover, patriarchy mythologizes the object of its dread, inventing ever new rationalizations in terms of "feminine psychology" for sustaining the status quo. Whatever the strategy, whether in terms of idealization, debasement, the association of women with nature, with matter, or even madness, the results are depressingly familiar. Culture, and hence the privileged access to power and authority, remains (in theory at least) a male preserve.

But suppose, once again, that language and culture do not revolve around the threat of castration emanating from the figure of a father, or his curiously disembodied stand-in, the phallus? A whole way of dichotomous thinking, based on the Oedipal/preoedipal hierarchy, breaks down under this assumption. Although Derrida has elaborated a philosophy and technique of deconstructing such polarized and necessarily oppressive categories of thought, he seems uninterested in its consequences for a feminism that also seeks to redeem the body of the mother from both its unnatural

7. Ellie Ragland-Sullivan speculates about the effects of patriarchy on women through her invention of the term "double Castration." According to this view, women, like men, are "castrated" as a result of separation from the mother. Women, however, bear the burden in cultural terms of the assumption of the split in identity occasioned by access to the Symbolic order. The term "secondary castration" refers to the effects of this process, which Ragland-Sullivan describes as follows: "The primordial (m)Other at the mirror-stage, structural base of the ego becomes confused with woman; and women are consequently seen as secretly powerful. The mother within both sexes therefore implies an unseen dominance. This makes woman—as her displacement—someone to be feared, denied, ignored, denigrated, fought, and conquered—or conversely worshipped and enshrined. But whether woman is generically feared or extolled, the individual's attitude toward women implies a position toward their own unconscious" (*Jacques Lacan and the Philosophy of Psychoanalysis* 297). The only problem with this position is that it offers no particular hope or rationale for social change.

prominence and its oblivion in psychoanalysis, that seeks, in addition, a material base for discussing the actual conditions of women's lives.[8] But if one can imagine the body of the (m)other as offering a model for the radical paradox of absence-in-presence which propels the process of signification, then perhaps one can also find some way in language of responding to, without attempting to marmorealize, the fleshly terms of our existence.

Speech itself, after all, is a bodily product, a result of a complex collaboration of heart, brain, lungs, and vocal cords, to which the tongue adds a special twist. And if our breath, like our speech, is always escaping, doesn't this tie the function of linguistic expression to the fate of the body, which houses that other evolutionary riddle we call consciousness? If we women, moreover, are no more alienated from language than men, why should we assume the burden of representing matter at the expense of spirit? Conversely, why should spirit strive to divorce itself (as if a man were author of himself) from flesh? Unless perhaps the body in its vulnerability and contingency reminds us too sharply of our state of tragic incompleteness—of the mournful function of memory, rooted in the sense of having been ripped untimely from oblivion. If, finally, we experience our condition of estrangement physically as well as metaphysically, we need a philosophy and a psychology that are adequate to this awareness. We need, in particular, a language of sexual difference which does not revolve around the terms of phallic presence and vaginal absence, one that maintains an allegiance to physical reality in all its stunning variety, without effacing the common ground of our existence.

We are, each of us, male and female, fallen out of that state of

8. In *Spurs: Nietzsche's Styles*, Derrida discusses woman as the figure of a truth that endlessly defers itself. "There is no such thing as the truth of woman, but it is because of that abyssal divergence of the truth, because that untruth is 'truth.' Woman is but one name for that untruth of truth" (51). The term "woman," however, must not be confused with the reality of individual women, as Derrida makes clear in the following passage: "That which will not be pinned down by truth is, in truth—*feminine*. This should not, however, be hastily mistaken for a woman's femininity, for female sexuality, or for any other of those essentializing fetishes which might still tantalize the dogmatic philosopher, the impotent artist or the inexperienced seducer who has not yet escaped his foolish hopes of capture" (55). Given this philosophic stance, it is hard to see how one *can* talk about women, as opposed to woman. For another view of this dilemma, see Teresa de Lauretis's *Alice Doesn't*.

fullness of Being which we sometimes imagine as paradise, which we seek falsely to identify with intrauterine existence. And yet each of us enters the world through the body of a woman—a carnal enigma that has virtually baffled our systems of understanding. Rather than fleeing, condemning, or idealizing the body of the (m)other, we need to recognize her in ourselves. "I am the lover and the loved," Adrienne Rich writes in "Transcendental Etude," "home and wanderer, she who splits / firewood and she who knocks, a stranger / in the storm" (*Dream of a Common Language* 76). If the sense of estrangement and familiarity which we choose to name subjectivity resides in our very flesh, then what we need is a whole new metaphysics beginning here.

Works Cited

Abel, Elizabeth. *Virginia Woolf and the Fictions of Psychoanalysis*. Chicago: Chicago UP, 1989.

Andreas-Salomé, Lou. *The Freud Journal*. Trans. Stanley A. Leavy. New York: Basic, 1964.

Bachofen, J. J. *Myth, Religion and Mother-Right*. Trans. Ralph Manheim. Bollingen Series 84. Princeton: Princeton UP, 1967.

Balmary, Marie. *Psychoanalyzing Psychoanalysis: Freud and the Hidden Fault of the Father*. Trans. Ned Lukacher. Baltimore: Johns Hopkins UP, 1982.

Becker, Ernest. *The Denial of Death*. New York: Macmillan, 1973.

Bernheimer, Charles, and Claire Kahane, eds. *In Dora's Case: Freud-Hysteria-Feminism*. New York: Columbia UP, 1985.

Carotenuto, Aldo. *A Secret Symmetry: Sabina Spielrein between Freud and Jung*. Trans. Arno Pomerans, John Shepley, and Krishna Winston. New York: Pantheon, 1982.

Chodorow, Nancy. *The Reproduction of Mothering: Psychoanalysis and the Sociology of Gender*. Berkeley: California UP, 1978.

Cixous, Hélène, and Catherine Clément. *The Newly Born Woman*. Trans. Betsy Wing. Minneapolis: Minnesota UP, 1986.

Clark, Ronald W. *Freud: The Man and the Cause*. 1980. London: Paladin/Grenada, 1982.

Clément, Catherine. *The Lives and Legends of Jacques Lacan*. Trans. Arthur Goldhammer. New York: Columbia UP, 1983.

Collins, Jerre, J. Ray Green, Mary Lydon, Mack Sachner, and Eleanor Honig Skoller. "Questioning the Unconscious: The Dora Archive." *A Fine Romance: Freud and Dora*. Ed. Neil Hertz. *Diacritics* 13 (Spring 1983): 37–42.

Works Cited

Coward, Rosalind. *Patriarchal Precedents: Sexuality and Social Relations.* London: Routledge & Kegan Paul, 1983.

Daly, Mary. *Gyn/Ecology.* Boston: Beacon, 1978.

Darwin, Charles. *The Descent of Man and Selection in Relation to Sex.* Princeton: Princeton UP, 1981.

Davidoff, Leonore. "Class and Gender in Victorian England: The Diaries of Arthur J. Munby and Hannah Cullwick." *Feminist Studies* 5 (1979): 87–141.

De Lauretis, Teresa. *Alice Doesn't: Feminism, Semiotics, Cinema.* Bloomington: Indiana UP, 1984.

Derrida, Jacques. "Coming into One's Own." Trans. James Hulbert. *Psychoanalysis and the Question of the Text.* Ed. Geoffrey Hartman. Baltimore: Johns Hopkins UP, 1978. 114–48.

——. *Of Grammatology.* Trans. Gayatri Chakravorty Spivak. Baltimore: Johns Hopkins UP, 1976.

——. "The Purveyor of Truth." *Yale French Studies* 52 (1975): 31–113.

——. *Spurs: Nietzsche's Styles/Éperons: Les Styles de Nietzsche.* Trans. Barbara Harlow. Chicago: Chicago UP, 1979.

Deutsch, Felix. "A Footnote to Freud's 'Fragment of an Analysis of a Case of Hysteria.'" *Psychoanalytic Quarterly* 26 (1957): 159–67.

Diacritics: The Tropology of Freud 9 (Spring 1979).

Dijkstra, Bram. *Idols of Perversity: Fantasies of Feminine Evil in Fin-de-Siècle Culture.* Oxford: Oxford UP, 1986.

Dinnerstein, Dorothy. *The Mermaid and the Minotaur: Sexual Arrangements and Human Malaise.* New York: Harper & Row, 1976.

Donn, Linda. *Freud and Jung: Years of Friendship, Years of Loss.* New York: Scribner's, 1988.

Eagleton, Terry. *Literary Theory: An Introduction.* Minneapolis: Minnesota UP, 1983.

Eisenstein, Hester, and Alice Jardine, eds. *The Future of Difference.* 1980. New Brunswick: Rutgers UP, 1985.

Erikson, Erik. "The Dream Specimen of Psychoanalysis." In *Psychoanalytic Psychiatry and Psychology: Clinical and Theoretical Papers,* ed. Robert P. Knight and Cyrus R. Friedman, 131–70. Austin Riggs Center, 1. New York: Hallmark-Hubner, 1954.

——. "Reality and Actuality." *Journal of the American Psychoanalytic Association* 10 (1962): 451–74.

Erlich, Iza S. "What Happened to Jocasta?" *Bulletin of the Menninger Clinic* 41 (May 1977): 280–84.

Evans, Martha Noel. *Masks of Tradition: Women and the Politics of Writing in Twentieth-Century France.* Ithaca: Cornell UP, 1987.

Fee, Elizabeth. "The Sexual Politics of Victorian Social Anthropology." In *Clio's Consciousness Raised: New Perspectives on the History of Women,* ed. Mary Hartman and Lois W. Banner, 86–102. New York: Harper & Row, 1974.

Ferenczi, Sandor. "A Little Chanticleer." In *The Development of Psycho-analysis*, 204–13. New York: Dover, 1956.

Flax, Jane. "Mother-Daughter Relationships: Psychodynamics, Politics, and Philosophy." In *The Future of Difference*, ed. Hester Eisenstein and Alice Jardine. New Brunswick: Rutgers UP, 1985.

Frazer, James George. *The Golden Bough*. Vol. 2: *Adonis, Attis, Osiris*. New York: Macmillan, 1935.

French Freud: Structural Studies in Psychoanalysis. Yale French Studies 48 (1972).

Freud, Ernst L., ed. *The Letters of Sigmund Freud*. Trans. Tania and James Stern. New York: Basic, 1975.

——. *The Letters of Sigmund Freud and Arnold Zweig*. Trans. Elaine and William Robson-Scott. New York: Harvest/Harcourt Brace Jovanovich, 1970.

Freud, Sigmund. *The Standard Edition of the Complete Psychological Works of Sigmund Freud*. 24 vols. Trans. James Strachey et al., ed. James Strachey. London: Hogarth, 1974; rpt. 1986.

——. "The Aetiology of Hysteria." 1896. *SE* 3:187–221.

——. "Analysis of a Phobia in a Five-Year-Old Boy" (Little Hans). 1909. *SE* 10:1–149.

——. "Analysis Terminable and Interminable." 1937. *SE* 23:209–53.

——. *Beyond the Pleasure Principle*. 1920. *SE* 18:1–64.

——. *Civilization and Its Discontents*. 1930. *SE* 21:57–145.

——. *The Ego and the Id*. 1923. *SE* 19:1–66.

——. "Female Sexuality." 1931. *SE* 21:221–43.

——. "Femininity." 1933 [1932]. *New Introductory Lectures*. *SE* 22:112–35.

——. "Fragment of an Analysis of a Case of Hysteria" (Dora). 1905 [1901]. *SE* 7:1–122.

——. "From the History of an Infantile Neurosis" (The Wolf Man). 1918 [1914]. *SE* 17:1–71.

——. *The Future of an Illusion*. 1927. *SE* 21:1–56.

——. *Inhibitions, Symptoms and Anxiety*. 1926 [1925]. *SE* 20:75–174.

——. *The Interpretation of Dreams*. 1900. *SE* 4:1–338.

——. *Leonardo Da Vinci and a Memory of His Childhood*. 1910. *SE* 11:59–137.

——. "Medusa's Head." 1940 [1922]. *SE* 18:273–74.

——. *Moses and Monotheism: Three Essays*. 1939 [1934–38]. *SE* 23:1–137.

——. "Mourning and Melancholia." 1917 [1915]. *SE* 14:237–58.

——. "Notes upon a Case of Obsessional Neurosis" (The Rat Man). 1909. *SE* 10:151–318.

——. "On the Universal Tendency to Debasement in the Sphere of Love" (Contributions to the Psychology of Love, II). 1912. *SE* 11:177–90.

——. "Preface and Footnotes to the Translation of Charcot's *Tuesday Lectures*." 1892–94. *SE* 1:129–43.

——. *Project for a Scientific Psychology.* 1950 [1895]. *SE* 1:281–397.
——. "Psycho-Analytic Notes on an Autobiographical Account of a Case of Paranoia" (Dr. Shreber). 1911. *SE* 12:1–82.
——. *The Psychopathology of Everyday Life.* 1901. *SE* 6:1–279.
——. "Screen Memories." 1899. *SE* 3:299–322.
——. "Some Psychical Consequences of the Anatomical Distinction between the Sexes." 1925. *SE* 19:241–58.
——. "A Special Type of Choice of Object Made by Men" (Contributions to the Psychology of Love, I). 1910. *SE* 11:163–75.
——. "The Taboo of Virginity" (Contributions to the Psychology of Love, III). 1918 [1917]. *SE* 11:191–208.
——. "The Theme of the Three Caskets." 1913. *SE* 12:289–301.
——. *Three Essays on the Theory of Sexuality.* 1905. *SE* 7:125–245.
——. *Totem and Taboo.* 1913 [1912–13]. *SE* 13:1–161.
——. "The 'Uncanny.'" 1919. *SE* 17:217–52.
Gallop, Jane. *The Daughter's Seduction: Feminism and Psychoanalysis.* Ithaca: Cornell UP, 1982.
——. *Reading Lacan.* Ithaca: Cornell UP, 1985.
——. "Reading the Mother Tongue: Psychoanalytic Feminist Criticism." *Critical Inquiry* 13 (Winter 1987): 314–29.
Garber, Marjorie. *Shakespeare's Ghost Writers: Literature as Uncanny Causality.* London: Methuen, 1987.
Gardiner, Judith Kegan. "Mind Mother: Psychoanalysis and Feminism." In *Making a Difference: Feminist Literary Criticism,* ed. Gayle Greene and Coppélia Kahn, 113–45. London: Methuen, 1985.
Gardiner, Muriel, ed. *The Wolf-Man by the Wolf-Man.* New York: Basic, 1971.
Garner, Shirley Nelson. "Feminism, Psychoanalysis, and the Heterosexual Imperative." In *Psychoanalysis and Feminism,* ed. Richard Feldstein and Judith Roof. Ithaca: Cornell UP, 1989.
——. "Freud and Fliess: Homophobia and Seduction." In *Seduction and Theory: Readings of Gender, Representation and Rhetoric,* Ed. Dianne Hunter. Urbana: Illinois UP, 1989.
——, Claire Kahane, and Madelon Sprengnether, eds. *The (M)other Tongue: Essays in Feminist Psychoanalytic Interpretation.* Ithaca: Cornell UP, 1985.
Gaudin, Colette, Mary Jean Green, Anthony Higgins, Marianne Hirsch, Vivian Kogan, Claudia Reeder, and Nancy Vickers, eds. *Feminist Readings: French Texts/American Contexts. Yale French Studies* 62 (1981).
Gay, Peter. *Freud: A Life for Our Time.* New York: Norton, 1988.
Gearhart, Suzanne. "The Scene of Psychoanalysis: The Unanswered Questions of Dora." *Diacritics: The Tropology of Freud* 9 (1979): 114–26.
Gilligan, Carol. *In a Different Voice.* Cambridge: Harvard UP, 1982.
Gilman, Sander. "Male Stereotypes of Female Sexuality in Fin-de-Siècle

Vienna." In *Difference and Pathology: Stereotypes of Sexuality, Race, and Madness*. Ithaca: Cornell UP, 1985.

Greene, Gayle, and Coppélia Kahn, eds. *Making a Difference: Feminist Literary Criticism*. London: Methuen, 1985.

Griggs, Kenneth. "All Roads Lead to Rome: The Role of the Nursemaid in Freud's Dreams." *Journal of the American Psychoanalytic Association* 21 (1973): 108–26.

Grinstein, Alexander. *Sigmund Freud's Dreams*. New York: International Universities Press, 1980.

Grosskurth, Phyllis. *Melanie Klein: Her World and Her Work*. New York: Knopf, 1986.

Hartman, Mary S., and Lois Banner, eds. *Clio's Consciousness Raised: New Perspectives on the History of Women*. New York: Harper & Row, 1974.

H.D. (Hilda Doolittle). *Tribute to Freud: Writing on the Wall*. Ed. Norman Pearson. New York: New Directions, 1984.

Hellor, Judith N. mays "Freud's Mother and Father." In *Freud as We Knew Him*, ed. Hendrick M. Ruitenbeck, 334–40. Detroit: Wayne State UP, 1973.

Hertz, Neil. "Dora's Secrets, Freud's Techniques." In *A Fine Romance*, ed. Neil Hertz. *Diacritics* 13 (Spring 1983): 65–76.

——. "Freud and the Sandman." In *Textual Strategies: Perspectives in Post-Structuralist Criticism*, ed. Josue V. Harari, 296–321. Ithaca: Cornell UP, 1979.

Hirsch, Marianne. "A Mother's Discourse: Incorporation and Repetition in *La Princesse de Clèves*." *Yale French Studies* 62 (1981): 62–87.

——. "Mothers and Daughters." *Signs* (Autumn 1981): 200–222.

Hogenson, George. *Jung's Struggle with Freud*. Notre Dame: Notre Dame UP, 1983.

Homans, Margaret. *Bearing the Word: Language and Female Experience in Nineteenth-Century Women's Writing*. Chicago: Chicago UP, 1986.

Horney, Karen. "The Flight from Womanhood: The Masculinity Complex in Women as Viewed by Men and by Women." In *Women and Analysis*, ed. Jean Strouse, 171–85. New York: Grossman/Viking, 1974.

Irigaray, Luce. "And the One Doesn't Stir without the Other." Trans. Helene Vivienne Wenzel. *Signs* 7 (Autumn 1981): 60–67.

——. *Speculum of the Other Woman*. Trans. Gillian C. Gill. Ithaca: Cornell UP, 1985.

——. "When Our Lips Speak Together." In *This Sex Which Is Not One*, trans. Catherine Porter with Carolyn Burke, 205–18. Ithaca: Cornell UP, 1985.

Isbister, J. N. *Freud: An Introduction to His Life and Work*. Cambridge: Polity, 1985.

Jacobus, Mary. *Reading Woman: Essays in Feminist Criticism*. New York: Columbia UP, 1986.

Works Cited

Janik, Allan, and Stephen Toulmin. *Wittgenstein's Vienna.* New York: Touchstone/Simon & Schuster, 1973.

Jardine, Alice. "Gynesis." *Diacritics* 12 (1982): 54–65.

——. *Gynesis: Configurations of Woman and Modernity.* Ithaca: Cornell UP, 1985.

Jones, Ann Rosalind. "Inscribing Femininity: French Theories of the Feminine." In *Making a Difference: Feminist Literary Criticism,* ed. Gayle Greene and Coppélia Kahn. London: Methuen, 1985.

——. "Writing the Body: Toward an Understanding of *L'Écriture Féminine.*" In *The New Feminist Criticism: Essays on Women, Literature, Theory,* 361–77. New York: Pantheon, 1985.

Jones, Ernest. *The Life and Work of Sigmund Freud.* 3 vols. New York: Basic, 1953.

——. "Mother-Right and the Sexual Ignorance of Savages." In *Essays in Applied Psycho-Analysis,* 2: 145–73. London: Hogarth, 1951.

Jung, Carl Gustav. *Memories, Dreams, Reflections.* Trans. Richard and Clara Winston, ed. Aniela Jaffe. Rev. ed. New York: Pantheon, 1973.

——. *Psychology of the Unconscious.* Trans. Beatrice M. Hinkle New York: Moffat, 1916.

Kahane, Claire. "The Gothic Mirror." In *The (M)other Tongue: Essays in Feminist Psychoanalytic Interpretation,* ed. Shirley Nelson Garner, Claire Kahane, and Madelon Sprengnether, 334–51. Ithaca: Cornell UP, 1985.

Kahn, Coppélia. "The Absent Mother in *King Lear.*" In *Rewriting the Renaissance: The Discourses of Sexual Difference in Early Modern Europe,* ed. Margaret Ferguson, Maureen Quilligan, and Nancy Vickers, 33–49. Chicago: University of Chicago Press, 1986.

——. "The Hand That Rocks the Cradle: Recent Gender Theories and Their Implications." In *The (M)other Tongue,* ed. Shirley Garner, Claire Kahane, and Madelon Sprengnether. Ithaca: Cornell UP, 1985.

——. *Man's Estate: Masculine Identity in Shakespeare.* Berkeley: University of California Press, 1980.

Kanzer, Mark. "The Motor Sphere of the Transference." *Psychoanalytic Quarterly* 35 (1966): 522–39.

Keller, Evelyn Fox. *A Feeling for the Organism: The Life and Work of Barbara McClintock.* New York: W. H. Freeman, 1983.

——. "The Gender/Science System: or, Is Sex to Gender as Nature Is to Science?" *Hypatia* 2 (Fall 1987): 37–49.

——. *Reflections on Gender and Science.* New Haven: Yale UP, 1985.

Kerr, John. "Beyond the Pleasure Principle and Back Again: Freud, Jung, and Sabina Spielrein." In *Freud: Appraisals and Reappraisals,* ed. Paul E. Stepansky. New York: Analytic Press, 1988.

Koestenbaum, Wayne. "Privileging the Anus: Anna O. and the Collaborative Origin of Psychoanalysis." *Genders* 3 (Fall 1988): 57–80.

Kofman, Sarah. *The Enigma of Woman: Woman in Freud's Writings.* Trans. Catherine Porter. Ithaca: Cornell UP, 1985.

Kristeva, Julia. *About Chinese Women.* Trans. Anita Barrows. New York: Urizen, 1977.

——. "A New Type of Intellectual: The Dissident." In *The Kristeva Reader,* ed. Toril Moi, 292–300. New York: Columbia UP, 1986.

——. "Revolution in Poetic Language." In *Kristeva Reader,* 90–136.

——. "Stabat Mater." In *Kristeva Reader,* 161–86.

——. "Women's Time." In *Kristeva Reader,* 188–213.

——. "Word, Dialogue, and Novel." In *Kristeva Reader,* 35–61.

Krüll, Marianne. *Freud and His Father.* Trans. Arnold J. Pomerans. New York: Norton, 1986.

Lacan, Jacques. *Écrits: A Selection.* Trans. Alan Sheridan. London: Tavistock, 1977.

——. "Encore." In *Feminine Sexuality: Jacques Lacan and the École Freudienne,* trans. Jacqueline Rose, 138–61. New York: Norton, 1985.

Lazarre, Jane. *The Mother Knot.* Boston: Beacon, 1986.

Lewis, Karl Kay. "Dora Revisited." *Psychoanalytic Review* 60 (1973): 519–32.

Lubbock, John. *The Origin of Civilization and the Primitive Condition of Man.* London: Longmans Green, 1870.

McBride, Theresa. "As the Twig Is Bent: The Victorian Nanny." In *The Victorian Family: Structure and Stresses,* ed. Anthony S. Wohl, 44–58. New York: St. Martin's, 1978.

Macey, David. *Lacan in Contexts.* London: Verso, 1988.

McGrath, William. *The Politics of Hysteria: Freud's Discovery of Psychoanalysis.* Ithaca: Cornell UP, 1986.

McGuire, William, ed. *The Freud/Jung Letters.* Trans. Ralph Manheim and R. F. C. Hull. 1974. Cambridge: Harvard UP, 1979.

McLennon, John. *Primitive Marriage: An Inquiry into the Origin of the Form of Capture in Marriage Ceremonies.* Edinburgh: Adam and Charles Black, 1865.

Mahler, Margaret. "On the First Three Subphases of the Separation-Individuation Process." *International Journal of Psycho-Analysis* 53 (1972): 333–38.

Mahony, Patrick. *Freud and the Rat Man.* New Haven: Yale UP, 1986.

Maine, Henry Summer. *Ancient Law: Its Connection with the Early History of Society, and Its Relations to Modern Ideas.* London: J. Murray, 1870.

Malcolm, Janet. *In the Freud Archives.* 1984. New York: Vintage/Random House, 1985.

Mantegazza, Paolo. *The Physiology of Love.* Trans. Herbert Alexander, ed. Victor Robinson. New York: Eugenics, 1936.

Marcus, Steven. "Freud and Dora: Story, History, Case History." In *Repre-*

sentations: Essays on Literature and Society, 247–309. New York: Random House, 1976.

——. *Freud and the Culture of Psychoanalysis*. 1984. New York: Norton, 1987.

Masson, Jeffrey Moussaieff. *Against Therapy: Emotional Tyranny and the Myth of Psychological Healing*. New York: Atheneum, 1988.

——. *The Assault on Truth: Freud's Suppression of the Seduction Theory*. New York: Farrar, Straus & Giroux, 1984.

——, trans. and ed. *The Complete Letters of Sigmund Freud to Wilhelm Fliess 1887–1904*. Cambridge: Belknap/Harvard UP, 1985.

Mayer, Elizabeth Lloyd. "'Everybody Must Be Just Like Me': Observations on Female Castration Anxiety." *International Journal of Psycho-Analysis* 66 (1985): 331–47.

Miller, Nancy K., ed. *The Poetics of Gender*. New York: Columbia UP, 1986.

Mitchell, Juliet. *Psychoanalysis and Feminism*. New York: Pantheon, 1974.

—— and Jacqueline Rose, eds. *Feminine Sexuality: Jacques Lacan and the École Freudienne*. Trans. Jacqueline Rose. New York: Norton, 1985.

Moi, Toril. "Representation of Patriarchy: Sexuality and Epistemology in Freud's Dora." *Feminist Review* (October 1981): 60–73.

——. *Sexual/Textual Politics: Feminist Literary Theory*. London: Methuen, 1985.

——, ed. *The Kristeva Reader*. New York: Columbia UP, 1986.

Morgan, Lewis Henry. *Ancient Society*. 1877. Ed. Leslie A. White. Cambridge: Belknap/Harvard UP, 1964.

Morrison, Toni. *Beloved*. New York: Knopf, 1987.

Muller, John P., and William J. Richardson. "Toward Reading Lacan." *Psychoanalysis and Contemporary Thought* 1 (1978): 325–72.

Muslin, Hyman, and Merton Gill. "Transference in the Dora Case." *Journal of the American Psychiatric Association* 26 (1978): 311–28.

Obholzer, Karin. *The Wolf-Man Sixty Years Later: Conversations with Freud's Controversial Patient*. Trans. Michael Shaw. New York: Continuum, 1982.

Olsen, Tillie. *Silences*. New York: Delacorte, 1978.

Peters, Uwe Henrik. *Anna Freud: A Life Dedicated to Children*. New York: Schocken, 1985.

Pfeiffer, Ernst, ed. *Sigmund Freud and Lou Andreas-Salomé Letters*. Trans. William and Elaine Robson-Scott. 1966. New York: Norton, 1985.

Quinn, Susan. *A Mind of Her Own: The Life of Karen Horney*. New York: Summit/Simon & Schuster, 1987.

Ragland-Sullivan, Ellie. *Jacques Lacan and the Philosophy of Psychoanalysis*. Urbana: University of Illinois Press, 1986.

Ramas, Maria. "Freud's Dora, Dora's Hysteria: The Negation of a Woman's Rebellion." *Feminist Studies* 6 (1980): 472–510.

Rank, Otto. *The Trauma of Birth*. New York: Robert Brunner, 1952.

Rich, Adrienne. "Compulsory Heterosexuality and Lesbian Existence." *Signs* 5 (1980): 631–59.

———. *The Dream of a Common Language*. New York: Norton, 1978.

———. *Of Woman Born: Motherhood as Experience and Institution*. New York: Norton, 1976.

Rieff, Philip. *Freud: The Mind of the Moralist*. 3d ed. Chicago: University of Chicago Press, 1979.

———, ed. *Dora: An Analysis of a Case of Hysteria*. New York: Crowell-Collier, 1963.

Roazen, Paul. *Freud and His Followers*. 1971. New York: Meridian/NAL, 1976.

Robinson, Marilynne. *Housekeeping*. 1981. New York: Bantam, 1982.

Rogow, Arnold. "A Further Footnote to Freud's 'Fragment of an Analysis of a Case of Hysteria.'" *Journal of the American Psychoanalytic Association* 26 (1978): 331–56.

Roithe, Estelle. *The Riddle of Freud: Jewish Influences on His Theory of Female Sexuality*. London: Tavistock, 1987.

Rose, Jacqueline. "Dora—'Fragment of an Analysis.'" *m/f* 2 (1978): 5–21.

Rudnytsky, Peter. *Freud and Oedipus*. New York: Columbia UP, 1987.

Ruitenbeck, Hendrick M., ed. *Freud as We Knew Him*. Detroit: Wayne State UP, 1973.

Sayers, Janet. *Sexual Contradictions: Psychology, Psychoanalysis, and Feminism*. London: Tavistock, 1986.

Schatzman, Morton. *Soul Murder: Persecution in the Family*. 1973. New York: Signet/NAL, 1974.

Schneiderman, Stuart. *Jacques Lacan: The Death of an Intellectual Hero*. Cambridge: Harvard UP, 1983.

Schorske, Carl E. *Fin-de-Siècle Vienna: Politics and Culture*. 1980. New York: Vintage/Random House, 1981.

Schur, Max. *Freud Living and Dying*. New York: International Universities Press, 1972.

———. "Some Additional 'Day Residues' of the 'Specimen Dream of Psychoanalysis.'" In *Psychoanalysis—a General Psychology: Essays in Honor of Heinz Hartman*, ed. Rudolph M. Loewenstein, Lottie M. Newman, Max Schur, and Albert J. Solnit, 45–85. New York: International Universities Press, 1966.

Sedgwick, Eve Kosofsky. *Between Men: English Literature and Male Homosocial Desire*. New York: Columbia UP, 1985.

Showalter, Elaine, ed. *The New Feminist Criticism: Essays on Women, Literature, Theory*. New York: Pantheon, 1985.

Works Cited

Signs: French Feminist Theory 7 (Autumn 1981).

Smith, Paul. *Discerning the Subject*. Minneapolis: University of Minnesota Press, 1988.

Spielrein, Sabina. "Die Destruktion als Ursache des Werdens." *Jahrbuch für Psychoanalytische und Psychopathologische Forschungen* 4 (1912): 465–503.

Sprengnether, Madelon [Gohlke]. " 'I wooed thee with my sword': Shakespeare's Tragic Paradigms." In *Representing Shakespeare: New Psychoanalytic Essays,* ed. Murray Schwartz and Coppélia Kahn, 170–87. Baltimore: Johns Hopkins UP, 1980.

——. "(M)other Eve: Some Revisions of the Fall in Fiction by Contemporary Women Writers," 298–322. In *Psychoanalysis and Feminism,* ed. Richard Feldstein and Judith Roof. Ithaca: Cornell UP, 1989.

Stanton, Domna. "Difference on Trial: A Critique of the Maternal Metaphor in Cixous, Irigaray, and Kristeva." In *The Poetics of Gender,* ed. Nancy K. Miller, 157–82. New York: Columbia UP, 1986.

Stoller, Robert. "Facts and Fancies: An Examination of Freud's Concept of Bisexuality." In *Women and Analysis,* ed. Jean Strouse, 343–64. New York: Grossman/Viking, 1974.

Strouse, Jean, ed. *Women and Analysis: Dialogues on Psychoanalytic Views of Femininity*. New York: Grossman/Viking, 1974.

Suleiman, Susan. "Writing and Motherhood." In *The (M)other Tongue,* ed. Shirley Nelson Garner, Claire Kahane, and Madelon Sprengnether, 352–77. Ithaca: Cornell UP, 1985.

Sulloway, Frank J. *Freud: Biologist of the Mind*. New York: Basic, 1979.

Swales, Peter. "A Fascination with Witches." *Sciences* 22 (1982): 21–25.

——. "Freud, Martha Bernays, & the Language of Flowers." Privately published paper, copyright 1983.

——. "Freud, Minna Bernays, and the Conquest of Rome: New Light on the Origins of Psychoanalysis." *New American Review* 1 (Spring/Summer 1982): 1–23.

Swan, Jim. "*Mater* and Nannie: Freud's Two Mothers and the Discovery of the Oedipus Complex." *American Imago* 31 (1974): 1–64.

Thornton, E. M. *The Freudian Fallacy: Freud and Cocaine*. 1983. London: Paladin/Collins, 1986.

Todd, Jane Marie. "The Veiled Woman in Freud's '*Das Unheimliche*.' " *Signs* 11 (Spring 1986): 519–28.

Todd, Janet. *Feminist Literary History*. New York: Routledge & Kegan Paul, 1988.

Van Herik, Judith. *Freud on Femininity and Faith*. Berkeley: University of California Press, 1982.

Wehr, Gerhard. *Jung: A Biography*. Trans. David M. Weeks. Boston: Shambhala, 1987.

Willis, Sharon. "A Symptomatic Narrative." In *A Fine Romance*, ed. Neil Hertz. *Diacritics* 13 (Spring 1983): 46–60.

Winnicott, D. W. *The Child, the Family, and the Outside World*. Reading, Mass.: Addison-Wesley, 1987.

——. "Mirror-Role of Mother and Family in Child Development." In *Playing and Reality*, 111–18. New York: Basic, 1971.

Young-Bruehl, Elizabeth. *Anna Freud: A Biography*. New York: Summit/ Simon & Schuster, 1988.

Index

Abel, Elizabeth, 34n, 89n, 101n
Andreas-Salomé, Lou, 82n, 106, 231n
Androgyny, 7, 77, 195, 214
Anglo-American theory, 8. *See also* Object relations theory
Anna O. *See* Pappenheim, Bertha
Antigone, 176–78

Bachofen, J. J., 4, 97–98, 101–3, 110–14, 122, 126, 141–42; and matriarchy, 88–89, 101; and matrilineality, 89, 107; and mother-right, 88, 101–2
Balmary, Marie, 13n, 15, 17
Becker, Ernest, 123n, 150n
Bernays, Judith Heller, 21n
Birth trauma, 121, 136–52, 229
Bisexuality, 34; in Dora case history, 53; and *écriture féminine*, 202–3, 206; and femininity, 154–57; in girls, 163–65
Breuer, Josef, 39
Burlingham, Dorothy, 178n

Carotenuto, Aldo, 92n
Castration: and Eckstein, 31; and femininity, 53, 148–49, 153, 155, 164–65, 183; of girl, 207; and mother, 37, 59, 145, 155, 159, as separation from mother, 8–9, 63, 121, 144–53, 176, 182, 228–30, 243
Castration anxiety, 26, 54
Castration complex: and civilization, 4, 117; and femininity, 157; and Fliess, 37; and *Golden Bough*, 104; in Little Hans case history, 56; and masculinity, 144–45, 156; and Oedipus complex, 35; and renunciation of mother, 9; and

separation from mother, 5; and sexual difference, 63
Castration threat: and birth trauma, 140, 142; and civilization, 114, 243–44; in Leonardo case history, 79; and masculinity, 188; of mother, 85; and sexual difference, 157; in Shreber case history, 71; in *Totem and Taboo*, 105; in Wolf Man case history, 72–74; of woman, 82–83
Chodorow, Nancy, 6, 8, 190–94, 220, 222, 227
Chora, 213
Civilization: and birth trauma, 140; and masculinity, 227; and Oedipus complex, 40, 87; and patriarchy, 8; and transcendence of mother, 3; and woman, 116–17
Cixous, Hélène, 201–6, 222
Clark, Ronald, 13n, 15n, 87n
Clément, Catherine, 196n, 201

Daly, Mary, 48n
Darwin, Charles, 89, 96
Death instinct: and aggression, 115, 117; and birth trauma, 136; and civilization, 118; and eros, 128; and masculine development, 182; and mourning, 237; and patriarchy, 244; and preoedipal mother, 5, 127, 135, 137, 219, 231–32; and repetition compulsion, 132–35; and Spielrein, 124, 126
Derrida, Jacques, 9, 129n, 236, 244; *Of Grammatology*, 236–39, 243; "Purveyor of Truth," 236n; *Spurs*, 245n; and supplement, 237–38, 243

259

Index

Index

Todd, Janet, 223n
Toulmin, Stephen, 14n

Van Herik, Judith, 103n, 150n

Willis, Sharon, 43n
Winnicott, D. W., 183–85

Wolf Man, 72–74

Young-Bruehl, Elizabeth, 166–68n, 176n, 178n

Zajic, Monica, 14. *See also* Nannie

Library of Congress Cataloging-in-Publication Data

Sprengnether, Madelon.
  The spectral mother : Freud, feminism, and psychoanalysis/
Madelon Sprengnether.
    p. cm.
  Includes bibliographical references.
  ISBN 0–8014–2387–2 (alk. paper).—ISBN 0–8014–9611–X (pbk. : alk. paper)
    1. Women and psychoanalysis. 2. Freud, Sigmund, 1857–1939. 3. Mother and
child. 4. Oedipus complex. I. Title.
BF175.S643 1990
150.19′52′082—dc20   89–39688